PRAISE FOR SELL WITH A STORY

"A must-read for anyone who wants to captivate attention and win business."
—Lisa McLeod, sales consultant and author of
Selling with a Noble Purpose

"Incredibly insightful and practical beyond words. A must-read for anyone who wants to be more persuasive."
—Dr. Jeffrey Docking, president, Adrian College

"A game-changer essential to taking your sales skills to the next level."
—Michael Miller, president and CEO of Primo Solutions, LLC and author of *Selling at Combat Speed* and *Stop Selling and Start Caring*

"Anyone who thinks that storytelling can't be learned hasn't read this book. Sell with A Story will teach you how to persuade your prospects with the same techniques that Hollywood screenwriters use to captivate audiences."
—Logan Strain, digital content specialist, NextGen Leads

"There are a lot of books out there telling the reader what storytelling is. Paul not only does that, but he tells you the how's, the why's, and the when's to use storytelling. As a salesperson, you will finally get what storytelling is, and how to use it to create transfer of ownership and shorten the sale."
—Skip Miller, author of *ProActive Selling*

SELL
WITH A
STORY

HOW TO CAPTURE ATTENTION, BUILD TRUST, AND CLOSE THE SALE

PAUL SMITH

AMACOM

American Management Association

New York * Atlanta * Brussels * Chicago * Mexico City * San Francisco
Shanghai * Tokyo * Toronto * Washington, D. C.

Bulk discounts available. For details visit:
www.amacombooks.org/go/specialsales
Or contact special sales:
Phone: 800-250-5308
Email: specialsls@amanet.org
View all the AMACOM titles at: www.amacombooks.org
American Management Association: www.amanet.org

This publication is designed to provide accurate and authoritative information in regard to the subject matter covered. It is sold with the understanding that the publisher is not engaged in rendering legal, accounting, or other professional service. If legal advice or other expert assistance is required, the services of a competent professional person should be sought.

Library of Congress Cataloging-in-Publication Data

Names: Smith, Paul, 1967 July 3- author.
Title: Sell with a story : how to capture attention, build trust, and close
   the sale / by Paul Smith.
Description: New York, NY : American Management Association, [2016] |
   Includes bibliographical references and index.
Identifiers: LCCN 2016017357 | ISBN 9780814437117 (hardcover) | ISBN
   9780814437124 (ebook)
Subjects: LCSH: Selling. | Storytelling. | Sales management. | Communication
   in management.
Classification: LCC HF5438.25 .S6425 2016 | DDC 658.85–dc23 LC record available at
https://lccn.loc.gov/2016017357

About AMA

American Management Association (www.amanet.org) is a world leader in talent development, advancing the skills of individuals to drive business success. Our mission is to support the goals of individuals and organizations through a complete range of products and services, including classroom and virtual seminars, webcasts, webinars, podcasts, conferences, corporate and government solutions, business books, and research. AMA's approach to improving performance combines experiential learning—learning through doing—with opportunities for ongoing professional growth at every step of one's career journey

Printing number
10 9 8 7 6 5 4 3

To my father, Robert Smith, who spent more time listening to sales stories than anyone I know.

CONTENTS

PART II

How to Craft Sales Stories   103

FOREWORD

PAUL SMITH'S FIRST book, *Lead with a Story—A Guide to Crafting Business Narratives That Captivate, Convince, and Inspire,* dramatically increased my effectiveness as a speaker and consultant. So you can imagine my excitement upon learning that Smith was applying his storytelling expertise to a new book on my favorite topic—selling.

I spend my days helping sales leaders and salespeople develop new business and acquire new customers. More than any other topic or sales skill, the area where sellers require the most help is with *telling their story*. Almost every day I tell anyone who will listen that "your story is your most critical sales weapon." Yet, executives and salespeople tend to be awful at storytelling. Just awful. Their stories are boring, confusing, often pointless, and almost always self-focused. In fact, as you'll read in Chapter 1, many lack the essential components to even qualify as a "story."

A great sales story changes everything. It causes buyers to put down their defenses. It helps them relax. It engages their minds and their hearts by appealing to both their intellect and emotions. A great story builds credibility and properly positions you in the eye of the buyer. Instead of being viewed as a pitchman (see the pearls of wisdom Smith has pulled from procurement people), a compelling story helps you come across as the value-creator, professional problem-solver, and consultant you so badly want to be.

Possibly even more important, your powerful story allows buyers to open up and share theirs. Nothing encourages prospective clients to answer your probing questions and reveal their problems, needs, desired results, frustrations, and opportunities better than your ability to tell a relevant story, in the appropriate way, at just the right time! Too often, we blow quickly through the discovery phase because buyers are not forthcoming when it comes to sharing information. Typically, our probing isn't effective because we haven't warmed up the prospect, built credibility, or earned the right to ask provocative questions—all things a great story can accomplish for us.

Sell with a Story delivers on the promise of its subtitle, *How to Capture Attention, Build Trust, and Close the Sale,* by showing how real salespeople tell stories throughout every stage of the sales process. These authentic stories of how sellers deploy their own stories when building rapport, making presentations, handling objections, closing sales, and servicing customers afterward are worth the price of admission alone.

One of the most interesting facets of this book is that while it's highly entertaining and easy to read (because it's filled with intriguing stories!), it also helps you put these valuable principles to use. Treat this as a workbook: keep a pen and pad handy; download the templates; identify the narratives you need and then craft them into compelling stories you can use. The author did his homework interviewing hundreds of people, and he has earned the right to ask you to do yours.

If you're serious about increasing your effectiveness as a communicator and looking to transform your sales results, *Sell with a Story* is for you. This book empowered and energized me, and I know it will do the same for you.

MIKE WEINBERG
Consultant, Speaker, and Author of the AMACOM Bestsellers
New Sales. Simplified. and *Sales Management. Simplified.*

ACKNOWLEDGMENTS

FIRST, I'D LIKE TO thank the people whose names and stories grace the pages of this book. I'm grateful to all of you for sharing your experience and wisdom so that others could benefit from them.

For most, your names are already included elsewhere in the book, so I won't repeat them here. But I am just as humbled by those who contributed their time and expertise in lengthy interviews and conversations but whose names do not show up as characters in one of the stories. You include: Ray Brook, Kevin Canfield, Charlie Collins, Jeff Docking, Dan Dorr, Elliott Feldman, Paul Johnson, Tim Linehan, Mark McKay, James Mounter, Kristin Pedemonti, Rudy Pollan, Ed Tanguay, Andrew Tarvin, and Paul Wesselmann.

Thanks also to the amazing staff at AMACOM Books who continue to be fabulous partners, specifically my editor, Stephen S. Power; the publicity director, Irene Majuk; and the rights and international sales director, Therese Mausser. Also thanks to my copyeditors at Neuwirth & Associates, and to my literary agent, Maryann Karinch, for connecting me with such a great team.

Last, thank you to my wife, Lisa, and sons, Matt and Ben, for your constant love and support as I continue to follow my dreams.

SELL
WITH A
STORY

INTRODUCTION

I**N MAY 2015,** my wife, Lisa, convinced me to attend a juried art fair with her at Coney Island in Cincinnati, Ohio. As an artist herself, she has a sophisticated appreciation for fine art that I don't. She can spend hours on end lazily drifting from one booth to the next, studying each piece and talking to the artists about their inspiration, medium, and techniques. Me, I just like to look at the pictures.

As the day dragged on, we arrived at the booth of Chris Gug (pronounced "Goog"), a photographer known for his awe-inspiring images of marine life. His gallery is full of breathtaking underwater shots of anemones, corals, sea turtles, and whales. On a mission to find a piece for our boys' bathroom at home, Lisa eyed a picture that looked about as out of place as a pig in the ocean. It was a picture of a pig in the ocean. She described it as inspired genius—a cute little baby piglet, up to its nostrils in the salt water, snout covered with sand, dog-paddling its way straight into the camera lens. I thought it was a picture of a pig in the ocean.

The artist joined us as we admired his piece—Lisa admiring it in her way while I admired it in mine. I asked him what on Earth that pig was doing in the ocean. And that's when the magic started.

Gug explained that the picture was taken in the Caribbean, just off the beach of an uninhabited Bahamian island officially named Big

Major Cay. He told us that years ago, a local entrepreneur brought a drove of pigs to the island to raise for bacon. Gug went on:

> But, as you can see in the picture, there's not much more than cactus on the island for them to eat. And pigs don't much like cactus. I guess in typical laid-back Bahamian fashion, the entrepreneur failed to plan that far ahead. So the pigs weren't doing very well. But at some point, a restaurant owner on a nearby island started bringing his kitchen refuse by boat over to Big Major Cay and dumping it a few dozen yards off shore. The hungry pigs eventually learned to swim to get to the food. Each generation of pigs followed suit, and now all the pigs on the island can swim. As a result, today the island is more commonly known as Pig Island.

Gug went on to describe how the pigs learned that approaching boats meant food, so they eagerly swim up to anyone arriving by boat. And that's what allowed him to more easily get the close-up shot of the cute little sandy-nosed, dog-paddling piglet.

I handed him my credit card and said, "We'll take it!"

Why my change of heart? The moment before he shared his story (to me at least), the photo was just a picture of a pig in the ocean, worth little more than the paper it was reproduced on. But two minutes later, it was no longer just a picture. It was a story—a story I would be reminded of every time I looked at it. The story turned the picture into a conversation piece—a unique combination of geography lesson, history lesson, and animal psychology lesson all in one.

In the two minutes it took Gug to tell us that story, the value of that picture increased immensely. Perhaps for an art aficionado like my wife, it was already a valuable piece. But for me, my interest in and willingness to pay good money for that picture increased exponentially as a result of the story.[1]

Stories sell. And the people who can tell a good sales story sell more than people who can't.

This book will help you tell better sales stories.

PURPOSE OF THIS BOOK

If you're looking for a comprehensive book on selling, this is not it. Nor does this book offer an entirely new selling process to replace the one you're using today.

What it does offer is a new skill to add to whatever process you're currently using. That skill is storytelling.

Many people assume that a talent for storytelling is the kind of thing you're either born with or you'll never have. And while it's true that some people are born with a natural ability to tell stories, it's not true that you can't learn it. Storytelling is like any other skill, such as playing music. Some people are natural-born musicians. But even if you're not one of them, if you take guitar lessons for a few months, you could probably learn to play a few songs.

Treat storytelling like any other professional skill. If you invest the time to learn how to do it well, and then practice it, you can master it. This book is your first step in that journey. It's designed to answer the following questions: What is a sales story, why should you tell them, which sales stories should you tell and when should you tell them, how can you come up with these stories, and how can you craft and deliver them for maximum impact.

HOW THIS BOOK WAS WRITTEN

This book is the third in a series designed to bring the power of storytelling to bear on some of the most important work we do as humans. The first was *Lead with a Story*,[2] to help harness the power of storytelling for leadership. The second was *Parenting with a Story*,[3] to help parents teach their children character and life lessons through storytelling. And now *Sell with a Story*, to help all of us persuade and influence more effectively with storytelling.

This book, like its two predecessors, draws on four primary sources of knowledge and expertise. First, over the last six years I've personally conducted more than 250 in-depth, one-on-one interviews with people from 20 countries and all walks of professional and personal life.

I've documented more than 2,000 personal stories and dissected them to uncover what works and what doesn't.

For this book in particular, I interviewed sales and procurement professionals from a diverse set of 50 organizations, including Hewlett-Packard, Costco, Abercrombie & Fitch, Microsoft, Huntington Bank, Xerox, Cushman & Wakefield, Bulgari, Amway, Ghirardelli, DataServ, and Children's Hospital Los Angeles.

With the salespeople, I obviously asked questions about their selling process and where storytelling fit into it. But I also asked them questions like, "How do you come up with your stories? How do you practice them? And how true do they have to be?" Most importantly, throughout the interview I prompted them to share their most effective (and least effective) stories.

It's worth pointing out why I also chose to interview procurement managers for a book about sales. My logic was that there are no people better positioned to understand which sales stories work and which don't than the professional buyers on the receiving end of those stories. These are people who spend their days listening to one sales story after another and deciding which ones compelled them to buy something and which ones did not.

I specifically asked this group to recall the best (and worst) sales stories they ever heard and what made them so effective (or ineffective). I also asked what kind of stories they want to hear (and don't want to hear) from salespeople, what stories they find themselves telling salespeople and why, and—perhaps most interestingly—what makes a sales pitch sound like a sales pitch.

Second, this book is also informed by a thorough reading of the best academic and trade books on storytelling for business in general and for selling in particular. You'll see dozens of those works referenced in the text, the Endnotes, and the Additional Reading section.

Third, as a professional storytelling coach and trainer, I have the privilege of working with a diverse set of dozens of clients from large Fortune 50 companies to small sole-proprietorships. Each engagement gives me the opportunity to see the communication, leadership, and selling struggles my clients are facing and help them craft better stories. Doubtless I learn as much during these sessions as they do, and you'll see that wisdom reflected in these pages as well.

Last, I also drew on my own seven years of experience working on Procter & Gamble's global sales teams that called on corporate buyers at Walmart, Sam's Club, Costco, and BJ's Wholesale Club.

So this is not a theoretical treatise revealing the results of new academic studies. It's a practical guide for leveraging the best thinking on storytelling to the business of selling.

HOW TO USE THIS BOOK

This book isn't meant to be skimmed or perused or looked at occasionally. It's not a reference manual or a coffee-table book. It's a workbook. Don't just read it. Use it. Chapters 1 and 2 cover what a sales story is and why you should tell them. Part I identifies the sales stories you need and when to tell them. If you're like most salespeople, you're using storytelling in only a fraction of the selling situations you could be. This section will help you identify the 25 sales stories you need to have in your storytelling repertoire. Each chapter has Exercises at the end designed to help you find the selling narratives you need.

The majority of the book is Part II: How to Craft Sales Stories. This section includes several "Story Clinics" designed as case studies to help you apply the techniques to a real story. It also refers to templates and lists in the Appendixes that you'll need to craft those narratives into compelling stories. Feel free to make copies and use them each time you craft a new story. You have my permission. Electronic copies are available to download at www.leadwithastory.com/resources. If you already have a good feel for the stories you want to tell and are eager to learn how to tell them better, you can skip to this section. But once you've done that and have your stories in top shape, come back to Part I and see what other stories you might benefit from having.

If all you do is read this book, you'll have missed out on most of its value. Put all these tools and techniques to use. You'll get more value out of it if you do.

Let's get started.

1

WHAT IS A SALES STORY?

IT'S 9 O'CLOCK on Monday morning, three days before a big sales call with a new prospect. The entire team is assembled in a conference room ready to start planning the sales pitch. At 9:02, the sales VP walks in the room and calls the meeting to order with a clap of her hands. She remains standing, puts her hands down on the conference table, leans out over the surface, and says, "Okay, people, what's our story?"

Do you think she's asking for an actual story in the traditional sense? Almost certainly not. She's probably asking for the logical series of facts and arguments and data the team should lay out for the prospect, probably in a PowerPoint presentation, that will have the greatest odds of leading to a sale. That would certainly be a reasonable request. But it's not something anyone would have called a story 10 years ago. It would have been called a message track, or talking points, or presentation slides, or simply a sales pitch.

In the business world, it's become popular in many circles to consider just about any meaningful series of words a story. Our strategy document is a story . . . the mission statement is a story . . . our co-marketing programs are stories . . . our brand logo is a story . . . and so on.

If using the word *story* for all those purposes helps people find or create more meaning in their work, then that's obviously a good thing.

But for the purposes of this book, these are not stories. Not every set of words that has meaning is a story, just like not all collections of words constitute poetry. A story is something special.

So, how can you distinguish a story from other narratives that are not stories? We need some practical tips to recognize a story.

The most sensible attempt I've seen to do this is by business storytelling consultant Shawn Callahan. He even created a 10-story quiz at www.thestorytest.com to help people practice identifying general business stories from nonstories. I encourage you to try the quiz yourself.

SIX ATTRIBUTES OF A STORY

Inspired by Callahan's work, here are my top attributes that distinguish a story from all other forms of narrative. Stories, as I will discuss them in this book, typically have the following six identifiable features, listed in the order you're likely to encounter them in a narrative: (1) a time, (2) a place, (3) a main character, (4) an obstacle, (5) a goal, and (6) events. When you find these features in a narrative, it's a good indication that what you're experiencing is a story. It might not be a good story, but it's a story. We'll get to what makes stories good or even great later in the book. But for now, let's just figure out how to recognize a story when we come across one. Stories generally have:

1. A *time indicator.* Words like "Back in 2012" or "Last month" or "The last time I was on vacation" are all indications of when something happened. And since in a story something has to happen, these time indicators are a clue that something is about to happen.

2. A *place indicator.* A story sometimes starts with words like "I was at the airport in Boston" or "It all started in the cafeteria at our office" or "On my way home." Again, since stories relay events, those events have to happen somewhere. Try telling a story about something specific that happened to you without mentioning where it happened. It's not impossible, but it feels awkward, which is why most stories have a place indicator.

3. *A main character.* This should be obvious, but as discussed above, much of what passes for "a story" these days are things like mission statements or talking points that have no characters at all. For a narrative to be a story, there has to be at least one character, and usually more. In the context of sales stories, the character is almost always a person, but it could be an animal, a company, or even a brand.

4. *An obstacle.* This is the villain in the story. It's usually a person, but it doesn't have to be. It could be a company that's your main competitor, the disease you're designing medicine to combat, or the faulty copy machine you finally got your revenge on.

5. *A goal.* The main character in a story must have an understood goal, particularly one that's worthy or noble in the eyes of the audience. Don't confuse your goal in telling a sales story with the goal of the main character in the story. Your goal in telling the story may be to close the sale. But the goal of the pigs in the Pig Island story, for example, was to find food to survive. It's hard to get much more worthy than that.

6. *Events.* If there was a single most important identifier that a story is happening, this would be it. For a story to be a story, something has to happen. Statements about your product's amazing capabilities or your service commitment, or testimonials about how awesome your company is, are generally not stories because they don't relay events. Nothing happens in them. They're just someone's opinion about something. If nothing happens, it's not a story. Those kinds of narratives can be very compelling and effective and are an essential part of any salesperson's tool kit. They just aren't stories.

SALES STORY TEST

Let's give these criteria a test drive and see how they work. Similar to Shawn Callahan's story test, below are four narratives that may or may not be rightly called a story, but specifically in a sales context. Your job is to decide which are and which are not stories, and why. We'll score your answers after the narratives.

Narrative #1: Are your teeth stained or yellow? Are you embarrassed to smile at parties or in pictures or videos, especially next to your friends with movie-star smiles? Have you tried teeth whitening systems but given up after a few days because they made your teeth too sensitive? If so, Ultra-White is right for you. It's the revolutionary new teeth whitening system designed by Hollywood dentists to give you star-quality whiteness without all the pain and discomfort. Ultra-White involves a two-step process that alternates applications between a high-impact whitening paste and a desensitization gel. The result is sparkling white teeth without any discomfort that would keep you from showing off your new Hollywood smile.

Narrative #2: A couple of years ago, Dave Neild, the network service leader at the University of Leeds in the UK, realized he had a problem. He was getting cease and desist orders and copyright violation notices from all over the world as a result of students using file-sharing services like BitTorrent. In addition, many of the students were showing up in his office with computers infected by viruses. It took his staff up to an hour to clean up each one. Dave agreed to do a test with Hewlett-Packard's TippingPoint network security device to see if that could help. When the test was over, he told us, "As soon as we installed TippingPoint, we instantly stopped receiving copyright notices. That protected our students from getting threatened by lawyers, and it protected the reputation of the university." The university also got about 30 percent of its lost bandwidth back from the reduction in file sharing.[1]

Narrative #3: You should be using your shoppers' planned purchases of toothpaste to sell more toothbrushes. Currently, shoppers buy toothbrushes only about every six months, despite the fact that dentists suggest replacing a toothbrush every three months. But your shoppers are already in your Oral Care aisle every two months to buy toothpaste. If you co-merchandised toothbrushes with toothpastes, you could close more of your shoppers with toothbrushes. And toothbrushes help sweeten the profits for you as a retailer. The average toothpaste category profit margin is only X percent, but the profit margin on toothbrushes is usually double that. And your own sales data show a dramatic increase in toothbrush sales when merchandised with toothpaste. Our February co-merchandising event delivered a 22 percent sales increase on toothbrushes over three weeks. That was $YY million in incremental sales. This was by far the best toothbrush sales month of the year. Even bigger than Christmas![2]

Narrative #4: I had just spent way too much money on my new road bike, which was white with bright orange highlights all over it. I unloaded it off my truck last week and was standing at the elevator doors of my loft. As the doors opened, I saw a girl from my building already standing inside. I'd been wanting to meet her for some time. She gave a friendly smile as I entered. I see this girl all the time and she runs and bikes constantly, so I knew she was going to comment on the new bike. I was just waiting for her to speak up. She kept looking my direction, clearly about to say something. When she finally opened her mouth, she said, "Is that a wood watch?" I had totally forgotten I was wearing my Sully Green Sandalwood watch from Jord that day. "It's really cool," she said. At that moment, the elevator stopped on her floor and she got out. Didn't even notice the bike. Might as well have been invisible. That watch gets so many comments, it's crazy. Thanks, Jord!

Okay, let's see how you did.

First off, admittedly none of these are earth-shatteringly great stories. But some of them are stories, and some of them are not.

Narrative #1 (Ultra-White): *Not a story*—Let's walk through all six criteria. There is no time and no place mentioned. There's also not a clear main character, although "you" is mentioned several times. There does appear to be a main obstacle (yellow teeth and the discomfort of most teeth whitening systems). And there is clearly a goal (whiter teeth). Finally, and most tellingly, there aren't any events that occur in the narrative. Nothing happens. Net, this narrative contains only two or three of the six criteria. It might make for a good advertisement. But it's not a story.

Narrative #2 (TippingPoint): *Story*—There is a time (two years ago), a place (University of Leeds), a main character (Dave Neild), an obstacle (cease and desist orders), a goal (stopping the orders), and events (students sharing files and the university running the TippingPoint test). This has all the indicators of a story.

Narrative #3 (Oral Care): *Not a story*—This one is tricky. It's exactly the kind of narrative professional salespeople use all the time, and they might easily refer to it as a story. But let's look at the criteria. There are time references to February and Christmas, but most of the text doesn't involve those times. There is no place mentioned. It's confusing who the main character is. Sometimes it appears to be "you," and sometimes it appears to be the shopper. It goes back and forth. The obstacle appears to be the current merchandising practices, and the goal is clearly to sell more toothbrushes. But the events are a hodgepodge of things the shopper does, things the buyer did, and things the buyer and seller did together. This one meets two of the six criteria well, and it's muddled at best on the other four. This narrative is best described as a persuasive sales pitch, and it's a pretty good one at that. But it's really not a story.

Narrative #4 (wood watches): *Story*—This is perhaps the easiest narrative to identify as a story. It's a narrative about something that happened to somebody. Even a 10-year-old would recognize this as a story. It has a time (last week), a place (the elevator in the loft), a main character (the unnamed author), an obstacle (difficulty meeting the woman in the elevator), a goal (to finally meet the woman in the elevator), and events (all the activity and conversation on the elevator).

So, now we know what a story is and how to recognize it. That was the hard part. Now for the easy part. What's a *sales* story?

A sales story is any story that's used in the process of earning a sale and maintaining a customer. That's it. As you'll see in Part I, stories can be used in any phase of the sales process, from stories you tell yourself prior to the sales call, to building rapport with the buyer, to the sales pitch itself, to negotiating price, to closing the sale, and even after the sale to manage the customer relationship. For our purposes in this book, all of these are sales stories. You'll see examples of and learn how to develop all of them.

2

WHY TELL SALES STORIES?

COMPARED TO OTHER forms of communication used in sales, storytelling has a number of unique abilities. It can help capture your buyer's attention and build your mutual relationship. It connects with the decision-making areas in your buyer's brain and makes you and your product easier to remember. It can literally increase the value of your product or highlight your main idea by moving it to another context. Stories are contagious and spread by word of mouth. They let you be more original and stand out from your competition. And unlike a presentation, your buyers actually want you to tell them stories. Last, compared to clicking through the slides of a sales pitch, telling stories is just more fun—for you and your buyer.

This chapter briefly discusses the 10 compelling reasons why storytelling is a master sales tool. If you want to go deeper into the academic research and science behind why storytelling works, see the list of books in the Additional Reading section at the end of the book.

•   •   •

1. STORIES HELP THE BUYER RELAX AND JUST LISTEN

It's similar to the response college students have when the professor stops writing formulas on the board and starts sharing a personal anecdote or analogy. The students relax their shoulders for a minute, stop taking notes, lean back in their chairs, and just listen.

In his book *The 60-Second Sales Hook*, sales expert Kevin Rogers observes of most buyers, "One glance that a sales pitch is being slung your way, and your 'mental door' slams shut."[1] Storytelling works well precisely because it doesn't sound like a sales pitch to a buyer, just like a story doesn't sound like a lecture to a student. So in both cases, the buyer and the student open up their minds and just listen.

2. STORIES HELP BUILD STRONG RELATIONSHIPS

Storytelling almost magically builds trust, which is the foundation of good relationships. A 1999 *New York Times*/CBS survey asked, "Of people in general, how many do you think are trustworthy?" The average answer was 30 percent. Then it asked, "Of people you know, how many do you think are trustworthy?" The average answer shot up to 70 percent![2] What does that suggest? It suggests that people who don't know you default to not trusting you. But people who do know you default to trusting you unless you've given them a reason not to.

Telling a story can move you from the 30 percent to the 70 percent, because it provides a personal, intimate, and perhaps vulnerable glimpse into your world. Reading the facts on your resume doesn't really let someone get to know you, and spending enough time together could take months or years. A story is the shortest distance between being a stranger and a friend.

How important is it to move from the 30 percent to the 70 percent? Apparently quite a bit. Mike Parrott, vice president and general merchandise manager at Costco Wholesale, has been on the buyer's side of the desk for 15 years. He says, "If all other things are equal, buyers will buy from a salesperson they like best and trust the most. It breaks the ties. And there are a lot of ties in this business."

Telling stories is also the most reliable way to get the buyer to open up and tell you their stories. After hearing someone tell you one of those genuine, personal stories, it's almost impossible to not share a story in return. It's like extending your hand for a handshake. It would be rude to not respond in kind.

3. STORYTELLING SPEAKS TO THE PART OF THE BRAIN WHERE DECISIONS ARE ACTUALLY MADE

Much of the cognitive science in the past two decades tells us that human beings often make subconscious, emotional, and sometimes irrational decisions in one place in the brain, and then justify those decisions rationally and logically in another place. So if you're trying to influence buyers' decisions, using facts and rational arguments alone isn't enough. You need to influence them emotionally, and stories are your best vehicle to do that.

Veteran salespeople know this from experience. Rick Rhine is the owner of Tailwind Marketing, an Arizona-based company that sells telecommunication services door-to-door. He says, "The least effective moment in those doorstep conversations is when my sales rep is the most factual—when they stop talking about the experience and start talking numbers. When we say, 'I'm gonna get you 20-meg Internet service for $29.95 a month and I can have a tech out here in two days to hook that up, how does that sound?' the customer doesn't care and you can see it in their eyes."

But when his reps tell customers a story about how their neighbors are enjoying the new service, or lets customers tell their own stories about the problems they're having with their current service, things work out better.

As NYU social psychologist Jonathan Haidt observes, "The human mind is a story processor, not a logic processor."[3]

4. STORIES MAKE IT EASIER FOR THE BUYER TO REMEMBER YOU, YOUR IDEAS, AND YOUR PRODUCT

Many studies show that facts are easier to remember if they're embedded in a story than if they're delivered in any other form.[4] For example, Stanford University Professor Chip Heath asked his students to give one-minute speeches about crime. The average student used 2.5 statistics in his speech, while only one in ten students told a story. But when students were asked to recall the speeches, 63 percent remembered details of stories. Only 5 percent remembered any individual statistic.[5]

But you don't even have to believe these studies. You can prove this to yourself right now with a little test German storytelling coach Andrea Heckelmann uses with her clients.[6] Try to remember this series of facts: Two legs sit on three legs, eating one leg. Then along comes four legs and steals one leg from two legs. Two legs then hits four legs with three legs and gets his one leg back.

You could do it, but it would probably take you several minutes of repeated effort and practice to remember it correctly. Now try to remember the same series of facts shared as a story with characters, goals, and obstacles: A young boy (two legs) sits on a stool (three legs), eating a chicken bone (one leg). Then along comes a dog (four legs) that steals the chicken bone (one leg) from the boy (two legs). The boy (two legs) then hits the dog (four legs) with the stool (three legs) and gets his chicken bone (one leg) back.

Chances are you can now recite the list of facts perfectly and after reading through the story only one time. The story creates a meaningful scene in your mind that the simple list of facts doesn't. That scene is easier for your mind to remember than the list of facts. Stories create scenes. Facts don't.

Last, you inherently know stories are easier to remember than facts. Each of you reading this book right now knows that by this time tomorrow, you won't remember more than two or three items on this list of 10 reasons why storytelling works in sales. But you will remember the story of Pig Island at the very beginning of the book. And next week, next month, or even next year, most of you won't remember this list at all. But all of you will remember most of the facts in the Pig Island story and probably be able to tell it almost as well as Chris Gug does.

5. STORYTELLING ACTUALLY INCREASES THE VALUE OF THE PRODUCT YOU'RE SELLING

In July 2009, journalist Rob Walker and author Josh Glenn conducted a remarkable experiment.[7] They purchased 100 ordinary used objects from thrift stores and garage sales—a jar of marbles, a meat thermometer, a wooden mallet, a toy pink horse, a bottle opener, a Santa Claus nutcracker, etc. Each item cost on average $1.29.

They then asked volunteers to write short, fictional stories about each item. For example, to accompany a ceramic piggy bank, one author wrote a story from the perspective of a little girl who thought the piggy bank was cursed. Her father would come home each payday and put half his pay in the piggy bank, only to watch during the week as the paper money in the pig turned into coins and then eventually disappeared.

Walker and Glenn then placed each item for sale on eBay. But instead of putting a simple description next to the picture of each item, they put only the fictional story that had been written for it. Care was taken to make sure it was clear that the story was purely fictional so as not to suggest that the object being sold was somehow more special than the common household item it appeared to be.

Within five months, all 100 items had been sold. The experimenters originally paid a total of $128.74 for the items, but the resale price paid on eBay totaled $3,612.51, or a 2,800 percent increase in value. In the words of Walker and Glenn, their experiment showed that "Narrative transforms insignificant objects into significant ones." In other words, stories turned cheap objects into valuable ones.

Now, is it possible that those same items, if listed on eBay with a simple description instead of a story, could have sold for more than the thrift store prices they were acquired at? Of course. But experiences like buying Chris Gug's picture of a pig in the ocean only after hearing his story convince me that much of that 2,800 percent increase in value is indeed due to the story. In fact, we'll see in Chapter 7 that this is one of the key purposes of sharing a story in a sales call.

6. STORYTELLING HIGHLIGHTS YOUR MAIN IDEA BY MOVING IT TO ANOTHER CONTEXT

In a wonderful and underappreciated book, *Soft Tales and Hard Asses*, Paul Lanigan and Denis Goodbody describe this aspect of storytelling working like a photographer uses a cyclorama—that curved white background you see in a studio for the main attraction to stand in front of. "Everything they photograph in front of it is pin-sharp and clear. Every detail is visible because there are no distractions. In our case, we need the story backdrop to give a context in which the action can take place. By making it alien, surreal, or fantastic, we remind the listener that the part at the center is the bit they need to focus on."[8]

Someone who's seen the context-shifting power of storytelling for years is Mike Figliuolo. Mike is the founder of *thought*LEADERS, LLC—an executive training firm in Columbus, Ohio. Since founding the company in 2004, he's taught leadership, influence, and problem-solving skills to thousands of business leaders around the world. His classes are typically a full day with 15 to 30 executives in a classroom setting. To help with the learning, Mike creates simplified fictitious case studies for the participants to practice on using the new techniques he teaches them. Importantly, he intentionally invents examples from outside the industry of the participants he's teaching. Occasionally a client asks, "Why can't we invent a case study based on our business? Won't that make the learning more relevant?"

Mike's answer is compelling. He says:

> I've learned from experience that when I use examples familiar to the people in my class, two things happen. First, participants tell me everything that's wrong with the *fictitious* case study, saying things like "That's not how we really do it" or "You're using outdated numbers." That's understandable; people want things to be right and when they're not, they obsess with what's "wrong" even though the case study is made up. Second, they spend too much time trying to crack the case

and get the "right" answer, instead of focusing on the new tools and techniques I'm trying to teach them. Using an unfamiliar context forces them to focus on the methods I want them to learn instead of getting mired in industry-specific fictitious data.

7. STORIES ARE CONTAGIOUS

Make a great sales pitch and it stays in the room where you made it. But when you tell a great story, it can travel around the world. In his book *What's Your Story?*, sales guru Craig Wortmann observes: "Salespeople are rarely able to reach all of the decision makers at once. This is where stories are also useful, because they more readily spread from client to client."[9]

Wortmann explains by asking when was the last time you heard anyone say, "Wow! You're never going to believe the PowerPoint presentation I just saw!"[10] Probably never. But people say that about a good story all the time.

Even if you've been on the receiving end of a great sales pitch, it's hard to repeat it to someone else in your office without having all the same materials and slides on hand that the salesperson had when she made the pitch to you. But anyone can easily repeat a story without prompting, notes, or even a single slide—and they do. And that's the point.

8. STORYTELLING GIVES YOU AN OPPORTUNITY TO BE ORIGINAL

Let's face it: most professional buyers have seen it all. They've heard every pitch, tactic, and attempted close line in the book. They've heard them from you, your competitors, and the last two people who had your job. And as storytelling expert Doug Stevenson observes in his book *Story Theater Method*, "People are yearning for someone to tell them something they don't know already."[11] Your story lets you give that to them.

Storytelling gives you a way to stand out in the crowd with something interesting and original to say. It distinguishes you not only from your peers and competitors but also from your predecessors, because the stories you tell won't be the ones cooked up by the marketing department, your ad agency, or even the sales manager. They're your stories. Nobody else will have them unless you decide to share.

9. YOUR BUYERS WANT MORE STORIES FROM YOU

Forrester Research conducted a study in 2013 asking 319 executive-level buyers in North America and Europe how frequently the salespeople who call on them are prepared in certain ways. The buyers responded that 62 percent of the time the salespeople were knowledgeable about the company and products they represented; 42 percent of the time they were knowledgeable about the buyer's industry; but only 21 percent of the time (the lowest in the survey) did they have relevant examples or case studies to share.[12] In other words, only one in five sales calls include enough stories to satisfy the buyer.

My own qualitative research supports this. One of the questions I asked procurement professionals was "What kind of stories do you want to hear from salespeople?" Among the most consistent answers were stories to help them understand:

1. Why and how your company was founded,

2. who you are and what your values are,

3. how and why the product you're selling was invented,

4. stories about how the product is made, and

5. the level of integrity they can expect from you and your company.

For example, Mike Parrott of Costco is quick to relay the story about how in 1975, Dan Huish was frustrated with the low quality and high price of laundry detergents. So, in true entrepreneurial fashion, he started making his own detergent in his garage and began selling it to neighborhood grocers. His company, Huish Detergents, now known as Sun Products, eventually became the largest maker of retailer-branded detergents in North America, including the Kirkland Signature brand sold at Costco today. Mike says stories like that tell you a lot about the company trying to sell you something. Why they do what they do is sometimes as important as what they do. And the story communicates that in a far more memorable and compelling way than being told, "Huish Detergents was founded to make high quality and affordable laundry detergent."

10. STORYTELLING IS MORE FUN THAN DELIVERING A CANNED SALES PITCH, FOR YOU AND THE BUYER

Jennifer Doherty is the chief procurement officer for the Commonwealth of Pennsylvania. She says, "You can tell when a salesperson has delivered the same sales pitch over and over again and they're bored with it. They quickly flip through a standard PowerPoint deck, without a lot of voice inflection or stopping to see if you have any questions."

And if you think delivering a monotonous, canned sales pitch is boring, how exciting do you think it is to be on the receiving end of one? Telling stories gives you an excuse to go off script and keep the conversation organic and flowing—which, as Jennifer points out, is critical because buying and selling "is like dating. If it's not organic and flowing, it's probably not going to work out."

Storytelling humanizes us and therefore creates more meaningful bonds. It makes us laugh and can make us cry. Storytelling delivers surprises that open our eyes and describes awkward moments that make us cringe. Storytelling is the most natural and enjoyable form of human communication. If you doubt that, try taking the plot of a novel or movie and converting it into an outline with bullet points and see how quickly it becomes neutered of any chance to make a difference in the world again.

I share this reason last because if I'd included it as one of the first reasons, some readers would surely take this entire effort less seriously. Why? Because "fun" doesn't sound like a legitimate reason to make a change in how you go about making your living. But it should be. If you're planning to spend three decades or more engaged in any activity, you'd damn well better enjoy it, or you won't last half that long before you quit to take on something you do enjoy. And you'll also be making it more enjoyable for the hundreds of potential buyers whose three decades of time will be spent in meetings with people like you. They'll thank you with more business anyway.

Now that you know why you should be telling more sales stories, let's move on to what sales stories you need to tell.

PART I

WHAT SALES STORIES YOU NEED AND WHEN TO TELL THEM

MOST PROFESSIONAL SALESPEOPLE consider the selling process a long and multiphased activity that spans from well before a sales call ever occurs to long after the sale has been made and the product delivered. An amalgam of the most common components looks something like this: The early stages include defining an ideal prospect, putting themselves in a position to meet new prospects (say, networking at an industry conference), and planning for the sales call. Then comes building rapport with the prospect, discovering what their needs are, qualifying them as a desirable customer, defining the best product or solution to offer, making the sales pitch itself, handling objections, negotiating price, and closing the sale. The final stages include customer service after delivery and long-term ongoing customer relationship management.

It turns out that storytelling is being successfully used in every stage that involves contact with the prospect or customer. A few salespeople I interviewed intentionally use storytelling in all customer-contact stages. Most, however, concentrate their storytelling in only one or a few of those stages. Which stage they use storytelling in varies by person, providing further evidence of storytelling being successfully used across all customer-contact stages.

In the chapters that follow, you'll find examples of real stories used by professional salespeople (and in some cases procurement managers) arranged by stage of the selling process. My purpose in sharing them is threefold. The first reason is to serve as a springboard to give you ideas for developing your own stories for each stage of your selling process. I found that most of the people I interviewed were open to using more storytelling. They just didn't have good story ideas to use in each stage.

The second reason is to give you some experience with solid, effective selling stories prior to getting to Part II, where we'll discuss how to craft your own compelling stories. As we saw in Chapter 1, most of what passes for a story today is not. As you read through the stories in Part I, begin to take note of what common elements they have, what you like and dislike about each one, and what the difference is between a good story and a great one.

The third reason for sharing these stories is that I'll refer back to some of them as examples to help illustrate the storytelling techniques in Part II.

You'll also find ideas from many of my interviewees about how to navigate these stages of the sales process by using your stories. It's the kind of wisdom you come across when you interview people with more than 1,000 collective years of experience in professional sales.

3

INTRODUCING YOURSELF

THE EARLIEST OPPORTUNITY you have to tell a story is the moment you introduce yourself to a potential new customer. It could be in an email you're sending or a phone call you're placing for the purpose of introducing yourself. Or it could be face to face at a networking event as you're exchanging business cards with someone who may or may not turn out to be a prospect. Whatever the venue, the question you're answering is likely the same: "So, what do you do for a living?"

The way you answer that question will determine how much interest your prospects have in listening to anything else you have to say before deleting the email or making an awkward escape to the cocktail bar.

EXPLAINING WHAT YOU DO SIMPLY

There are generally two types of stories used at this stage of the relationship. The first type explains what you do for a living in a way that's meaningful if your audience happens to be a prospect, but without putting them to sleep if they're not.

In other words, the story avoids this kind of corporate yawner that's guaranteed to leave you standing alone at the hors d'oeuvre table: "I represent a company that's best in class at optimizing the distribution channels between the core manufacturing center and the desired consumer experience."

In his book *Unique Sales Stories,* Mark Satterfield offered the following story for exactly the purpose I'm talking about. Instead of the eye-roller presented above, imagine if our distribution channel expert had answered the question like this:

> Well, suppose you're in the chicken business. They're pretty perishable things and I don't know if you've ever unwrapped a chicken you've bought at the grocery store that's gone bad, but it's not an experience you want to repeat. Anyway, the tricky part is, how do you get the chicken from the farm to the retail store, in less than three days, all ready for cooking and smelling nice? That process has a lot of moving parts, a lot of people involved, actually a lot of different companies, and if one thing breaks down from farm to grocery store, the whole thing turns into an enormous, foul-smelling hair ball real quickly. So basically what I do is to look at all the steps in the process and try to figure out if there is some way we can do them faster, better, less expensively, or more efficiently.[1]

See how much more clear and interesting that was. Sure, it took a little longer (30 seconds longer, by my estimation). But so what? Who would rather endure 10 seconds of unhelpful, overly scripted boredom than 40 seconds of a genuine, conversational, and even entertaining story that actually answers the question? More important, which of those two types of answers is likely to get you invited to the buyer's office for a sales call? Exactly.

So, if your "what I do for a living" answer sounds more like the first response above, you have some work to do. Fortunately, this is one of the easiest stories to develop that you'll come across in this book. (We're starting simple.) The reason it's so easy is that—as you might have noticed—it's completely made up. It's a fictional story based on a hypothetical situation. So, unlike the typical stories we'll be discussing in this book, you won't need to rack your brain to remember the details or hunt down the exact facts of the case. Just rely on your knowledge of the business and the typical type of problems your company tends to solve, and create a plausible storyline around it.

You know you've got it about right when you can tell the story to your mom, your spouse, or your kids and they can understand what you do for a living. So, your first homework assignment is to develop this kind of story for yourself. Here's how. Start by inventing a main character who's in a typical industry you serve ("Suppose you're in the chicken business"). Then describe a plausible series of events ("get the chicken from the farm to the retail store") that results in the problem your product or service is designed to fix ("the whole thing turns into an enormous, foul-smelling hair ball"). Finish with a one-sentence description of what you do to solve that problem ("So basically what I do is to look at all the steps in the process and try to figure out if there is some way we can do them faster, better . . ."). Don't worry about the structure and format of your story yet. You'll learn all of the nuts and bolts of how to craft compelling sales stories in Part II. For now, just get some of the details and ideas down on paper. You'll come back to them later to turn them into a great story.

Once you get some experience telling this kind of story, you can start ad-libbing the details based on the industry of the person you're talking to. When they ask you what you do for a living, start by asking them what business they're in. Then build your story around it: "Oh, you're in the pharmaceutical business. Then you've got super-expensive product in your inventory chain all the time, and if a customer has too much, some of it could expire and have to be thrown away."

EXPLAINING WHOM YOU'VE HELPED AND HOW

The second type of story generally told at this stage of the relationship goes deeper than the first one. It provides real examples of customers you've helped and how you've helped them. As sales consultant Mike Weinberg explains, "Your goal with stories at this stage is to entice the prospect into meeting with you—to give them a glimpse of what they'll miss out on if they don't talk to you later."

Here's a real example of what that looks like when it's done well from the perspective of a prospect. In this case, that prospect is Quave Burton, a global procurement executive at Abercrombie & Fitch.

In July 2015, Quave attended a strategic sourcing forum in Newport

Beach, California. Part of the conference included a networking exercise the attendees jokingly refer to as "speed dating." Buyers and sellers chose whom they'd most like to meet during the networking period. Then they got 30 minutes with each one at a table before rotating to the next one. One of Quave's six "dates" that day was Ben Koberna, CEO of Electronic Auction Services, Inc. (EASI). EASI runs reverse auction services for buyers. The company essentially gets multiple suppliers to bid on the contract to supply whatever it is the buyer needs. Quave's responsibilities are primarily buying indirect goods and services for Abercrombie. That's everything Abercrombie buys for its stores that does *not* become a part of the clothing: utilities, travel services, IT software and hardware, etc. And that's exactly the kind of items EASI has the most experience with, which is why Ben wanted to meet with Quave.

But that day, Quave wanted to know if the same kind of reverse auction could work for services or direct materials. EASI had almost no experience with the direct side. So, in order to convince her it would be worth her time to meet with him later, Ben would have to take one of the only experiences EASI had with direct materials auctions and make it work for him. As a result, he told her about his experience with a world-famous luxury clothier headquartered in New York:

> They normally deal with three suppliers for their cashmere program—two in Scotland and one in Italy. But this year, they received a fourth bid, from a manufacturer in China. Their normal suppliers usually bid between $165 and $175 per roll. But the Chinese supplier's bid came in at $125 a roll. On a $3 million program, that 30 percent savings would be huge, so it was going to be almost impossible to turn down.
>
> They place a premium on quality, not just price. In fact, they have a rigorous process to test all the raw materials they buy. The "spinners" at the suppliers send them a sample of cashmere. Then they take it to their knitters to make it into something. And the knitters then test it for wear to see how quickly it pills. They'd already tested the Chinese fabric and it tested very well. What they couldn't know was if that quality would be reliably delivered.
>
> But with a $1 million savings staring them in the face, that consideration was at risk of getting pushed to a smaller part of the equation.

What they needed to know was what were the best prices available from all their suppliers so they could determine if the risk of going with the Chinese supplier would that be worth the savings.

So that's exactly what we helped them do. Since the Chinese supplier was obviously going to be the low bidder, we ran a reverse auction that really just included the other three bidders. We put in the $125 bid once at the beginning so they would all know there was another supplier that had a low bid. But the goal was really to get the other three to sharpen their pencils. We contacted all of the suppliers and explained how the process would work. Then over the course of about 45 minutes, we ran the auction. Each supplier had several chances to bid and rebid as the price dropped.

At the end of the time, all three suppliers had lowered their bids, but not enough to match the Chinese bid. But that didn't matter. The auction had given them a true picture of the market pricing. Plus, EASI's process also collects other information about the suppliers their client might not normally have access to. And that's when their procurement director really got to earn a seat at the decision-making table. In a normal situation, the product people and the CFO might have negotiated among themselves. But the auction process gave procurement a bigger role to play than usual.

And that's all Quave needed to hear. She made arrangements to meet with Ben the next week for a full demonstration of EASI's service. And she still had 15 minutes of her "speed date" left to grab a coffee.

If you don't have your own story like this, get one. It's the shortest path from "Hello, nice to meet you" to "When's a good day for me to stop by your office?"

EXERCISES

1. Invent a "What I do, simply" story.

   a. Use the "Suppose you're in the chicken business" story from earlier in this chapter as a guide to model your story after.

b. Choose a fictional main character in a typical industry you serve.

c. List a plausible series of events that leads to the problem your product or service is designed to fix.

d. Briefly describe what that problem looks like to the customer.

e. Write one sentence to describe what you or your company does to help fix that problem.

2. Develop a "Whom I've helped and how" story.

a. Use Ben Koberna's story about the cashmere auction from earlier in this chapter as a guide.

b. Choose an actual client in a typical industry you serve. (You don't need to reveal the client's name.)

c. Sketch out a brief outline of the events that led up to the client's needing your product or service—in other words, the background and the problem or opportunity the client encountered. (Include just the basic facts for now. In Part II, you'll work on turning it into a proper story.)

d. List the main steps of what you or your product did for the client.

e. Explain the outcome in terms of how it benefited the customer (e.g., "And that's when the procurement director really got a seat at the decision-making table").

4

STORIES YOU TELL YOURSELF

I N 2008, ADAM Grant, a Wharton management professor and social psychologist, conducted a very telling study.[1] He and two research assistants went to an outbound call center where a fund-raising organization was raising money for a major university. They divided the callers into three random groups. Ten minutes prior to starting their shift, the first and second groups were asked to report to the break room, where they were asked to read stories. The third group (the control group) was left to report to work on time as usual.

The first group, which we'll call the "benefit to others" group, read stories that were written by students at the university who'd received scholarships funded by the money raised at the call center. For example, one story was by an engineering student who wrote about how the scholarship allowed him to pursue his education and participate in a number of extracurricular activities.

The second group, which we'll call the "benefit to me" group, read stories written by previous call center employees describing how their jobs at the call center had made a difference in their careers. For example, one story was about how the call center experience helped an employee get a lucrative job in the real estate business.

These story sessions were conducted two nights in a row. Each caller's success in fund-raising for a week following the intervention was recorded and compared to how the caller did a week prior to reading the stories. The results showed that both the control group and the "benefit to me" group had no significant change in the number of pledges or the total money raised. But the "benefit to others" group more than doubled both the number of pledges and the total money raised.

The obvious conclusion Grant and his team reached was the power of storytelling on the sales performance of the fund-raisers. However, not just any stories will do. Stories that highlight how important their job is to them personally had no effect. But stories about how much good they were doing for other people—stories that gave their work a noble purpose—had a tremendous effect.

Many professional salespeople have learned this lesson on their own. So, unlike every other chapter in this book, this one is not about stories salespeople tell during meetings with the buyer. Instead, it's about stories people tell during meetings with themselves. Many of the salespeople I interviewed admitted to this kind of self-storytelling, usually through inner monologue, that helped them in several ways. The most notable reason was to motivate themselves to do well in their next sales call, just like the call center fund-raisers who benefited from Grant's stories in his study. A beautiful case in point follows.

STORIES FOR MOTIVATION

In her inspiring book *Selling with Noble Purpose,* sales consultant Lisa McLeod recounts a conversation she had with a top sales rep at a major biotech company.[2] Lisa asked the rep, "What do you think about when you go on sales calls? What's going on in your head?" Lisa writes that the rep sheepishly admitted the following:

> When I go on sales calls, I always think about this particular patient who came up to me one day during a call on a doctor's office.
>
> I was standing in the hallway talking to one of the doctors. I was wearing my company name badge, so I stood out. All of a sudden this elderly woman taps me on the shoulder.
>
> "Excuse me, Miss," she said. "Are you from the company that makes drug x?"

"Yes, ma'am."

"I just want to thank you," she said. "Before my doctor prescribed your drug, I barely had enough energy to leave the house. But now I can visit my grandkids; I can get down on the floor to play with them. I can travel. So thank you. You gave me back my life."

Lisa writes that the sales rep told her, "I think about that woman every day. If it's 4:30 on a rainy Friday afternoon, other sales reps go home. I don't. I make the extra sales call because I know I'm not just pitching a product. I'm saving people's lives. That grandmother is my higher purpose."

FINDING YOUR PERSONAL MOTIVATION STORY

Motivational speaker and sales guru Zig Ziglar reminded his audiences that "Sales isn't something you do *to* someone. It's something you do *for* someone." In other words, if you do your job properly, you're doing people a great service. In fact, Ziglar went further to suggest salespeople "think of themselves as an assistant buyer," helping buyers find what they need and what's best for them.[3]

If you don't have one already, you need your own personal motivation story like the biotech rep's story above—one that can remind you that you're actually doing your clients a great service. Here's how to get started:

Think about a time when you made a real difference for one of your customers. This would be a time you went above and beyond what was expected of you or when what was expected of you resulted in an extraordinary success for your customer.

Recall the situation that surrounded it. What problem did the customer come to you with? What was your first reaction? Your second? How did you solve the problem for them? What did they say to you when you delivered the solution? How did it make them feel?

Finally, think about the moment when you realized that what you had done made an extraordinary difference to the customer. Was it the words that they said to you? The tone of their voice? The sincere look in their eyes? The complimentary note they wrote to your boss? The "supplier of the year" award that was handed to you on stage? Something else? And how did you feel at that moment? Close your eyes and think through that moment. That moment is the climax of the story you're going to create. Write down all of the events leading up to that moment and how it felt to know in that instant how important you were to that customer. This is your personal motivation story.

STORIES TO RELAX AND TAKE THE STRESS OUT OF THE CALL

Another purpose of self-storytelling is to relax and take the stress out of the sales call. I came across the most amusing and perhaps most effective example of this in authors Paul Lanigan and Denis Goodbody's *Soft Tales and Hard Asses.* Their fictional main character observes:

> Over the years I've learned to focus on all the positives and remind myself why I'm there in the first place. One of the most valuable techniques I have—it sounds a bit crazy at first, but it makes sense—is to tell myself that I am financially independent and I don't need this deal. I've found that, by adopting this mindset, I relax more and care less. Instead of living with the burden of the whole company's future, and that of its workforce, on my shoulders, I become a gentleman of means indulging in some sport.[4]

I've tried running that story through in my head myself before a sales call with a potential speaking or training client. It really does create a different attitude and tone in your voice. Instead of sounding like a desperate salesperson, you sound like a trusted consultant and adviser. It's perhaps another way of following Zig Ziglar's advice to become the assistant buyer, not the salesperson. Both are more relaxed and stress-free roles.

This doesn't have to be your story. But if it's not, what would work for you? What story can you ruminate on before a sales call that will help you relax and take the stress out of selling?

EXERCISES

1. *Find your own motivational sales story.* Think about a time you went above and beyond what was expected of you and made an extraordinary difference for your client. Turn that into a story you tell yourself before every call.

2. *Think of a story that helps you relax and takes the stress out of selling.* An example would be stories that help you think of yourself as the assistant buyer instead of the salesperson (as Zig Ziglar suggested). Lanigan and Goodbody's story about a "gentleman of means" is another good example.

5

GETTING BUYERS TO TELL THEIR STORY

YOUR FIRST OBJECTIVE in a sales call should be to get buyers to tell you their stories, not the other way around. If you don't hear their stories first, how will you know which of your stories to tell?

Sales guru Mike Weinberg explains with a memorable analogy: "You wouldn't trust a physician who walked into the examining room, spent an hour telling you how great he was, and then wrote a prescription, would you?"[1] Of course not. Then why would a buyer accept the recommendation of a salesperson who did the same thing?

So you need to get buyers talking early on. You want them to do some of that talking in the form of stories, and for many of the same reasons we discussed in Chapter 2: It will help you relax and listen better, help you build a better relationship with them, and help you better remember what they say. And when the story they tell is about the problem they're facing, it helps you understand the context, characters, and complications so you'll have a better idea of the opportunity you're up against.

The good news is that getting buyers to tell their story won't be hard since people want to tell their own stories. Even so, there are some successful strategies top salespeople use to draw those stories out. But first let's talk about what kind of stories you need them to tell. In talking to procurement professionals, I learned that there are three main kinds of stories they think you should want buyers to tell you.

First are personal stories about them to help you get to know them better as people. I'll elaborate on these in the next chapter when we discuss stories you need to tell to build rapport.

The second type of story is about the biggest problems buyers are facing that you might be able to help them with. These stories not only get them to identify the kind of solution they want you to sell them—they also give you most of what you need to know how to sell that solution to them. If they just tell you, "I'm looking for a more efficient warehousing network," you really know very little about what they need. But if they tell you a story about how the last shipment they made went out late because they couldn't find the right product in their warehouse so they had to run a custom production schedule and then ship the product express delivery, only to then find the original product right where it was supposed to be all along, etc., well, now you know what you're dealing with.

The third type of story you want to hear from buyers is about how a particular supplier became their favorite supplier. This is where you really start to learn something of long-term value to your relationship. Anyone can tell you that he wants his suppliers to be flexible and available and responsive. You were already planning on being those things. The story, though, gives you a glimpse into how to go from good to great in his mind—a tangible example of what excellence looks like to him.

One procurement manager remarked, "Nobody is going to tell you their favorite supplier is the one who caves on price more than all the others." Instead, you're going to hear a story like the following one.

On May 21, 2011, Iceland's Grímsvötn volcano had its largest eruption in 50 years and continued erupting for four days.[2] The plume of ash and smoke rose 12 miles high and eventually spread across much of Europe. Air travel to and from cities across the northern half of the continent were canceled, delayed, or diverted to alternate destinations.

Iceland closed its airports almost immediately after the eruption. Denmark closed its airspace below 21,000 feet the next day. By the third day, more than 1,600 flights were canceled in Scotland, England, Wales, Sweden, and Ireland. Day four saw 600 more affected flights in Germany. All told, it was more than a week before many stranded passengers reached their destinations, making this one of the largest natural disruptions to global air traffic on record.

While all of this was occurring in Europe, 6,000 miles away in Redmond, Washington, Microsoft was just concluding a sales planning meeting with more than 200 of its leaders from around the world. Many of those leaders were now stranded and couldn't get home. And as long as the volcano continued erupting, there was no way to tell how long the problem was going to last. All of a sudden, Microsoft's travel department had a huge problem.

Working with their main travel consultants, they went to work on the situation. John Stephens, Microsoft's senior director of strategic sourcing, described the work this way: "First, find out who's stranded (about 180 different people). Second, let them know we're on it. Third, extend their local hotel reservations so they don't get thrown out while they're waiting for flights home. Fourth, get them office space nearby to remain productive during the delay. And last, but most importantly, figure out how to get them home as quick as possible."

All of that, of course, would be an administrative nightmare. After quickly taking care of priorities one through four, the travel department turned their attention to number five. But with flights to northern Europe canceled, and flights to southern Europe overbooked, they had to find a third alternative. Their solution? They chartered a Boeing 767 aircraft to fly all 180 stranded travelers to Madrid, Spain, where the airports were still open.

Then, while the passengers were en route, the travel department arranged 180 separate ground transportation packages to individual cities across Europe by car, bus, train, and boat. By the time the plane landed, every passenger had received a text with his or her ground transportation itinerary. Microsoft's travel team leader and the head of its travel supplier happened to be in Paris at the time. The pair rented a car and drove twelve hours straight to be in Madrid when the plane touched down to make sure everything went smoothly.

John recalls not sleeping for a full 48 hours that week working to make sure everyone got home safely. And he recalls his travel consultants doing the same. Perhaps most tellingly, he said of that travel partner, "They did all of that amazing round-the-clock work without ever once mentioning the fees they would need to pull it all off. They just said, 'We'll figure all that out later. Let's get your people home first.'"

John tells this story to salespeople at existing suppliers as well as potential ones—even suppliers not in the travel business. Why? "Because it communicates to them what real partnering looks like," he says. It also shows a supplier what it looks like to have the right focus on priorities (getting people home) and to demonstrate trust that the money will all work itself out. Of course, he could just tell salespeople that Microsoft values all those attributes in a supplier. But the story does a much better job of explaining it.

After hearing a story like that, potential suppliers are in a much better position to understand what success looks like to the customer. And therefore, they're in a much better position to win the business.

FIVE WAYS TO GET BUYERS TO OPEN UP AND TELL YOU STORIES

Getting your buyers to talk is easy. Getting them to tell you stories requires a little more work. Here are five tactics being used effectively by successful salespeople.

1. Shut Up and Listen

This is probably the most obvious but underutilized tactic to elicit stories from buyers. Human beings abhor silence in a conversation like nature abhors a vacuum. We're desperate to fill the void with *something*. If you can resist the temptation for that something to be your voice, you have a near certain chance of that something being the buyer's voice. And the more space you give buyers to talk, the more likely they are to tell you a story. When buyers are fighting to get a word in edgewise between the lines of your sales pitch, they'll offer short statements and commentary. Give them room to tell a story and they probably will.

2. Ask Questions That Require a Story for an Answer

If you ask yes or no questions, you'll get yes or no answers. Just asking questions isn't enough. You have to ask the right kind of questions. Here are some tips.

First, *ask mostly open-ended questions instead of closed-ended questions*. Closed-ended questions can be answered with a simple, specific piece of information. Such questions include yes or no questions but aren't limited to them. Open-ended questions require lengthier, more full discussions, and they usually lead to a story.

For example, "What's your number one problem area right now?" is a closed-ended question. The answer would be given in the form of a word or two, like "productivity" or "employee morale." So then you'd have to probe more deeply and say, "Tell me about that." That would get you perhaps a full sentence, like "Well, our employee satisfaction scores have been going down for six months." That forces you to dig more and say, "Really, why do you think that is?" and so on. There's nothing wrong with that line of questioning. You should use it often. But just don't expect it to yield a story.

Compare that to an open-ended question designed to elicit a story: "When did you know for sure that you had a real problem on your hands?" That question is more likely to elicit a story: "Oh, that would have to be the day that Frank walked out and took two of my best engineers with him. You see, everyone knew he'd been hoping for the shift supervisor job for over a year. But then . . ."

Second, *ask about specific events in time*. Having conducted literally hundreds of in-depth, one-on-one interviews with executives when I was looking for stories, I've learned that simply asking people to tell you stories is not an effective strategy. That's because most people don't think of their best stories as "stories." They think of them as events in their lives. That became clear to me early in the research process for my first book.[3] After spending an hour or two in an interview with an executive, I would write a draft of one of the stories I had heard and send it to her for feedback. One of the most insightful responses I got was, "Oh, I didn't know that's what you were looking for. That's not really a story. That's just something that happened to me one time."

Exactly—that's what a story is. If you want to hear a story, don't ask someone to tell you a story. Ask her to tell you about something that happened: "Tell me about how you ended up in your current job . . . What led up to losing your last major customer? . . . Really, the board fired the CEO? What led up to that?"

Third, *use "problem prompts."* Ask about specific problems you think your prospects might have with their current supplier. For example, as Rick Rhine of Tailwind Marketing explains:

> If you're selling high-speed Internet service, asking "Do you like your current Internet service?" won't get you any stories. But if you ask "Have you ever noticed that your Internet slows down after dinner?" your prospect is likely to launch into a story about the last time that happened: "Oh yeah, it does! Last Monday night I had all the guys over for the football game. In the middle of the first quarter, it started to buffer every few seconds. It got so bad, we had to go to Jim's house to finish the game. It was embarrassing for me, and Jim's wife wasn't too happy with us either . . ."

Fourth, *ask "day in the life" questions.* These work for stories about the past, present, or future. For example, "Tell me what a typical day is like for your junior team members. What did they do yesterday?" or "A year from now, if everything is going perfectly, what would your day be like? Walk me through that." This is also a great way to get a glimpse of the buyer's vision for the future and how you might be a part of it.

3. Ask About Something Personal in the Buyer's Office

This is perhaps the oldest and most leveraged method for eliciting (and telling) stories. People generally reserve their shrinking desk and wall space for items of high personal value. Each one likely has many stories behind it that people are eager to tell. Sometimes it's as simple as saying "Tell me about that" when pointing to one of them, and a story comes pouring out.

4. Get Buyers Away from the Office

Jeff Strong is executive vice president of Sun Products and has close to three decades of experience in sales. He explains that when buyers are in their office, they're busy and have their game face on. They're worrying about hitting their numbers this month and are already starting to think about the meetings they'll have with the next three salespeople who'll walk in today after you leave. They're more likely to have time and mental space to share stories if they're out of the office.

In the old days, the solution that most salespeople could count on was plenty of time on the golf course with their prospects to share stories and close deals. In some circles, that's still the case. But the faster pace of business today and stricter conflict-of-interest policies have cut down on a lot of that.

Now, a day on the golf course can be replaced by more business-focused time spent with you on a market visit, walking retail stores, taking manufacturing plant tours, or attending industry conferences. Plus, there are the hours of time you both spend in cars, trains, and planes getting to and from those places.

5. Tell Your Stories First

If all else fails, lead by example. If you want to get buyers to tell personal stories about where they grew up, you tell a personal story about where you grew up. If you want them to tell a story about a problem they're having with their computer, you tell a story about a problem you're having with your computer. You know this works because it works on you. When people tell you a story, the most likely thing that's running through your head is "Hey, something like that happened to me once," and now you can't wait to tell them about it. Just remember, when the buyer interrupts and starts telling you his story, refer back to tactic #1 above. Shut up and listen.

EXERCISES

1. *Create a list of questions* to elicit the following stories from your buyers. In your next meeting, ask them for:
   - Personal stories to help you get to know them better
   - Stories about the biggest problems they're facing, so you can get a concrete idea of how you might help them
   - Stories about how their favorite suppliers became their favorite suppliers, so you can become the next one

2. *Draft planning notes for your next meeting* to get your buyer to open up and tell you stories instead of facts. These notes should include:

> a. *Shut up and listen.* Leave some silent space in the conversation with room for the buyer to fill with a story.

> b. *Require a story for an answer.*
>> ▪ Ask open-ended questions instead of short-answer or yes/no questions.
>> ▪ Ask about specific events in time (What happened last year when . . . ?").
>> ▪ Use "problem prompts" ("Have you ever noticed that your Internet slows down after dinner?").
>> ▪ Ask "day in the life" questions ("Tell me what a typical day is like for one of your team members today? A year from now?").

3. *Plan to get your buyer away from the office.* Think of three specific opportunities to do that this year (for example, a market visit, a tour of retail stores or manufacturing plants, or attending a conference with you).

4. *Create a list of your own stories* that demonstrate the three stories you want to hear from the buyer. Your buyer will respond to hearing your story by telling a similar one of her own:
> ▪ Personal "get to know you" story
> ▪ "Biggest problem" story
> ▪ "Favorite supplier (or customer)" story

6

BUILDING RAPPORT

NOW THAT YOU'VE gotten buyers to tell their stories, it's time to share yours. These include stories about you personally, as well as stories about your company. Buyers tend to do business with people they like and trust—people they're comfortable with. That's why building trust and rapport with a potential buyer is usually the earliest objective a salesperson has. And as discussed in Chapter 2, storytelling is the quickest way to do that. It helps people get to know you more intimately than reading your resume, and more quickly than spending a lifetime together. The chief sourcing officer at Huntington National Bank, Debbie Manos-McHenry, explains, "These kind of stories won't make me buy something I don't need. But they sure do take obstacles out of the conversation."

Telling these "stories about me" is not the same as telling people where you went to school or where you grew up. You don't need to read a book to tell you how to do that. You'll do that anyway. Rather, these are stories to take people beyond your bio. There are five of these stories you can, and should, have in your repertoire of stories to tell.

●　　●　　●

1. "WHY I DO WHAT I DO" STORIES

The major premise of Simon Sinek's bestselling book *Start with Why* can be summarized in his statement "People don't buy what you do; they buy why you do it."[1] It should make sense, then, that in order to know you well enough to trust you, a buyer needs to understand why you do what you do for a living. What drew you to the profession or the company you work for? The reasons say something about who you are as a person. And the passion you show, or lack thereof, will influence the buyer's natural affection for you. After all, who doesn't want to do business with someone who's passionate about what they do? As such, this should be one of your earliest stories. Here's an example.

Chris Powers had wanted to make partner at the public accounting and consulting firm Crowe Horwath since the day he joined the company. Eight years later, in 1998, his dream was about to come true. He'd made the cut. All the hard work and late hours had paid off. The promotion was scheduled to go through on April 1 of that year, a day he'd been waiting for with much anticipation. When it finally arrived, he walked into his boss's office . . . and resigned.

"What the hell? Are you crazy?" was the response. What could make him do such a thing? The answer was Keith Krach. Keith was the co-founder and CEO of Ariba, one of the early pioneers of using the Internet to streamline the procurement process. Keith met with Chris and offered him a job as one of Ariba's first sales reps. It obviously wasn't the job title that lured Chris away. So what was it? Chris explains:

> My dad was a high school basketball coach. He played for John Wooden in both high school and college. So I grew up loving sports, and I played them all. Once I started my career after school, I started to miss the fun and camaraderie of the team environment, of playing together as a team, and winning together.
>
> Keith must have had similar experiences, because in our first conversation, he convinced me of three things that made it impossible to say no to him. First, he said, "We're going to work hard, but we're going to have fun doing it." He made it clear that I was going to be part of a culture that sounded like the one I was missing from sports.

Second, he showed me that Ariba had game-changing technology that was really going to impact how businesses bought and sold from one another—and how we could help them do that faster, more reliably, and save them money at the same time. The Internet was still new and absolutely nobody was doing what they were doing. That was really exciting to me.

Third, he said I was personally going to be able to influence my customers and their business results like I was as a consultant, but that I would be doing it as part of a real team effort.

Chris explained that the sort of sales call he would conduct at Ariba wasn't the typical solo salesperson in the room with a buyer. It was usually two or three people from Ariba in the room with the buyer, all with specific roles to play, just like in sports.

"It was a no-brainer," Chris said. "I signed up and traded in my partnership to become employee #92 in a company that grew to over 2,000. And it was absolutely the best decision I ever made."

One of Chris's early customers was Debbie Manos-McHenry, then director of operations at KeyBank in Cleveland. She recalls listening to Chris tell his story in one of their first meetings. She described it as both inspired and inspiring (When's the last time a buyer described your opening words in a meeting as "inspiring"?), and explained Ariba's team selling effort in equally glowing terms. She said it reminded her of the E.F. Hutton TV commercials from the 1970s, where someone in a crowded restaurant starts to share with a friend what her E.F. Hutton adviser told her, and everyone in the restaurant turns silent and leans in to listen. But in this case, Debbie said, she was the one who felt like E.F. Hutton, because all the Ariba people in the room were intently listening to her. The team environment Chris was craving wasn't just working for him. It was working for Debbie, too.

More importantly for our purposes, their very successful business relationship started with a compelling story about why Chris Powers took the job he did.

What's your story?

2. "I'LL TELL YOU WHEN I CAN'T HELP YOU" STORIES

One of the things I learned from interviewing professional buyers was that there are two things salespeople can do to immediately earn buyers' trust and credibility. In the words one buyer used to explain it, "First, tell me when you can*not* help me. And second, tell me when you made a mistake before I find out from someone else."

Here's the logic behind the first one: If you're honest enough to tell buyers when your company is *not* well suited for a particular need they have, they're more likely to believe you when you tell them you *are* the best solution. The only problem with that situation is that it may not occur until after you and the buyer have been doing business together for a while. That's where storytelling comes in handy. Even if you haven't yet come across a problem they have that you can't solve, you can instill in them a sense of confidence that you would tell them if that situation does arise. You can't accomplish that by just telling them, "Of course, I'll always tell you when I'm not the best option for you." But you can do that through a story about a time you have done that with another customer.

Jamie Lancaster, vice president of indirect sourcing at Kroger, describes what that looks like in practice. Back in 2001 when he worked at Fifth Third Bank, they were wrestling with an IT problem and called in two suppliers to ask for potential solutions. Jamie says:

> The first guy answered every question I asked with, "Yeah, we can do that!" He thought his confidence was reassuring me. In fact, it was having the opposite effect. These weren't the most common problems. If he thinks he already has all the answers, maybe he doesn't really understand the questions.
>
> The second guy that came in was very different. He asked good questions, acknowledged how tough the problems were. And he said things like, "I've not seen that before. Let me see how we could fix it." I could tell he was actually trying to solve the problem in his head instead of focusing on closing the sale.

The other benefit of this humbler approach is that it acknowledged to Jamie that Fifth Third was on the cutting edge in some way. If the bank's problems stumped the expert solutions salesman, they must be out front. Paying your buyer an honestly deserved compliment like this usually doesn't hurt.

Not surprisingly, Jamie gave the business to the second guy.

If you've ever done anything like the second salesperson in Jamie's story, craft a story about it and have it ready to share with your next prospect. And if you haven't done anything like this before, you should start. Otherwise, you're the first guy.

3. "I'LL TELL YOU WHEN I MADE A MISTAKE" STORIES

The second way to immediately earn trust and credibility with your buyer is to admit you made a mistake before the buyer hears about it from someone else. If you admit your own mistakes, they're more likely to find out sooner when they have a problem.

Here again, you could just say, "Yeah, I've made mistakes before, but I always own up to them." But that's not believable. Through storytelling, though, you can show buyers that experience with a previous client, so they'll have good reason to believe you'd be just as honest with them.

If you've ever owned up to a mistake to a buyer, craft a story around it and have that "I'll tell you when I made a mistake" story ready to tell at your next sales call.

4. "I'LL GO TO BAT FOR YOU WITH MY COMPANY" STORIES

A fourth type of "stories about me" is one to convince buyers that, when necessary, you're willing to go to bat for them with your own company leadership.

Of course, that doesn't mean you should always cave in on every request from buyers. Although they might not complain about it, most buyers would admit that they wouldn't respect a salesperson who did that. But they won't do business long with someone who never does. The truth is that in disagreements between supplier and customer, sometimes one side has a better argument and sometimes the other does. Most buyers want a sales rep who can engage in a fair-minded assessment of the disagreement and passionately lobby on their behalf when the buyer is right.

Like not hiding from your mistakes, you can't just tell your prospects, "I'll go to bat for you." And if you wait around for them to learn that on their own, you might not ever land them as a client. The best solution is to share the story of when you've done that before. Here's a case in point.

In 2012, Xerox was in a sticky situation with Huntington National Bank. Xerox was in the middle of a five-year agreement to provide Huntington with its printer, copier, and paper needs. Huntington was looking for ways to save money on office expenses and asked Xerox for some ideas to reduce paper usage. The problem with that, of course, was that it would mean lower revenues for Xerox. So the Xerox people told Huntington that they would do so, but only after the end of the current contract.

So the folks at Huntington did what most people would do in that situation. They figured out a way to reduce their paper usage on their own—25 percent less, as it turned out. Facing a significant loss of income on that account, Xerox invoked a provision in the contract to raise the price per page if volume fell below a certain level. That, of course, didn't sit well with Huntington, which refused to pay the higher price and threatened to cancel the contract entirely.

The result was exactly the kind of stalemate that puts salespeople in a bad spot. What's a good account rep to do? Demand the customer abide by the contract and pay up? Or go to bat for the customer at headquarters and try to get the contract changed?

Well, the guy Xerox put in that spot was Eric Storey. Eric met with parties at both companies, investigated the facts, and made a fair-minded assessment of the situation. Among other things, he discovered that Xerox was already providing new customers with the kind of innovation that Huntington was asking for—the kind that reduces paper usage significantly. Xerox just wasn't offering it to Huntington yet because they were in the middle of the contract.

Both sides felt thoroughly justified in their position. But it was this last fact that convinced Eric that Xerox should back down. He went to his leadership, lobbied hard, and eventually convinced them that he was right. Xerox rescinded the price increase, and accepted the revenue reduction that came with it, earning the good will and respect of a valued customer.

When Eric shares this story with new prospects, they can be confident that when the situation calls for it, he'll go to bat for them, too.

5. "I'M NOT WHO YOU THINK I AM" STORIES

The last type of "stories about me" that professional salespeople often find useful is an "I'm not who you think I am" story. It helps get rid of negative preconceptions about you. And apparently just being in sales is sometimes enough to create negative preconceptions. A yearbook sales manager we'll call "Brad" is a prime example of why you might need such a story.

Prior to his yearbook sales job, Brad spent eight years teaching high school English and journalism in Nebraska. He was also the yearbook adviser, so he knew firsthand how big a role the publisher's sales rep plays in the yearbook publishing process and how much of a hassle it is to change to a new publisher or even just a new rep.

But when Brad moved out of state in 2004 to take the yearbook sales job, he learned how those facts would make it difficult for him to get off to a good start. Yearbook publishing is highly competitive, with four well-resourced players in the high school yearbook market. In his first two months on the job, Brad learned that his competitors had things like this to say about *him* to his customers and prospects: "You know, that new rep isn't going to be around long . . . He came from teaching, and he'll probably go back . . . He's from Nebraska; you know his kids will miss it and want to go back home soon . . . They won't like it here anyway . . . You really don't want to work with him. It'll be such a hassle for you when he quits next year."

Brad needed a way to combat that negative equity with anyone who'd heard it already. But perhaps even more importantly, he needed a subtle way to preempt its impact with anyone who hadn't heard it yet. Imagine trying to tell prospects in a meeting, "Hey, just in case anyone tries to tell you that I'm going to quit and go back to teaching, don't believe them." Not only would that sound paranoid and desperate, but it might plant a bad idea in their heads that they never would have had.

The better solution was the story that Brad started telling in his introductory meetings with new prospects. He said:

> I left an eight-year teaching career, not because I was unhappy. I just wanted a new challenge. And after serving as the yearbook adviser all those years, this seemed like a natural fit. Sure, it was a little scary for all four of us to move hundreds of miles away from home. But we found a house we really like. The neighborhood is great—a lot of other couples with kids the same age as ours. We got our kids enrolled in school and they love it. They're already making new friends. And we found a church that's similar to the one we used to attend in Nebraska. So that's comfortable for us.
>
> And for me, personally, I absolutely love this new job. The company's been great to me, and I love working in yearbooks. I've been in the shoes of the customers I call on, and I know what they're going through. So I know I can help them better than whoever they're working with now. Who wouldn't love that? I guess what I'm saying is that my whole family is all in. We love it here and we're not going back.

After hearing that story, nobody would think Brad would even consider going back.

When crafting your "I'm not who you think I am" story, first consider what the most likely negative preconceptions your new customers or prospects are likely to have about you. Can't think of anything? Ask your boss, your peers, your predecessor, and even your most trusted customers (that's how Brad found out). They'll know.

Then think of a situation that demonstrates the opposite conclusion and craft a story around it. Don't worry about getting it perfect now. Just get the basics down. We'll work on perfecting your stories in Part II.

6. STORIES ABOUT YOUR COMPANY

Once your buyers understand who you are and what you're all about, they'll want to know about the company you represent. Just like you, your company has a resume of facts. And just like you, your company should have stories for when you're ready to get past the facts—at least two of them.

1. Founding Stories

One such story that every salesperson should have is your company's founding story. It introduces your buyer to the person who started your company and helps them see and feel why it was started in the first place.

Imagine you work for the active travel company Backroads. Consider the following two ways you might try to explain to someone who that company is. Here's Version A:

> Backroads is the world's #1 active travel company. We've been in business for 36 years since our CEO, Tom Hale, founded the company in 1979. From our first trips in California, today we operate in 48 countries around the world. Each year, our 500 leaders take more than 29,000 guests on at least 2,000 exciting trips.
>
> You could be hiking or biking or kayaking, but wherever you are, you won't be bored. From our expert trip designers and engaging leaders to our skilled bike mechanics and stellar guest service team, quality is woven into the philosophy and fabric of our company. We call it guest focus, and we aim to be the most guest-focused company out there.

Now compare that to Version B:

> When our founder, Tom Hale, was a kid, he wasn't much of a fan of mass tourism. You know, big theme parks where people are shuffled around in herds and stand in line for hours just for a three-minute ride. He felt like he was trapped in an artificial, sedentary environment with a bunch of strangers.
>
> Then when he grew up, his first job out of college was in a big office building in Las Vegas. Six months into it, he realized his job was a lot like those vacations he never liked as a kid: trapped in a huge artificial city, working long hours in the same spot, surrounded by lots of people he didn't know.
>
> Then one night he woke up at 2 a.m. with an idea. And by 8 o'clock the next morning, he'd sketched out a plan for a more exciting career for himself, and a better vacation experience for everyone else. And that's when Backroads was born.

His idea was to thoughtfully plan out authentic, active, outdoor experiences, in naturally beautiful locations, in small groups that *you*
help select. That way, whether you're hiking, biking, kayaking, or
something else, it's never fake, you'll never get bored, and you'll always
be among friends.

Notice what neither of these versions do. Neither does a great job of
explaining exactly what Backroads *does*. That's intentional. This isn't
your product story. We'll cover that in the next chapter. This is just
supposed to introduce your prospects to your company, its purpose,
and its values, and to do so in a way that's interesting and leaves them
wanting to know more. Version B does that because it's a story. Version
A does not.

2. "How We're Different from Our Competitors" Stories

A second story about your company that salespeople need is one that
explains how your company is different from your competitors. Procurement people will tell you (like they told me) that competitors in
every space are so similar that it's difficult to tell them apart. They
need a "differentiation" story—which means *you* need a differentiation
story. For a good example of what that looks like, I turned to Joanna
Martinez, former chief procurement officer at Cushman & Wakefield
in New York, one of the world's largest real estate services companies.

Joanna has recommended lots of cleaning companies to service the
hundreds of buildings Cushman & Wakefield manages for its clients.
But for every one she's selected to recommend, there are dozens more
vying for those contracts that she didn't recommend. When asked for
an example of a story that makes one cleaning company stand out
from the rest, she tells the story she heard from Sharad Madison, CEO
of United Building Maintenance (UBM).

"To understand Sharad's story," she says, "you first have to understand that many of our clients have diversity programs for their purchases contracts. They're targeting a certain percentage of their
spending to go to minority-owned businesses. So I'm constantly on the
lookout for legitimate, professional, minority-owned suppliers to contract for those clients."

And many of those minority businesses understandably make it easy for her to recognize them. "Most will mention they're a 'minority supplier' several times in the first few minutes of a call, and have it prominently mentioned on their websites," she says. But Sharad Madison was different. Sharad never mentions that UBM is a minority-owned business, and you have to dig around quite a bit to find any reference to it on UBM's website.

What he does instead is tell stories about how his father, who founded the company, would get up in the middle of the night and visit their work sites at 3 o'clock in the morning to make sure nobody was slacking off. Or he tells stories about how nobody at his company is "too big for their britches." He explains how at many companies, once you make supervisor, you think you're too good to clean anymore. But neither he, his father, nor his mother is afraid to pick up a toilet brush.

But perhaps the most compelling differentiation story is about what Sharad does when UBM takes over a new client. For example, Sharad explains:

> When we took over the contract for the Verizon building in New Jersey, we had a 30-day transition period. We took that time to go walk the floors and observe what the current cleaning staff was doing—to find out if they're properly trained and have the right tools.
>
> It's a 1.7-million-square-foot property across several buildings. And the corridors are huge. We went to see the guy who vacuums the carpet and found him using a regular household vacuum cleaner. Those hallways are 12 feet wide and over half a mile long! Can you imagine trying to clean it with the same machine you use at home? It would take all night, and it still wouldn't be very clean. We ordered him a triple-wide, industrial-strength cleaner that will do the job in less than half the time and last forever.
>
> We found someone else shampooing those same carpets with a regular walk-behind shampooer. Again, that could take all night just to shampoo that one corridor. We put him in a high-speed riding shampooer that could do the job in a fraction of the time, with much better results. And it gets him off his feet.
>
> Then we got to the offices and started looking at the top of the file

cabinets. You could see half-moons swiped out on top of otherwise dusty cabinet tops. I know exactly what that means, so we went to find the people who dust those cabinets. When we found them, my suspicion was confirmed. Those cabinets were 5½ feet tall and several of the cleaners were shorter than that. They weren't lazy. They just couldn't reach high enough with their handheld rags to clean the whole cabinet top. That's what leaves the half-moon shape. The truth is, they'd be better off not cleaning it at all, since the contrast between the dusty part and the clean part makes it apparent that it's dirty. We gave them all extension wands so they could reach all the way to the back.

Sharad's goal obviously isn't to be the cheapest cleaning service in town. His goal is to be the best. Telling a prospect that UBM "aims for operational excellence in all that they do" won't communicate that very effectively. And announcing with fanfare that his is a minority-owned business won't communicate that at all. Telling this story does. And it's one of the main reasons Joanna Martinez picked UBM and not one of its many undifferentiated competitors.

ADVICE FROM THE PROS

Since these first few stories set the stage for the ultimate success or failure of the relationship you're trying to build, here's some additional quick advice on how to make the most of them.

Look for Clues to Story Selection

As mentioned in Chapter 5, the most commonly used tactic for identifying story topics is looking around the buyer's office for clues to common interests. As Eric Storey explained, "When I enter a buyer's office, I look around. What personal items are on the desk and wall? Pictures of family, race ribbons, diplomas? All are clues to potential connections we have."

But today, technology helps make it even easier. Scroll to the bottom of your prospect's LinkedIn profile, past all their jobs and degrees, and you'll find professional groups they belong to, people whose ideas they follow, news sources they trust, and companies they keep tabs on.

A more sophisticated technology is the app Refresh. It accesses your online calendar, identifies the people you have upcoming meetings with, puts together a dossier on their background and interests, and sends it to you prior to your meeting. Based on their public social media profiles, it can tell you what their interests are, pull recent headlines about the company they work for and their top competitors, and access their most recent public posts online. Even better, it identifies commonalities for you, like which influencers you both follow on Twitter or if you went to the same university.

Sales and marketing strategist Kristin Luck swears by it. For example, she said that prior to a recent call, Refresh let her know that the person she was meeting with had golden retrievers. Kristin has three dogs of her own, so she changed her presentation to include a couple of stories about her dogs. "Until I got to that point," she said, "the woman I was meeting with seemed distant. But as soon as I got to the part about my dogs, she warmed up to me. Now we had something in common."

Toot Your Own Horn Without Sounding Like You're Doing It

Debbie Manos-McHenry wants the salespeople she meets with to understand that she's driven, focused, and has a strong work ethic. But saying that about herself, or even telling stories about herself that will lead her audience to those conclusions, would make her appear arrogant.

Instead, she tells them stories about her mother who divorced at 48, raised five kids, passed the bar exam at 64, and is now 76, has 350 clients, and works 80 hours a week and loves it. What comes through in these stories is that Debbie has enormous respect for her mother and those traits in particular. She is a reflection of her mother. And those stories communicate that to her audience without her having to toot her own horn.

Tap into Common Fears

Author and professional speaker Christy Demetrakis advocates tapping into common fears in your storytelling. For example, she relates the story of how she started her communications skills training company, The Empowered Speaker, while still a full-time salesperson at a Fortune 50 company. She was deathly afraid she'd get fired if anyone found out, so she kept the whole effort a secret for months. It turns out that's a fear lots of entrepreneurs have when they start to pursue their dream job on the side while still holding down a full-time corporate gig. How does she know? Her audiences tell her that they did the same thing with their first business. And that story helps them bond over that common fear.

Allow for Three Degrees of Connection

Exactly how much personal information should you share in these early "stories about me"? Barry Blake, senior managing director at a major New York investment bank, thinks about it this way: "I think of professional relationships in three phases. At first, I'm just getting to know you. Then we have to earn each other's trust. Over time, we'll build a lasting relationship and friendship."

So he thinks of his storytelling along the same lines. He shares some of the personal stories right up front with a new customer or prospect. He might talk about growing up in Sheridan, Arkansas, and how he still hasn't been able to shake his Southern accent (despite his Ivy League education and blue chip resume).

Later on, he might go a little deeper into his past, about how he grew up poor and was the first person in his family to go to college. And then, as the relationship progresses, and he and his new customer are spending lots of time together in boardrooms working on deals, he opens up a bit more and might share the stories of how he lost his father at a young age and lived on his own as a high school senior.

How quickly a relationship moves through those phases can vary. Just know that you don't have to open all the way up the first day.

Be Aware of Cultural Differences

Last, a comment on cultural differences. The amount of time spent in a sales call on these rapport-building elements can vary drastically depending on where you are. Irmaliz Perez has spent a dozen years in sales management for organizations including Bulgari, Elizabeth Arden, Pernod Ricard, and Procter & Gamble, working with customers across both North America and Latin America. She's noticed that out of a one-hour sales call in Latin America, it's not uncommon to spend thirty minutes sharing personal stories and asking each other about family and personal lives. In contrast, the same sales call with a North American customer might include only a handful of minutes on similar topics. Each time she has to adjust her storytelling to what's comfortable and interesting to the prospect. Some salespeople would feel abruptly cut off after only four minutes of that repartee. Others might feel awkwardly inappropriate, and desperate for material, if rapport building continued for a full thirty minutes.

So, how long should rapport building last? As long as the customer wants it to. Be prepared for either end of the spectrum.

EXERCISES

1. Brainstorm ideas for these five stories about you. You'll flesh them out in Part II.

    a. "Why I do what I do" story. Consider the job interview that inspired Chris Powers to give up his partnership. What moment inspired you to do what you do?

    b. "I'll tell you when I can't help you" story. Think of a time you were honest enough to tell a buyer you're not their best solution.

    c. "I'll tell you when I made a mistake" story. Think of a time when you made a mistake and owned up to it with the buyer before they heard about it from anyone else.

d. "I'll go to bat for you" story. This could be similar to Eric Storey's tale about going to bat for Huntington National Bank.

e. "I'm not who you think I am" story. What negative preconceptions are your prospects likely to have about you? Make a list of them, along with an idea for a story to demonstrate that you actually possess the opposite quality.

2. Brainstorm ideas for these two stories about your company:

a. Your company's founding story. If you don't already know it, interview your company's founder, CEO, oldest employee, or corporate historian and find out.

b. "How we're different from our competitors" story. Consider Sharad Madison's story of walking the halls at Verizon to see how the cleaning was being done. What story could you tell to show how your product or service is unique?

3. Identify promising topics or common interests to build stories around.

a. Check out your buyer's LinkedIn profile for interest groups, education, previous employers, authored posts, companies followed, etc.

b. Try the Refresh app to get a common interest profile on all your prospects.

c. Make a note for your next visit to your buyers' offices to look around for diplomas, pictures, and art, etc. Think of your own stories that relate to what you find.

4. Find out what your buyer's greatest fears are. (Getting fired? Not getting promoted? A poor performance rating?) Create a lasting bond by telling your own story surrounding that same fear.

7

THE MAIN SALES PITCH

FOR **MOST SALES** calls, this is the heart of the matter—where most of the traditional selling is done, and where most of the time in a typical sales call is spent. So there's room for lots of stories, and successful salespeople often use more than one. Here are the five most typical kinds I found being used in this part of the selling process.

1. YOUR PRODUCT'S INVENTION OR DISCOVERY STORY

This is similar to the founding story of your company covered in the last chapter, except it's about the origin of the particular brand, product, or service you're offering at the moment. It answers the question "What situation gave rise to the inventor creating this product?" Consider the following example from Leah Jewell.

In the mid-1990s, Leah was managing the Higher Education English team at the publishing company Prentice Hall. Part of her job entailed selling the idea for new books, first to her own internal management, then to the sales reps, and finally to the college English departments that were the target audience. The main component of one particular sales pitch was the following story.

She started by simply asking, "Do you know Mickey Harris or the Purdue Online Writing Lab?" Since her external audience was made up of English professors, they nearly always did. Muriel "Mickey" Harris was fairly well known as the Purdue University English professor who in 1976 created the school's first writing lab to give students personal assistance with their writing projects. Harris eventually expanded access to the lab and its resources online, establishing one of the world's earliest online writing labs (OWLs).[1]

Leah continues by explaining that Mickey and her team had personally helped thousands of students with their writing in the previous two decades. And with over half a million words in the English language and more than a thousand grammar rules,[2] Mickey might have expected to be addressing a huge number of students' questions and issues. But after a number of years, she was surprised to observe that most of the students coming to her writing lab were showing up with a remarkably similar set of questions and writing problems. They were so consistent that her team developed handouts to address the most common problems. In fact, she ultimately concluded that the majority of issues were represented by only 20 unique topics.

Mickey had the data and experience to narrow down the most common writing errors and FAQs she encountered, and Leah and her team figured out a way to organize a book around this information to make it easier for students to find what they were looking for. That way, if students are having problems trying to figure out how to properly use semicolons, they can find the answer quickly and easily without wading through advice on em dashes versus en dashes. None of the current handbooks on the market was organized that way. And Mickey already had a good head start on the material with the reference handouts she'd been writing.

Everyone understood the value of Mickey Harris and her idea. It was easy to get approval to move forward with the project, the sales reps had a compelling, unique story to tell, and English professors saw that the approach solved a problem for them—how to get students to use a handbook effectively. The *Prentice Hall Reference Guide to Grammar and Usage* by Muriel Harris was born. Prentice Hall named Leah's team the "product team of the year." And today, the book is in its ninth edition and is still one of the bestsellers on the market.

2. PROBLEM STORIES

These are stories about people who encountered exactly the kind of problem your product is designed to solve. They're especially helpful if buyers don't even know they have a problem. Importantly, such a story allows buyers to understand the problem in a more personal, visceral way than just being told, "I'll bet you have this problem." Here's an example.

Kevin Moulton is director of sales for a technology company specializing in online security. When meeting with prospective clients in the banking industry, he's likely to tell them about a trip he made a few years ago to Las Vegas. He was there for a corporate event, but like everyone else, he made it a point to take in some of the Vegas night life.

"About 1 a.m.," he explains, "I realized I was out of money, so I found the nearest ATM. I put in my card and password, but the machine denied the transaction. Apparently, my bank thought it might be fraudulent. I don't have a problem with that. I like that my bank looks out for that kind of thing."

What the bank personnel did about it, however, did create a problem for Kevin. They called his wife.

"So it's 4 a.m. in New Jersey where we live, and they call and wake up my wife. And you have to imagine what she's hearing on her end of the phone. It must have sounded something like, 'I'm sorry to bother you, ma'am, but your husband is trying to get cash in Las Vegas at 1 o'clock in the morning. Do you approve?' How pissed do you think I was at my bank?"

What bothered Kevin even more was that the bank had an emergency phone number for him on file, which was his cell phone number. "But did they use it?" he grumbles. "No! They called my home instead. I called the bank the next day and reminded them that they had my cell phone number. They said, 'It's our policy to call the home number.' Well, then, why do they even have it?"

Kevin ends with this frustratingly unanswered question, appropriately delivered in an exasperated tone. The story establishes the problem that in their zeal to protect their customers from fraud, banks sometimes make it too difficult for their customers to do legitimate business with them. They can even, as this story illustrates, cause strife in their customers' personal lives. At this point, after telling this story, it's very easy for Kevin to ask if his prospects might have a few protocols that could similarly frustrate a customer. And since they almost always do, he goes on to share ways his company can help fix that. "For example," he says, "you could send a onetime password to your customer's cell phone. That way, you avoid the fraud without disrupting your customer's life."

The "problem story" is a critical part of a sales pitch and is a must-have in your repertoire of stories.

3. CUSTOMER SUCCESS STORIES

This type of story shows someone successfully using your product or service and being satisfied with the result. Don't confuse it with a testimonial, which can be as simple (and uninspiring) as quoting one of your existing customers saying, "I use this product and it works great." Customer success stories are stories, not statements.

What a success story does have in common with a testimonial is that they're both highly effective, which accounts for why success stories are perhaps the most ubiquitous type of sales story in use. There are two main reasons testimonials and customer success stories are so effective.

First, as Casey Hibbard points out in her book *Stories That Sell*, "We trust what others say much more than what a business says."[3] As evidence, she cites a 2007 Bridge Ratings survey where 3,400 respondents were asked to rank on a scale of 1 to 10 what their most trusted sources of information were.[4] At the top were family and friends (8.6). Somewhere in the middle were journalists (6.1). Not surprisingly, the bottom two sources on the list were advertising (2.2) and telemarketers (1.8).

As a result, customer success stories are most effective when they're written or recorded in first-person perspective, told by the customers themselves. However, in practice, most are told in the third person, by the salesperson. Yet these stories still benefit greatly from the credibility of the successful third-party experience.

The second reason testimonials and customer success stories are so effective is what psychology and marketing professor Robert Cialdini calls "social proof" or the "like me" factor, in his bestselling book *Influence: The Psychology of Persuasion*.[5] His finding is that people make decisions by (unconsciously) asking themselves, "What would someone like me do in this situation?" Your story shows them exactly what someone like them does—they buy your product. Therefore, the more similarities the character in your customer success story has to the prospect you're telling the story to, the more likelihood the story will work.

Doubtless you're already well acquainted with this kind of story, so I won't include a complete one here. I'll just reference some prominent examples you're likely already familiar with.

OnStar plays actual recordings from emergency calls in its advertisements. eHarmony almost went out of business until 10 couples went on James Dobson's radio program to share their relationship success stories. Casey Hibbard also cites Microsoft, Visa, Geico, HP, Accenture, Pfizer, Dell, Dow, IBM, Verizon, the Humane Society, and Ford Motor Company as all heavily leveraging success stories.[6]

If you already have customer success stories, you'll learn how to make them better in Part II of this book. If you don't have any yet, get some. Interview your best customers and get them to tell you their success stories with your product, and write them down. Better yet, ask if you can videotape the interviews. You can go to YouTube for an example of what it looked like when HP asked people at the University of Leeds in the UK to share their success story with HP's TippingPoint product [7] (discussed in Chapter 1).

Success Stories That Aren't Even Yours

Finally, in an interesting twist, some salespeople tell customer success stories about companies that aren't even their customers and whose success they had nothing to do with. And it isn't the least bit dishonest. It's actually quite brilliant—and it works.

Here's a case in point. Shane Skillen is cofounder and CEO of Hotspex, an innovative market research firm in Toronto. One of the success stories he tells prospective clients is about Febreze air freshener, a brand he's never worked on. Procter & Gamble launched Febreze in 1996 after inventing a new spray technology that actually removes odors from fabric instead of masking them with stronger and more pleasant smells. It was perfect for young socialites whose clothes smelled of smoke after a night at the bar, or any house with pets, sweaty socks, or teenage boys.

The brand was launched in lead markets with an aggressive marketing campaign: two flights of television commercials, product samples and advertisements mailed to homes, and huge displays of product in grocery stores. The result? It was a complete flop. The question, of course, was why.

The problem turned out to be that people who are constantly in the presence of bad odors become desensitized to them and don't notice them anymore. If they don't notice Fluffy's stinky litter box, they don't need Febreze.

The Febreze team decided to conduct more research, as best described in Charles Duhigg's book *The Power of Habit*. One of the people they interviewed was a woman in her 40s living in a suburb near Scottsdale, Arizona. She did have teenage boys, but nobody in the house smoked and there weren't any pets, so she didn't seem like the kind of person they expected to be such a heavy Febreze user. Even more interesting, she said she didn't use Febreze for specific smells. She said, "I use it for normal cleaning—a couple of sprays when I'm done in a room. It's a nice way to make everything smell good as a final touch."[8]

They asked if they could watch her clean her house, and they videotaped the whole event. They watched as she vacuumed the living room and then sprayed Febreze on the just-cleaned carpet. "It's nice, you know?" she said. "Spraying feels like a little mini-celebration when I'm done with a room."

That was the beginning of the breakthrough insight. Back at the home office, looking through thousands of hours of videotape of people cleaning their homes, the team confirmed their intuition. They saw a 26-year-old woman making a bed, smoothing the sheets, adjusting a pillow, and then smiling as she left the room. "Did you see that?" one of the researchers asked. Then they saw another woman cleaning the kitchen and wiping the counter before taking a nice relaxing stretch. "There it is again!" These women were enjoying a moment of satisfaction for a job well done when finishing a cleaning task. And—as the team learned from the woman in Scottsdale—Febreze could be a great way to give whatever someone was working on a just-cleaned smell, one worthy of celebrating.

It turns out P&G had been trying to sell Febreze to solve a problem people didn't have. Two years after the original launch, the company restaged the brand's positioning to be a reward—that nice smell at the end of a cleaning job well done. Sales doubled in the first two months.[9] And today Febreze is a billion-dollar brand.

As Shane Skillen describes it, P&G had at first been focusing on the wrong consumer "need-state." And only through the second round of creative research did the P&G team find a better strategy for the brand. Shane's company has a proprietary need-state discovery model that uses some of the same techniques the Febreze team used, plus some unique ones, to help companies find the right need-state the first time.

Shane could tell his prospective clients about his own customers that he actually has helped with Hotspex's need-state model, and sometimes he does. But he still finds value in telling the Febreze story because it's a better-known example of the kind of problem his company works on and the kind of solution he provides. He also doesn't have to worry about accidentally sharing any confidential client information with the Febreze story—because he doesn't have any.

If you're having trouble coming up with your own customer success stories—or even if you're not—spend some time brainstorming the most widely recognized success stories in your industry that you think bear a plausible resemblance to the experience your customers have with you. Share those stories, and connect the dots.

4. "TWO ROADS" STORIES

I've named this type of story after the Robert Frost poem "The Road Not Taken" that begins "Two roads diverged in a yellow wood."[10] As the name suggests, it's actually two stories, not just one. The first story is essentially a "problem story" as discussed above—the narrative of a person's encounter with the problem your product or service is designed to address. The second is a "success story" that follows the events of the same (or a similar) person when encountering the same situation, but showing that person making use of your product or service instead, thus leading to a presumably better outcome.

These can be true stories just like most of the others in this book. But this type of story is one where many salespeople tend to use hypothetical examples, so I'll share an example of that kind here.

One of Logan Strain's first jobs out of college was taking inbound calls at an online sporting goods store.[11] When someone called to ask about a basketball hoop, his sales objective was to get the caller to consider the company's top-of-the line model that was higher quality but of course also more expensive. It seemed like an easy task to him. These people already wanted to buy a basketball hoop. He just needed to get them to buy the best one.

During customer calls, he walked the caller through all the benefits of the premium model. "I emphasized the more durable pole, the wider backboard, the more comprehensive warranty—all the benefits I learned from the manufacturer."

But after months of effort, he admitted his success rate was dismal. That didn't change until he stopped talking benefits and started telling "two roads" stories to put those benefits in the context of a person's life. In this case, that person is the caller and perhaps the caller's children. Logan would say:

> This is a fine basketball hoop. But let's say it's two years from now and your kid is a lot better at basketball, because they've been practicing. But they can't make bank shots like they can do at their school because the backboard is too narrow. Maybe they even lower the hoop and try to dunk and wind up breaking the backboard. Unfortunately, you'll have to get a whole new one because dunking isn't covered under its warranty.
>
> But what if you get [Model B] and it's two years from now? They'll still be able to practice at home, because it's much closer to the pro systems that they use at the school games. And if they lower the hoop, dunk, and shatter the whole thing? The manufacturer will ship you a replacement. If you plan on living at your house for a long time and want a hoop that will last you, this is what I recommend.

Notice that Logan wasn't using any different facts or selling any different benefits. He was just explaining the impact of those differences in the context of the prospect's life, one story at a time. In his words:

> They weren't just bullet points on the manufacturer's spec sheet anymore. They represented real experiences. They told a better story. "A wider backboard" suddenly became a kid practicing his bank shot at home so he does better during his games at school. "A sturdier pole" suddenly became a durable system that can handle as much abuse as you're willing to give it. "A better warranty" suddenly became having a hoop to play on for years, instead of just doing without a basketball system because it broke. And rejecting all those things told a different story entirely—a worse story. By telling these two stories, I forced my prospects to think about which story they want to live with.

5. VALUE-ADDING STORIES

These are stories that actually add to the value or attractiveness of the product. Chris Gug's story of Pig Island at the beginning of this book is an example. But let me share an example from a more traditional B2B environment.

Andy Smith is senior vice president of an investment broker/dealer that serves the financial industry. His primary work is selling bonds to banks. Listening to a bond salesperson talking to a banker can sound like a foreign language to an outsider: "Hey, I've got an agency bond, it's got a five-year maturity, 2 percent coupon, and the price is one-eighth of a percent above par. You interested?"

Sometimes that's enough information for the banker to make a decision to buy a bond. But even to a banker, there's nothing sexy or unusually effective about that sales pitch. Andy prefers to sell what he calls "story bonds." As the name suggests, these are bonds with stories behind them that make them of more interest to the banker.

He explains with this example: "We sell a lot of mortgage-backed securities. Those are bonds made up of pools of hundreds or thousands of Fannie Mae or Freddie Mac home loans.[12] Bankers know they're pretty safe, liquid investments, that pay principal and interest every month. I might have one to sell that's made up of 30-year Fannie Mae 3.75 percent interest mortgages that pay a 3 percent coupon, and that's about all I can say about it."

But sometimes Andy gets a bond that consists entirely of what are called relocation mortgages. It might also be made up of 30-year Fannie Mae 3.75 percent mortgages with a 3 percent coupon. But he'd sell this one by telling the banker a story about his brother. Andy says the conversation typically goes like this:

> My brother's a couple of years older than me. He did a short stint in consulting, went Ivy League for his MBA, and then he took a job in corporate finance at a Fortune 50 company. Like a lot of those big global firms, they like their executives to have leadership experiences from all over the company. So they move their top performers to a new location every three years or so. He's relocated five times already.
>
> And every time they ship him off somewhere else, they hire a realtor to sell his house, move all his stuff, *and* they buy out his mortgage and pay it off when the house sells. Then three or four years later, they do it all over again. So his mortgages are typically getting paid back early. And even if they stop moving him, he's getting promoted so quickly and his salary's going up so fast that he'll want to upgrade to a bigger house fairly often. So either way, that mortgage is likely to get paid off early.
>
> So these relocation bonds are the same as all the other mortgage-backed bonds, except all the home loans are to people like my brother who are getting relocated for their job. So you expect them to pay off quicker and more reliably than the others.

And with that story, the appeal of what Andy's selling has now just gone up significantly. Let's look at how that worked. I'd argue two separate things are going on here.

One is that the story helped the banker come to the conclusion that these bonds are actually different from the other bonds in the same class. She can be more confident that these bonds won't default, because multibillion-dollar companies are often paying off the loans, not just individual borrowers. Plus, if interest rates go up, she isn't going to be stuck with this bond as long as she would the others because they generally get paid off sooner.

The other thing going on is the Pig Island effect. The story allowed Andy to humanize the collateral that these bonds are based on. The banker can now picture a human being on the other end of that mortgage pool, just like I could picture Chris Gug trolling up in his boat to a shoreline full of swimming piglets. And like the Pig Island story, that banker now has a story to reflect on every time she looks at her reports on that bond. Perhaps most important, that banker has a story to tell to the bank president, the board members, or her depositors when they ask how she's investing their money. Having that story to tell other people helps her sleep better at night and feel better about her investment, just like the Pig Island story makes me feel better about my investment in that picture every time I tell it to someone else.

EXERCISES

Develop stories for the five most common uses of storytelling during the main sales pitch.

1. *Your product's invention or discovery story.* What situation gave rise to the inventor creating this product? This is a personal story from the inventor's perspective, not an impersonal "corporate" story.

2. *Problem story.* Like the bank calling Kevin Moulton's wife in the middle of the night, think of a real situation where someone experienced the quintessential problem your product or service is designed to solve.

3. *Customer success stories.* Think of the most inspiring or engaging example of someone using your product or service and having a fabulous experience.
   - Interview your best customers to get all the details. (See tips on interviewing in Chapter 24.)
   - Better yet, videotape the interview and show it to your prospects instead of telling the story yourself.

- Since this is the most common sales story you'll tell, develop several of them with various customers. Then, use the one that involves a customer most similar to the prospect you'll be telling it to.
- Consider using borrowed success stories. What are the most recognizable examples of customer success stories in your industry? Share them and draw the similarities to the experiences your customers have.

4. *Two-roads stories.* Invent a problem story and a success story about the same hypothetical customer. The first describes his experience without your product or service, and the second describes his experience with it. (See Logan Strain's example earlier in this chapter as a model.)

5. *Value-adding stories.* What kind of story could you tell that actually increases the value of what you sell, like the Pig Island story or Andy Smith's "relocation bond" story? What can you say that makes your product or service interesting or unique?

8

HANDLING OBJECTIONS

AS MOST SALESPEOPLE have learned, the real selling doesn't
start until the buyer says no. As a result, salespeople use a number of time-tested models for handling objections, such as LAIR (Listen, Acknowledge, Identify Objection, Reverse It), LACE (Listen,
Accept, Commit, Explicit Action), LAARC (Listen, Acknowledge,
Assess, Respond, Confirm), and Feel-Felt-Found.[1] Some sales experts
swear that if you just stay quiet for a few seconds, prospects will answer
their own objections.[2]

These can all be very effective, and you certainly shouldn't jettison
whichever one is working for you. But if you're not using stories as part
of those methods, or in addition to them, you're missing out on a very
powerful tool. That's because your buyers' objections often take the
form of a story—whether it's shared with you that way or just carried
around in their head in that form. The story experts at Anecdote—a
company that helps business leaders develop their strategic story—refer
to them as "anti-stories" and observe, "You can't beat a story with a
fact. You can only beat it with a better story."[3] Here's an example of
exactly that from Tiffany Lopez.

Tiffany is a senior account executive at DataServ, a company that
helps businesses go completely paperless and manage all their payables,
receivables, and human resources processes and documents online.

One of the more common objections she gets during a call with a new prospect goes something like this: "I know your system would save us some time, and we're really busy right now. But I'm just not sure the return on that time savings would be worth the investment." When she digs a little deeper to find out what's behind the objection, Tiffany often finds the following story playing out in the prospect's head: "If I didn't have to spend so much time on paperwork, I guess I could finally clean up our vendor master files. That would allow me to really understand how much we're spending with each vendor and put me in a better position to negotiate for discounts. But that's not going to be a very big number."

In response, instead of a fact or set of arguments, Tiffany shares a story of one of her recent prospects that had the same objection—the local municipal zoo.

In one of my early calls with the zoo, I found out they were extremely busy, like you. They were spending a lot of time keying in documents to their internal system, just like you do, and shipping off hard copies of documents to off-site storage facilities just to have to go searching through a warehouse for them later. I explained how with our system, they wouldn't have to do any of that anymore and would save a significant amount of time. So I asked them, "What could you do if you had all that time back?"

Their eyes got really big at that point and they said, "We'd be able to do more research and apply for more grant money."

So I said, "Isn't grant money how you pay for most everything around here? Like that new gorilla exhibit you've been working on for months?"

They said, "Yes."

So I said, "Let me get this straight. All this administrative paperwork is actually holding you back from pursuing your number one revenue source?"

"Yeah, I guess it is."

"Well, then, it sounds like a no-brainer to me."

That's when Tiffany stops telling her story and provides a little silence for it to do its work. She tells the story because it's hard for most people to think of the most profitable way to spend a bunch of extra time they don't have yet—because they don't have it yet.

Apparently, it's not uncommon for prospects to come up with a few small issues to work on, like cleaning up the vendor master files. But after they hear her story, it's easier for prospects to think of much higher value work they could be doing—either because the story prompted them to think outside the box for a minute or because they just don't want to appear small-minded in comparison to Tiffany's other prospects. Either way, they quickly think of more valuable ways to spend their time. Her story immediately, and legitimately, drives up the value of the product Tiffany is selling. Just asking them to "think harder" about how to spend that extra time doesn't work nearly as well.

Notice something else interesting about this story. This isn't a sales success story where it ends with the zoo signing on the dotted line and becoming Tiffany's newest client. That hasn't happened yet (though she's confident that it will). Tiffany doesn't limit her stories to current clients. She knows there's also wisdom to be found in her calls with prospects that didn't work out and those that just haven't worked out yet. You should keep your mind open to these unexpected sources of story material, too.

NEGOTIATING PRICE

One of the most common—and often final—objections buyers bring up is price, so it warrants a special mention here.

If you're at the point that you're negotiating price, congratulations. You have a prospect interested in what you're selling, and you've probably resolved every other objection they have. Often, negotiating price is simply part of the game, and most salespeople have an explicit method for navigating it. Storytelling isn't meant to replace that, but it can augment it. As Rick Rhine from Tailwind Marketing explained, "If I can keep the stories flowing while we talk about price, I'm going to be more successful."

For example, if you discover the main reason for the price objection is the buyer's lack of appreciation of why your product is any different from lower-priced competitors on the market, then you need to tell your "How we're different from our competitors" story that you developed in Chapter 6. Here's an example specifically related to price that's instructive on many levels.[4]

"If you have to pay for anything up front in this industry, it's a rip-off!" So goes a familiar but unfortunate saying in the modeling and talent business. It's familiar because it's been floating around for decades. It's unfortunate because it isn't true—at least it's not if you want the best odds of success. Many an aspiring model naively thinks she can land a lucrative contract with no training, experience, or understanding of the business. "All I need," she might think, "is an agent to represent me." Not surprisingly, that rarely works. As in any industry, those with relevant skills and experience are in a better position to succeed. And one of the best places for that aspiring model to get that skill and experience is Excel Models & Talent. For 25 years, owner Melissa Moody has been placing models in women's magazines like *Vogue, Elle,* and *Cosmopolitan,* and on runways in New York, Paris, and Milan. The singers and dancers she represents have claimed prestigious awards, including a Grammy, an American Music Award, and a Teen Choice Award.

Unlike a traditional talent agency, Excel doesn't just match clients with models and collect a commission for brokering the deal. Instead, it trains its students in modeling, acting, professional etiquette, and the business side of the industry. And Melissa personally takes them to competitions in New York, Los Angeles, and Paris every year to get experience. Of course, she sometimes books them directly with clients. But she can also find them engagements all over the world through a network of international agents she works with.

So it's understandable that she needs to charge her students for these services. But still, she often gets the objection that "you shouldn't have to pay for anything up front in this industry" from a potential client, which is typically a 14-year-old girl accompanied by her parents.

In these situations, Melissa has three responses. First, she asks them to look around the office. "What do you see? How do you think I pay for the classrooms, the furniture, the lights?" she asks. If that doesn't work, she asks the prospective model, or her parents, what they do for a living. "Oh, good, you're an accountant," she might respond. "Because I really need my taxes done. But I don't want to pay for it unless

I get a refund. Will you do them for me?" Of course not.

If those two responses don't resolve the objection, Melissa pulls out her biggest gun: a story. This story is about Kristine, a 17-year-old, brown-haired, long-legged beauty with high cheekbones. She had the makings of a world-class model and was one of Melissa's best students. During one of the annual New York competitions, Kristine came in first runner-up out of 1,200 girls. Back home the next week, she got an unprecedented 42 callbacks from agents and clients. Melissa helped her pick the best opportunities, and Kristine and her parents were off to New York again to sign a deal.

The day of the big meeting, Melissa got a call from Kristine, who was on her cell phone, sitting in the backseat of a cab heading to the client's office to sign the contract. Kristine was in tears. "What's wrong?" Melissa asked.

Kristine was having second thoughts. Being a model was never really her idea. It was her mom's. Kristine wanted to be successful—just not in this business. "Melissa, I graduated at the top of my class. I don't want to make my living off my looks," she said. She wanted to go to business school and run a company. "What should I do?"

At this point in the story, Melissa pauses and explains to her prospect how she would have answered the question if Kristine hadn't paid for the training and experience she'd gotten from Excel. "I would have told her, 'Kristine, I've got $15,000 invested in you and a contract. Get your butt in that office and sign those papers so I can get my money back!' But because I don't work that way, what I actually told her was this: 'Kristine, follow your heart. Come home and pursue your dream.' " And that's exactly what Kristine did.

There are two lessons in Melissa's method of resolving the objection about payment. First, she knows her biggest and best weapon is a story, not a fact or an argument. Second, this particular story allows her to highlight the benefit of her pricing policy for the customer, not for her. That's very different from her first two attempts. The need to pay for lights and furniture is a reason *Melissa* needs to charge a fee. The analogy of the free tax service also explains why *Melissa* needs to charge up front. But the story about Kristine shows a benefit to the student. Paying up front gets you an agent who has your best interests in mind and keeps you out of a commitment you might not want to have later on. As far as Melissa's concerned, anything less would be a rip-off.

If you find yourself defending your pricing, think of a similar story about how the price you charge is good for the customer, not you. What would happen badly for customers if they paid less and your product was commensurately cheaper in quality?

BEING PROACTIVE WITH OBJECTIONS

Here are a couple of techniques to help you be more proactive with your stories to resolve objections. Both come from highly unlikely sources.

A Journey of Discovery Story

The first technique isn't from a traditional salesperson at all. It's from the global market research director at Amway, Randy Locke. Randy's job isn't to sell products. He traffics in ideas. It's his job and the job of his team to recommend strategic courses of action to senior management, often when that recommendation conflicts with the personal opinion of one of those senior managers. And it's those instances when Randy's pushing an unpopular idea that he's learned the most about selling and about storytelling.

The most straightforward way to bring up his disagreements with management, of course, is to simply state them and explain them. For example, he might say, "I've looked at the most recent strategy document and I disagree with points #2 and #4, and here are my reasons why . . ." But human beings, being what they are, tend to not like being told that they're wrong about something, especially in front of their peers. We can get defensive and inadvertently put up more of a barrier to the new ideas than is warranted, throwing out objection after objection in more of an attempt to rescue our pride than make the best decision.

Randy's found it to be more effective to tell a story about how his team started out in complete support of a new plan, and how they came to find their point of disagreement. That might sound like this:

"We were excited to get the new strategy document and went to work immediately to help flesh out the ideas with our best consumer insights. But as we were doing that, we came across some research that made us question points #2 and #4. We were surprised to find out that . . ." And from there, Randy launches into his journey of research that led to the epiphany in the first place.

All of the same points that would be brought up in the more straightforward approach would be mentioned in the storytelling approach. The difference is that the straightforward approach is set up from the beginning as an adversarial conversation: "I'm right and you're wrong, and here's why."

But the second approach, using storytelling, is set up as a journey of discovery. It starts in the same intellectual place as the audience. Instead of feeling confrontational or adversarial, the audience feels more of a sense of adventure and is eager to see where the journey leads. As a result, Randy is more likely to end up with an agreement than a headache.

If you have ideas to share with your prospects or buyers that are likely to be seen as contrary to their opinion on something, develop your own "discovery journey" story to explain how you came to your controversial position. You'll have much more success.

Resolve Objections Before They're Even Brought Up

Finally, one of the most powerful uses of storytelling to resolve objections is to settle them before they're brought up in the first place. An unlikely but illustrative example comes from the hip-hop movie *8 Mile*. The main character, B-Rabbit (played by Eminem), enters a rap battle where competitors hurl insults at one another. Rabbit is upset when he gets to the finals and realizes his opponent, Papa Doc, is the leader of a gang that recently beat him up and intimidated his best friend into shooting himself in the leg with his own gun.

Knowing that such embarrassing information gives Papa Doc an advantage, Rabbit has an epiphany just before walking on stage. Instead of launching into his insults, he starts his rap by unashamedly telling his own humbling life story, including: "I know everything he's 'bout to say against me . . . I do live in a trailer with my mom . . . I do got a dumb friend named Cheddar Bob who shoots himself in his leg with his own gun . . . I did get jumped by all six of you chumps."

Rabbit left his opponent with no ammunition. When it's his turn, Papa Doc simply hands the microphone to the emcee and walks off stage in defeat.

While the context might be unusual, Rabbit's strategy is a brilliant one that can also be used in sales calls. Here's an example from Ben Koberna at EASI, whom you met in Chapter 3. Ben explains, "Prospective clients always ask the same question, 'Do vendors like reverse auctions?'" His response always brings a laugh: "Well, we've run the numbers. And vendors get mad in about 100 percent of the cases."

Even though the humor diffuses some of the tension around the question, it doesn't resolve the underlying objection. His prospects don't relish the thought of hiring him because of the adverse reaction they know it will bring out of their suppliers. After getting that objection in many sales calls, Ben now uses the following story preemptively:

> One of my earliest clients was a midsize city government in central Florida. They'd been paying $250,000 a year for a contractor to remove sludge from a wastewater treatment plant when they hired us to do a reverse auction. We found several sludge removal companies to compete for the contract and invited them all to a pre-bid meeting so we could explain the process. The incumbent, accompanied by his lawyer, showed up with a tirade. He started yelling and screaming and at one point kicked over a chair. He insisted the whole process was illegal and claimed my team was going to be arrested.
>
> We eventually got him settled down and started the bidding process. His first bid was $250,000, of course. When more aggressive bids started coming in, he lowered his to $240,000, then $200,000, then $150,000. The next bid we saw from him was for $0. Obviously, that was a mistake. Somebody must have clicked the wrong button. So we paused the auction and called him on the phone. We explained his mistake and offered to delete that bid before we resumed the auction. He responded calmly, "I didn't make a mistake. I've been selling the sludge to local farmers for the last twenty years to use as fertilizer. I'll just come pick it up for free." And that's exactly what he's been doing ever since.

Having finished his story, Ben explains to his prospect, "You and I both know that vendors will be mad. But they'll yell and scream at me, not you. Part of my job is to shield you from all that. You just get to save money."

If there are objections you find you get in nearly every call, find a story to resolve them before it's ever asked.

EXERCISES

1. *What are the three most common objections you get during sales calls?* For each objection, think of an occasion involving a current or previous customer (or even another prospect) that demonstrates the fallaciousness of the objection. Ask your customers or other salespeople in your office for help identifying such an occasion.

2. *Think of an idea or concept you discuss in a sales pitch that's most likely to raise an objection.* Outline a "discovery journey" story about how you personally came to hold the point of view you're advocating. It should go something like this: "I used to think the way you did . . . But then I did some research . . . which led me to find out this . . . and this . . . which obviously changed the way I think about it."

3. *What is the single most common objection you get?* (See your list from Exercise #1 above.) Does it come up in almost every sales call? If so, think of ways you could use it preemptively instead of waiting to handle it defensively.

9

CLOSING THE SALE

AS MENTIONED AT the beginning of Part I, every salesperson I interviewed had an explicit sales process they followed, and almost all of the processes were different in some way. Some were long and complicated and some were short and simple. But there was one step, and only one step, every single one of those processes had in common: closing the sale (sometimes called "asking for the sale"). I can say that with confidence because the shortest and simplest sales process contained only one step, and "closing the sale" was it. You see this one-step sales process yourself every time a 10-year-old girl shows up on your doorstep and the only words out of her mouth are, "Would you like to buy some Girl Scout cookies?"

It would be easy to argue, then, that this is the most important step in the sales process, and the only one that can't be skipped. However, it's not the first step that comes to mind when thinking of appropriate uses for storytelling—or at least it wasn't the first step that came to mind for the majority of salespeople I interviewed. Building rapport with the buyer, the main sales pitch, and resolving objections were much more quick to come to mind.

But the salespeople who did use storytelling at this stage did so in some very unique and effective ways. As such, these stories warrant being added to any salesperson's repertoire. The three most promising ways are discussed below.

CREATING A SENSE OF URGENCY

Even after you've convinced your prospects that they would benefit from your product or service, that yours is superior to your competitor's, and that the price is acceptable, salespeople often face a final barrier that might be articulated this way: "We'll definitely place an order, but now's not the right time."

In this situation, salespeople often find themselves reiterating, in vain, the same benefits they already explained earlier. What many find more effective is helping the prospect understand the unique problem created by waiting. DataServ's Tiffany Lopez, whom you met in the last chapter, offers an instructive example.

In late 2013, Tiffany closed a sale with a prospect she'd been working with for almost two years—or so she thought. They agreed to buy DataServ's accounts payable software solution, but they didn't want to begin implementation until March. They explained that December and January were very busy months for the payables department when they're closing the books, and February is audit season. So March would be the earliest the A/P staff would be freed up for an installation project like this. "Come back in January and we'll sign all the paperwork, and then start work in March," they said.

January came, and Tiffany called the client. And called. And called. No response. Then she figured out why. She saw a news report that the company had just announced an acquisition of one of their competitors and were beginning work immediately to consolidate the new company. She knew what that meant. As she explains, "Typically in an acquisition, the acquiring company takes over the accounts payables for the acquired company. That means they might double the volume of payments they have to make, but with the same staffing. Plus, there's a big onetime effort needed to set all those new vendors up in their A/P system."

That's why Tiffany's calls weren't getting returned. They were swamped, working overtime on nights and weekends to keep up. In fact, to make matters worse, she found out that one of their key A/P managers had quit in the middle of it all, probably as a result of her excessive workload. That just increased the burden on the remaining staff. They had to hire more than one person to replace her, and training them was a job in itself. It's a vicious cycle Tiffany has seen before. Workload goes up, morale goes down, people quit, so workload goes up, etc.

When Tiffany finally heard from her client, it was no surprise that they couldn't even begin to consider taking on the implementation of the new A/P software now. They were just too busy and had no relief in sight.

The unfortunate and ironic thing about this story is that if they'd implemented Tiffany's solution when they originally discussed it the previous year, they'd be in a much better position now. The new system is much more efficient than their current system, so when the acquisition happened, they wouldn't have had to put in nearly as much overtime to keep up. That meant their best A/P manager might not have quit, which also meant they wouldn't have had to hire and train any new people. Delaying was a decision they were certainly regretting now.

Tiffany shares this story with prospects when they start to drag their feet. It creates exactly the sense of urgency you might expect it to, and not just for prospects that see an acquisition looming in their future. They know that any unexpected project that drops in their lap can result in the same series of unfortunate events, and that they'll be happier if they install the new system now and not wait.

Whatever your product or service is, there's likely a similar example of the unfortunate consequences of delay for the buyer. Find it, and create your own "sense of urgency" story.

ARMING YOUR SPONSOR WITH A STORY

A second unique use of storytelling in closing the sale comes in handy when the final decision-making will happen when you're not in the room. Every salesperson worth his salt does his best to get in front of the ultimate decision maker, but that's not always possible. Sometimes that's because the decision is being made too far up the hierarchy for the salesperson to get access (like by the president or CEO). Other times, it's because the final decision is being made by a group or committee the salesperson isn't part of—decisions taken by a board of directors, for instance.

In these cases, effective salespeople find an internal sponsor to champion their cause within the organization. Then they arm that sponsor with all the information needed to make the sale on their behalf. The more creative salespeople, however, also include a story, knowing it's more likely to be remembered and repeated in the meeting than any of the facts or arguments that make up the main sales pitch. They also know it's their most reliable way to inspire the sponsor with a sense of passion for the cause similar to their own. Here's an example of what that might look like from Tia Finn, global learning specialist at the publishing and education company, Pearson PLC, in London, England.

One of the things you learn quickly when you're selling textbooks and other educational solutions to schools is that the final decision is often made by the school board in a closed session. In those situations, Tia likes to tell what she calls a "future state" or "feeling" story.[1] Let's say she's talking to the superintendent of a struggling school district. The district's biggest problem is that the students aren't making the minimum scores on standardized tests to get into college. Tia has two programs she knows can help, and she's already showed the superintendent all the data documenting the results. She's hoping he'll represent those two programs on her behalf at the next school board meeting.

In her last meeting with the superintendent prior to the board meeting, she might say something like this:

> I really wish you could meet Mary Lou at Rover High School across town. You're familiar with that school, right? Well, she's just like you. Her students are very similar to yours, and they're struggling with the exact same issues. In fact, they've been facing it longer than you—more than a decade. Well, I got a call from her a few weeks ago and she said, "Tia, you won't believe it! Go get a copy of today's newspaper. There's an article about our school!" She was so excited.

Then she told me about the article. "It showed our newest test scores, and they're amazing! We're up fifteen percent since last year, and we had sixty more students placed in colleges. The programs you helped us put in place in the fall are really working. This is the biggest news about our school in a decade!"

Then Tia closes the story by asking this question: "Would you like to be able to make that phone call a year from now?"

The answer, of course, is always a resounding yes. And it sends her champion off to the school board meeting with an inspired purpose and a story to tell.

But why does such a simple story work so well? After all, it's less than 170 words long and can be told in about a minute. How is this story any different from just telling the prospect about the results at Rover High School—the fifteen percent increase in scores and the sixty additional college admissions? The answer is that the story isn't about the test scores and college admissions. The story is about Mary Lou and how those results made her feel. You can feel the excitement in her voice and her pride in the newspaper article and the accomplishments of her students.

Tia knows people don't buy a car because they're infatuated with the car. They buy a car because of how it makes them feel. It's the same with just about everything else. Tia's not just selling education programs. She's selling excitement and pride and accomplishment. And that's why Tia calls this a "feeling story." It's about how her programs make the customer feel.

Tia believes the key to having a great "feeling story" is the phrase "just like you." This makes the hero in the story relatable to the audience. If her prospect is a poor, rural school district struggling with elementary reading levels, telling them about a wealthy suburban school struggling with college readiness is not going to make a good story. That means Tia has to have a lot of stories so she can pull out exactly the right one when she needs it. And if you're going to do this well, you'll need several, too.

How are you going to find all these stories? We'll talk more in Chapter 24 about ways to do that in general. But for this particular purpose, notice that Tia's story is essentially a success story, like those discussed in Chapter 7. The difference is that in these success stories, the focus is not on the success itself but on how the success made the customer feel. To capture this kind of story, you might need to interview some of your better customers. Ask them to tell you about the moment that your product or service really started to feel like a success. Was it the aha moment when a report landed on their desk showing improved productivity? Was it when they got a call from their boss congratulating them on their good numbers? Was it when they received a department award? Or was it a simple smile from the production crew chief when he said he wouldn't have to work this weekend because the new machines were working more reliably than the old ones? Keep digging until you get to a real feeling worthy of building a story around.

COACHING THE BREAKUP

The last and most creative use of storytelling in closing the sale that I came across was from the yearbook salesperson in Chapter 6 who we called "Brad."

Imagine you're a high school English teacher and the adviser to the student yearbook committee. One of your jobs is to decide which publisher to produce your school's yearbook, and you've worked with the same one for years. The publisher's sales rep has always been easy to work with, has high integrity, and is a generally likable person. In fact, under other circumstances, you could easily see yourself being friends. But while her company does good work, you've recently come across another yearbook publisher that offers a better product at a more aggressive price. Now you have to fire the rep you've been working with for years. That's no fun. In fact, it can be downright daunting. How're they going to react? Will they be mad at you?

According to Brad, these are legitimate questions. He's heard it all. Some reps get offended, as if the buyer's being disloyal. Some lay on a guilt trip and complain that the buyer is taking food out of the mouths of their children. Some desperately offer to drop their price.

Some even start to cry. And while tears might be a little extreme, most of these reactions are no different from what you're likely to encounter in any industry. Business is personal when you're in sales and your livelihood depends on the revenue. As a result, getting dropped by a customer feels like getting dumped by your high school steady. And to anyone who's ever had to do it, you know that being the dump*er* is almost as painful as being the dump*ee*. And that's why firing your supplier can be a dreadful, guilt-ridden experience—so much so that a fair number of potential clients won't do it. They'd rather keep their current supplier and forgo a better one just to avoid the emotional turmoil.

And that's why one of the stories in Brad's bag is called "coaching the breakup." It's how he helps prepare a new client to end its existing relationship as painlessly as possible. In its most common form, the story he tells is about how one of his other clients navigated the breakup. It might start out something like this: "I'm looking forward to working with you. But I know you've got a difficult thing you have to do now—explain all this to your current publisher. And I can tell you're a little stressed about that. So I thought it might help if I told you how some of my other customers handled it."

Then Brad can walk the buyer through a few success stories of how other customers handled the offer to drop the price (by asking, for example, "Where has that discount been all these years?"), or handled the crier (by reiterating how this isn't personal, it's a business decision), or continued to work amicably with the old supplier for the rest of the school year before transitioning to the new supplier next year. The story he tells depends on what the customer thinks the most likely reaction will be.

If breaking up is hard for your prospects to do, develop your own breakup stories to help coach them through it successfully. This might also require some conversations with your better customers to find out how they did it. (You'll get some of your best stories that way. Don't be shy about asking. Think of it as a flattering excuse to schedule some time with your customers.) Your own company's procurement department is another great source for these kinds of stories. Who else has more experience firing suppliers than a professional buyer?

1. Think of a time when a prospect of yours delayed placing an order and then regretted doing so. Build a story around it and have it ready.

2. Interview your best customers and ask them to tell you about the moment that your product or service really started to feel like a success, and how that made them feel. Arm your sponsor with that story any time the final purchase decision will be made without you in the room.

3. Find out how your best clients handled firing your competitors before they started doing business with you. If breaking up with existing suppliers is a barrier to closing the sale with one of your prospects, share one of these "coaching the breakup" stories.

10

STORYTELLING
AFTER THE SALE

JUST **BECAUSE YOU'VE** closed the sale doesn't mean the need for storytelling has ended. Top salespeople continue to use storytelling after the sale in three primary ways: to deliver service after the sale, to generate loyalty, and to summarize the sales call. Let's talk about all three.

SERVICE AFTER THE SALE: "WHAT'S WORKED WELL IN THE PAST" STORIES

First, depending on the type of product or service offered, many times storytelling can help your existing customers make better decisions about how to use what they've already bought from you. And it's obviously in your best interest to help them do that so they become the most satisfied customers they can be. Here are some examples from Backroads, the active travel company you met in Chapter 6.

Let's say a typical trip with Backroads is six nights and five days. Each of those days might include three primary options for each person to choose from, decided over breakfast each morning. What decision people make can have an enormous impact on how much they enjoy the day. For example, on a biking day, if a novice biker chooses the longest, most difficult bike route, they'll be overwhelmed, late, and extremely tired when they return. If an experienced biker chooses the easiest path, they won't be challenged enough.

So, getting people to make the best decision is critical. The truth is, by the third day, the Backroads leaders know their guests well enough to tell them which option is best for them. But it would be insulting to say to a guest, "Bob, you're a slow rider, so you should take option #1 today." The Backroads leaders need to help guests make that decision for themselves, but make it in the most informed manner possible. That's where storytelling comes in.

Let's say our slow rider, Bob, has his heart set on taking the longest bike route today. The leader might share a story about a similar guest last week who made the same choice: "Last week, Sally picked the same route. But she knew it was going to be a long ride for her. So she got up an hour early, skipped breakfast, and headed out a couple of hours ahead of everyone else. We drove ahead and met her at the 15-mile mark and had a muffin and yogurt waiting for her. By 11 a.m., she was already over the mountain pass and had the rest of the day to make the easy part of the ride."

That short little story about Sally now helps Bob make a more informed decision about today's ride. He might choose to pick another option, or he can do what Sally did and leave early. Either way, he'll feel better about the experience than being told, "Okay, but you'll need to leave earlier than everyone else." That statement tells the guest what to do. The story empowers him to make a better decision for himself.

Storytelling can also help the trip leaders emphasize their flexibility by providing a concrete example. According to Jo Zulaica, global leadership development manager at Backroads, they might say something like the following: "Last week, we had a guest who was really interested in golfing and fishing even though that wasn't part of this trip. So on the layover days, he found a local operator who could take him fly fishing. And on a couple of other days, we set up a tee time for him at the nearest golf course. We drove him to the course right after breakfast to get started."

Compare that short story to the nonstory alternatives of just saying, "Hey, we set up a tee time for a guy last week who really loved golf," or the even less helpful, "Hey, anything you want to do, we can make it happen." The story is not only more interesting but gives the guest a concrete idea of how flexible "flexible" really is. If all you give people is a platitude, they don't really know what to do with it.

Jo Zulaica calls these "what's worked well in the past" stories. If you want to help your customers, in any industry, get the most use out of whatever it is you're selling, you need some of your own "what's worked well in the past" stories.

GENERATING LOYALTY

Storytelling after the call can also help build loyalty. Here's an example from author and speaker Mark Bowser.[1] If you had been in one of Mark's customer service training classes in Indianapolis in the late 1990s, the first words you would have heard him say as he stood at the front of the room to introduce himself would have been, "Hello. I'm Mark Bowser, and these are not my pants."

His explanation was just as entertaining.

His seminar was being held in the Hyatt Regency hotel, so naturally that's where he stayed the night before his early morning session. Apparently that evening, after he checked in and was safely ensconced in bed watching television, he started having a nagging feeling. As he tells the story:

> I kept hearing in my head "Check your suit, check your suit." So I crawled out of bed and looked in my bag. I found my suit jacket right away. And then I quickly realized, "Ahh, I don't have any pants!" Well, that sent me into a panic. "What am I going to do?" The only thing I could think of was to retrace my steps since I arrived. Maybe they fell out of my bag. So I went back through the parking garage, the lobby, and the stairs—no pants. As a last resort, I went to the front desk and sheepishly asked if anyone had found any pants and turned them in. They said no but told me the hotel had some clothing shops on the main floor that would be open in the morning if I wanted to buy some. They told me what time they opened, and of course it was too late for me to make it to the seminar on time.

I was just about to walk away when one of the other clerks who overheard the conversation interrupted. "Sir, did I hear you correctly that you need a pair of pants? Because I have some of mine in the back office. I just picked them up from the dry cleaners. You're welcome to borrow a pair for tomorrow." They didn't fit perfectly, but they were certainly better than nothing. I thanked him and wore them all the next day! It was the most amazing customer service I've ever personally experienced.

Mark never did find his pants. But as a motivational speaker and trainer in sales and customer service, he does find lots of opportunities to tell that story. It's the kind of over-the-top service story you might expect from Nordstrom. The most obvious use for such stories is to teach other employees within your company what great customer service looks like. But it's the not-so-obvious use that I'm more interested in here. If these stories can teach employees how to *deliver* customer service, they can teach existing customers what to *expect* from customer service. The purpose of doing that is to build loyalty—to keep your current customers from even considering going anywhere else.

Practically speaking, of course, only rarely would hotel guests realize they've lost their pants. A story like the one above isn't supposed to communicate to hotel guests that they should come down to the front desk to borrow a pair of pants. It just reinforces the notion that this hotel has unbelievable customer service. Why would you want to stay anywhere else?

Find your most outrageously positive customer service stories and share them with your existing customers on a regular basis—in sales calls, emails, newsletters, or notes slipped into invoices. You'll keep more of the customers you've worked so hard to earn.

To get some creative ideas for delivering your own over-the-top customer service, and to see a whole collection of great customer service stories, check out T. Scott Gross's book *Positively Outrageous Service: How to Delight and Astound Your Customers and Win Them for Life.*

SUMMARIZING THE CALL

A final purpose of storytelling after the sales call isn't found in a story you tell to the buyer, a story the buyer tells you, or even a story that you tell to yourself. It's a story that you craft for the benefit of other salespeople who work at your company. And it tells the story of the successful sale you just closed or the unsuccessful one you just failed to close. The purpose is to capture the wisdom you just gained in the call for your boss, your peers, or the next generation of salespeople calling on that customer.

We all know those wise old sales gurus who've been around and seen it all. We love hearing their "war stories" about what worked and what didn't work. Well, you don't have to have been around for 40 years to remember a few great war stories if you capture your stories as they happen. Here's an example from Steve Blair from his days as a salesperson for a major confectionery company.

In the summer of 2010, when Steve was about a year into the role, he was calling on the buyer at a major drugstore chain. The buyer, let's call him "David," was legendary in the business. Once you had his ear and earned his trust, you had it forever. But getting that trust was difficult. And neither Steve nor anyone at his company had earned it yet.

At one point, Steve and his boss (the CEO of the company) rented a suite at U.S. Cellular Field in Chicago and invited David and his boss to a White Sox baseball game. Their general purpose was to get to know their prospects a little better. But Steve also had a specific sales objective: get David to agree to carry at least one of their boxes of heart-shaped chocolates for Valentine's Day. Steve had been trying unsuccessfully for weeks to make that sale. David's objection each time was that he thought the price per ounce of chocolate was too high. Said another way, he thought there just wasn't enough chocolate for the price. Steve's response each time was that Valentine's Day chocolates are a gift. The person who receives the chocolate will appreciate the gift regardless of how much chocolate is in it.

Steve was hoping he could finally get David to see things his way during the White Sox game. Somewhere around the sixth inning, Steve saw his opportunity. He noticed that the server in the suite was a 20-something woman—exactly the demographic profile of someone who might be on the receiving end of a box of Valentine's Day chocolates. Steve thought David might understand his position if he could hear for himself how much a young woman would appreciate one of these gifts.

The next time she came through the suite, Steve pulled her over to ask her a question. He took out a sample of one of the boxes and held it in front of her. Making sure he had David's attention, he said to her, "What would you say if your husband or boyfriend gave you this for Valentine's Day?" Of course, Steve couldn't be sure how she'd respond. But who doesn't like a free box of chocolates?

The server opened up the box, looked inside, and then said, "Well, the first thing I'd probably say is 'Where's the rest of the chocolate?' "

David looked over at Steve and said simply, "Conversation over."

Steve was devastated. He thanked the server and sat silently for the remaining three innings of the game, knowing that his ill-conceived tactic to close the sale had not only failed but had actually backfired. David now had even more reason to not buy those chocolates, and he didn't for more than a year, until Steve had left for another job. The lesson Steve learned that day is that it's risky to employ a sales tactic when you can't predict the outcome.

Today, Steve is director of people and culture at the Harvest Group, a sales and marketing consultancy that specializes in helping consumer packaged goods companies sell their products to national retail buyers like David. Steve very generously shares this embarrassing failure story, as well as his many successes, with his coworkers. The reason, of course, is so that they can all benefit from the lessons and therefore make even more successful sales for their clients.

Not every one of your sales calls will result in a story this worthy of passing along. But many will. Don't let time rob them from your memory, and don't let your pride keep them from being shared. Write them down and share them as quickly and regularly as you would your expense report.

EXERCISES

1. *Who are your most satisfied customers?* What is it about how they use your offerings that makes them so satisfied? Find out, which might mean interviewing them. Then craft stories about how they do it. These stories can help your client make better decisions about how to best use your products or services.

2. *What are some of the most amazing customer service experiences in your company?* Develop them into well-crafted stories. Then you can build loyalty by sharing them in future sales calls, emails, newsletters, or notes slipped into invoices.

3. *What's the biggest lesson you ever learned about sales from conducting a sales call?* Develop it into a story worthy of sharing. Make it a habit of capturing what happened in your sales calls after each one. Do it as reliably and quickly as you turn in your expense reports.

PART II

HOW TO CRAFT SALES STORIES

NOW THAT YOU know what stories you need, let's turn our attention to finding and crafting the most compelling stories possible.

In order to do that, first we need to know what makes a great story a great story. We'll discuss that in Chapter 11. Armed with that, in Chapter 12, I'll describe a simple process to brainstorm and select the best stories to tell.

Then in Chapters 13 to 17, I'll cut through the dizzying array of story structures, from the overly simple to the unusably complex. I'll outline a seven-stage story structure that's more helpful than "beginning, middle, end" but easier to use than a 17-step Hollywood structure.

In Chapter 18, you'll learn how emotion is actually necessary for your buyer to make good decisions, plus five techniques to add more of it to your story. In Chapter 19, you'll learn how surprise helps your audience remember the lesson in your story, and specific techniques to create a surprise even if one doesn't naturally exist there.

In Chapter 20, we'll discuss the use of inner and outer dialogue, plus five good ways (and some bad ways) to add sensory detail to make your story come to life. We'll finish the chapter by answering the question "How long should my stories be?" And I'll show you how to cut a four-minute story down to a two-minute story or even a one-minute story.

Now your story is done and it's time to deliver it. In Chapter 21, I'll help you navigate the "ums" and "ers" of oral delivery, plus give you tips to keep your written story from reading like a boring business memo.

Wish you could tell a story with data and numbers instead of words? You can. Chapter 22 offers two techniques to do exactly that.

How true do your sales stories have to be? Chapter 23 discusses the ethics of storytelling, along with several techniques to help you maintain the integrity of your story.

In Chapter 24, you'll discover 14 places to look for great stories, five field-tested interviewing techniques, and great interview questions you can use when hunting for stories. And in Chapter 25, you'll learn how to save, practice, and remember your stories when you need them.

You'll also find several templates and case studies (called "Story Clinics") used throughout these chapters to help you practice and master each of the techniques. Use the templates each time you craft a story.

11

ELEMENTS OF A GREAT STORY

WHAT IS IT that makes a great story a great story? Is it a plot filled with drama and intrigue? A surprise ending? An emotional climax? Witty dialogue? Sensory detail that makes you feel like you were there? Or perhaps it's the authenticity of the storyteller or their performance skills at delivering an oratory.

Of course, all of those things are important. But above all else, these three things make a great story: a hero we care about, a villain we're afraid of, and an epic struggle between them. Any great story, not just a sales story, has these three elements at its foundation. And since business stories in general, and sales stories in particular, are told for a purpose and not just for entertainment, we can add a fourth element: that the audience learns a worthy lesson.

If this were a book on writing fiction, that would mean that we should invest the necessary time up front to invent a great hero, villain, and struggle, because everything else in the story hinges on them. But we're not writing fiction. For the most part, we're crafting stories out of actual events that happened in the lives of actual people. That means that the most important part of crafting a great sales story is choosing the right story to craft—choosing the right events in the lives of the right people to craft a story around.

It would be far better to tell the right story in a mediocre fashion than tell the wrong story with a stunning performance. The reason is that unless you're an actor or a professional speaker, your audience will forgive you if you stutter a little or tell the story slightly out of order or even butcher the surprise ending, as long as your story helps them. But if you deliver a magnificent story that's completely irrelevant or useless to them, they'll never forgive you for wasting their time. (And then, if they're smart, they'll file your magnificent story away in their memory to use at an appropriate time, which is what you should have done to begin with.)

So what does that mean for us? A *hero we care about, a villain we're afraid of, and an epic struggle* sounds a bit Hollywood. So let's turn that into more familiar language and explore the pieces a little.

In the business world, that translates into a relatable hero, facing a relevant challenge, and an honest struggle between them. And of course, we need the worthy lesson. Those are the four foundational elements of an effective sales story. Let's start with the most important one—the lesson.

A WORTHY LESSON

The first element to consider in choosing a story is the lesson the story teaches. In fact, a good argument could be made for it being the only element. Remember, sales stories aren't just told for entertainment. They're told for a purpose. If the story you choose to tell doesn't accomplish that objective, you've wasted your time and your prospect's time.

It may sound obvious, and it should be, but in my experience many businesspeople significantly underestimate the importance of the lesson in the story selection process. I can't tell you how many emails I get from people who ask, "I've got a big presentation next week; got any good stories I could use?," as if I could recommend a good story without having the slightest clue what their presentation is about or what their objectives are. When I explain that, I sometimes hear back, "Oh, I'm just looking for something emotional that I could use in a sales call."

It doesn't work that way. If you had a consultant who gave you advice without understanding what your goals are, you'd fire them, right?

Stories should be like every other set of words that come out of your mouth at work—intentional and productive. Even those "getting to know you" stories from Chapter 6 are what sales consultant Kristin Luck calls "chitchat with a purpose." If your story doesn't further your purpose, you chose the wrong story.

A RELATABLE HERO

In this context, the word "hero" doesn't necessarily mean the good guy who saves the day. It means the main character of the story, the protagonist, or more generally, the person from whose perspective the story is told.

The most compelling hero for your story is someone your audience can identify with. That means they can either imagine themselves in the same position or working with that person—in other words, a customer, a supplier, a boss, a subordinate, or even a competitor.

We saw a good example of that in Chapter 9. There you read about Tia Finn telling a school district superintendent a story about another superintendent in a different district. She even spent some time at the beginning of the story making it clear how similar the hero of her story was to her prospect. Her story began, "I really wish you could meet Mary Lou at Rover High School across town. You're familiar with that school, right? Well, she's just like you. Her students are very similar to yours, and they're struggling with the exact same issues."

Notice the key words "she's just like you," which Tia then backed up with some specifics of how they're the same. She did that for a reason. The more similar the hero in the story is to the audience, the more relevant the story will be to them, and the more likely they'll be to listen to the story, remember it, and learn from it. Tia surely has dozens of stories about other clients. But she chose that one to share with that particular prospect because the hero of the story would be more relatable than the others.

That doesn't mean stories can't be effective if they don't involve someone just like your prospect. It just means that as long as you're looking for a story to craft, pick one whose character resembles your audience as closely as possible.

▶ *Watch out:*

A typical problem I see is choosing a hero so aspirational that the audience can't see themselves in the character. I call this the "Superman" problem. If you tell me a story about how Superman saved the day, that might make for an entertaining story. But it won't make a good sales story because it doesn't help me much. After all, I can't fly, bend steel bars, or jump over a tall building with a single bound. How can I be expected to succeed like Superman?

Examples of Superman stories I hear a lot are corporate stories about Apple Computer or stories about the CEO of the company, sports superstars like Michael Jordan, or historical figures like Abraham Lincoln. Those stories definitely have a place in your repertoire of inspiring stories, but the majority of your stories should be more down to Earth.

When in doubt, choose a hero who's similar to your audience.

A RELEVANT CHALLENGE

The challenge is an obstacle or opportunity the hero confronts. The challenge plays the role of the villain in the story. Without a proper villain, it's hard for the audience to care about the hero or her struggle. Consider this example from Karen Dietz and Lori Silverman in *Business Storytelling for Dummies*:

- Mary goes to the store (we don't care)
- to buy some milk (we still don't care)
- for her baby (we care a little)
- who is sick (we care a little more)
- and hasn't eaten in days because a neighborhood bully stole most of her money on the way home from work (we care a lot).[1]

It's the challenge or villain that makes us care about our hero. But that doesn't mean the villain has to be a person. The obstacle could be:

- *An entire company* (like one of your competitors)
- *A thing* (like the mountain you're trying to climb)
- A *situation* (like Pig Island having no food for the pigs, or the Iceland volcano erupting in 2011)
- *You!*

Yes, you could be the obstacle in your own story. Consider Steve Blair's story about losing the Valentine's Day sale at the White Sox game in Chapter 10. (This is also the case in the "I'll tell you when I made a mistake" story that we discussed in Chapter 6.)

And the challenge doesn't necessarily have to have a negative connotation. For example, it could be:

- A *challenging goal* (like to grow sales by 50 percent)
- An *opportunity* (for example, the low Chinese cashmere bid for the clothing maker in Chapter 3 or the job offer Chris Powers got to work at Ariba in Chapter 6—both were exciting opportunities that the main character had to struggle with to make the right decision.)

But regardless of what the challenge is, it should be relevant to the audience. That means a challenge your audience is likely to run into themselves, or that they're at least familiar enough with to have empathy for the hero.

▶ *Watch out:*

Inexperienced storytellers often omit the challenge entirely. The result is a boring, useless story. These are stories where everything that happens is awesome! You've heard these before. You walk into the break room to find the office braggart saying something like, "Yeah, when I got here five years ago, nothing was going right. Sales were down, profits were down, employee morale was awful. But since I got here, sales really started picking up. Profits have doubled, and morale is through the roof!"

These stories are even worse than Superman stories because they won't help anyone. Their heroes didn't overcome any adversity. They didn't confront any challenge. They didn't learn anything valuable. In short, they got lucky. Telling a story about how you got lucky is no way to provide guidance since it can't be replicated.

AN HONEST STRUGGLE

The struggle between the hero and villain is the heart of storytelling. If there's no struggle, there's no story. That means it can't be easy for the hero to get what he's after.

In their book *The Ideal Problem Solver*, authors John Bransford and Barry Stein suggest, "A suitable story problem exists when there is a discrepancy between the initial state and a desired goal state, and when there is no ready-made solution for the problem solver."[2] That "no ready-made solution" is the key.

Here's an illustration: Bob desperately needed a ¾-inch socket wrench to finish his project. There was simply no way to complete the job on time without one. So he reached into his toolbox and grabbed one. The end.

Do you see how wrong that is? It's so wrong it's actually shocking, probably because it violates our core understanding of what a story should sound like. The story has a hero (Bob) and an obstacle (the lack of a socket wrench). But there's no struggle. It's too easy. We can't care about Bob or his project until we see him struggle.[3]

Imagine if the Microsoft executives stranded after the 2011 Iceland volcano eruption (as told in Chapter 5) had simply been able to book themselves on other commercial flights home the same day, or in some futuristic version of the story, simply walk into the transporter room and beam themselves home like on *Star Trek*. The story would have the same hero and the same obstacle, but no struggle. And it would have been useless as a story.

Make sure the stories you choose to tell involve a legitimate struggle and that your audience can see that struggle in the way you tell the story.

▶ *Watch out:*

Sometimes the struggle in a story is internal. And if you aren't the hero of the story, you might miss it or assume one didn't exist. Here's an example from David Hutchens in his book *Circle of the 9 Muses*, where he recounts a story told by one of his clients, Geoff: "There was one time when one of my coworkers—Marcela, who everyone here knows, because she manages the projects, and everyone loves her— made a mistake on our project plan. She came up and told everyone about the mistake and she didn't try to hide it even though it was a big deal. I thought that was really awesome. I wish more people would do that."[4]

As told, that story has a relatable hero (Marcela) and a relevant obstacle (a mistake she made). And as in the "I'll tell you when I made a mistake" story that we discussed in Chapter 6, she admits her mistake. But what's missing from this story is a struggle. Do we think that's because there really was no struggle? Of course not. It's just that the entire struggle took place inside Marcela's head as she debated with her conscience whether or not she should admit to the mistake.

With that insight, Geoff eventually expanded his story in the middle: "There were probably ways she could have covered her butt on this. She could have asked the client to change their timeline. Or she could have taken some resources from a different team. Or maybe she could have just put the blame on production or somebody. Because this was an expensive mistake!" We can all be certain Marcela thought about, and wrestled with, all of those options. Letting your audience see that wrestling is what having an honest struggle is all about.

12

CHOOSING THE RIGHT STORY TO TELL

SO, **HOW DO** you come up with the right story to tell? Now that we've discussed the most important components of a great story, we're in a position to know what we're looking for.

STEPS IN STORY SELECTION

Step 1: *Define your objective*—What do you want your audience to think, feel, or do as a result of your story?

Step 2: *Look for a relevant success, failure, or moment of clarity* surrounding that main idea.

Step 3: *Make one up*—This is if you strike out otherwise. Just make sure your audience knows you've made it up.

Step 4: *List and choose*—Pick the story that best delivers the main message. If all deliver it equally well, pick the one with the most relatable hero, most relevant obstacle, and most engaging struggle.

STEP 1: DEFINE YOUR OBJECTIVE

Since the most important element is that the story has a worthy lesson, we have to start by determining what lesson we want our audience to learn. In other words, step 1 of story selection is defining your objective in telling the story. Specifically, what do you want your audience to *think*, or *feel*, or *do* as a result of your story? What is your *main message*?

STEP 2: LOOK FOR A RELEVANT SUCCESS, FAILURE, OR MOMENT OF CLARITY

Once you've defined the objective, the most productive way to search for an appropriate story is to look for a relevant success, failure, or moment of clarity surrounding that objective. In other words, think of times in the past when you or someone else has done that thing very well or utterly failed to do it, or when you learned that lesson the first time.

Obviously, a story about someone successfully doing what you want your audience to do illustrates the behavior you're trying to encourage and probably also shows the benefits of doing it. A failure story can show the downside of not following your advice. We know that humans often learn more from our failures than from our successes. That's why they make good fodder for stories.

A moment of clarity could be a success or a failure, but often is neither. It's just a moment in time when something happened that taught you or the main character a meaningful lesson. And if it did such a good job of teaching that lesson when it actually happened, it can do a great job of teaching that lesson to others when it's recounted in a story.

You've seen examples of all of these in this book so far. Ben Koberna's narrative about the cashmere auction in Chapter 3 was a success story about how EASI ran a productive reverse auction even with direct materials. Similarly, John Stephens's recounting in Chapter 5 about getting all the Microsoft executives home safely after that Iceland volcano was a success story.

Kevin Moulton's story about the frustrating ATM experience in Las

Vegas (Chapter 7) was clearly a failure narrative, as was Tiffany Lopez's story (Chapter 9) about the acquisition that kept her client from implementing her software solution.

Two examples of moments of clarity are Chris Powers's story describing when he realized exactly what it was about Ariba that made him want to work there (Chapter 6) and Chris Gug's story of Pig Island (in the Introduction) that explained to him (and me) why on Earth there are pigs swimming in the ocean.

STEP 3: MAKE ONE UP

What happens if you can't think of a story? Do you just give up? Fortunately, you don't have to. You have another option. Step 3 is to just make one up. Seriously. You can fabricate the story you need. But you can only do it under one condition. That is that your audience knows you made it up. Otherwise, you risk losing all credibility.

You've seen this a couple of times in this book already. Recall the story from Chapter 3 that the distribution channel expert used to explain in simple terms what he does for a living. It began, "Suppose you're in the chicken business . . ." Everything in that story was completely made up, and yet it wouldn't even raise an eyebrow in conversation. The reason is that both the teller and the listener know that the story is made up, so they accept it as such. The first word, "suppose, . . ." makes it clear everything that follows is hypothetical.

You saw that again in Chapter 7 where you read Logan Strain's story about a child playing on two different models of basketball hoops. His words "Let's say it's two years from now . . ." are the clue to the listener that what follows is a hypothetical story.

For stories like this to be effective, however, they have to be plausible. In other words, they should be the kind of thing that could likely happen, or more pointedly, the kind of thing that probably does happen all the time. These might be one of the most underutilized kinds of stories discussed in this book, so let me provide another example.

David Gillig is a consultant to fund-raisers of philanthropic organizations and has spent most of his career raising money for hospitals. One of the services he's raised money for at Children's Hospital is something called trauma social services. When he's talking to potential donors at a fund-raising dinner, he explains it like this:

> I'd like to ask over the next minute for all of us in this room to be parents. And as a parent, I want to talk about how some of us might someday get that nightmare call that we all hope we never get. On the other end of the phone, someone says, "Your child has been hit by a car. She's been taken to Children's Hospital."
>
> In an instant, your entire world changes.
>
> You jump in your car and start racing to the hospital. You can't seem to focus or see straight because your emotions are running wild, just hoping your child is still alive when you get there.
>
> You arrive at the hospital, burst through the emergency room doors, and you're met by a trauma counselor who says to you calmly, "I know who you are. I know your daughter, and I know where she is. You can't go in to see her right now, but I'm going to stay with you. And I'm not going to leave you. I'm going to go in and check on her every few minutes and come back and let you know how things are going. And then I'm going to stay with you. And I will not leave you. No matter what happens, I'm going to stay with you and keep you up to date."
>
> That life-changing scene is going to happen three times today, and it's going to happen almost a thousand times this year. But without a trauma social service professional, what would probably happen when that parent gets to the emergency room is this. They'll be met by a security guard and told, "You can't go in. Just have a seat here in the lobby." And that's where they'll sit and wait. Scared. Worried. Grieving. Confused. And alone.
>
> Trauma counselors are a vital part of the hospital staff. Unfortunately, insurance companies won't pay for their services. Government agencies don't either. So it makes no financial sense for any hospital to employ someone like that. Yet it makes profoundly important human sense. The only way to pay for trauma social services is for people like you to make a donation. And that's what I'm asking you to do tonight.

Then, of course, with watery eyes and checkbook in hand, the audience does exactly as he asks. It's a very effective story. But also notice that it's a fictional one—a hypothetical situation that David asks his listeners to pretend for a moment was happening to them. What makes it work, of course, is that it's a highly plausible story. In fact, it's one that does indeed happen every day. But it's told without relying on the specific and very private details of any one family's personal ordeal.

Using a plausible but fictionalized story like this is perfect for situations where you know what generally happens in the situations you want to describe, but you don't have access to all the details that normally go into a specific story. Don't be afraid to craft and use hypothetical stories. Just make it clear to your audience that's what they are.

STEP 4: LIST AND CHOOSE

Using all this as a guide, think of as many potential events as possible to serve as the basis for your story—as many different successes, failures, and moments of clarity around this particular objective. List each of them on a piece of paper. The more you think of, the better. Just because you don't use each story this time doesn't mean your time's been wasted. Keep the list and use it again in the future. You may eventually use all of them for just the right situation.

Then you have to pick one to use. Obviously, if one of them does a better job than the others at communicating that lesson, go with that one. But assuming all of the stories you listed are equally well suited, make your choice based on how well your intended audience will identify with the hero, the obstacle, and the struggle: how relatable is the hero, how relevant the obstacle, and how engaging is the struggle.

At this point, don't choose based on which story is funnier or has the best surprise ending, or any of the other elements of storytelling we've yet to discuss. You'll learn how to create or improve all of those elements with the tools you'll learn in the next few chapters. [Note: Appendix B (Selling Story Roadmap) lays out all of the steps for selecting a story, plus the story crafting techniques you'll learn in the remaining chapters of the book. Make a copy or download an electronic version (at www.leadwithastory.com/resources) and use it each time you're ready to craft a new story.]

Once you've chosen, you're ready to move on to the next phase: story structure.

13

STORY STRUCTURE

"TELL THEM WHAT you're going to tell them. Tell them. Tell them what you told them." That's the advice most of us were taught in grade school for how to give a speech or presentation. And it's probably just as effective today as it was then. But as we've discussed, a story isn't the same as an entire speech or presentation. A story is typically just one part of those things. So that grade-school advice isn't well suited for the structure of an individual story, nor would it be very helpful. After all, the entire story is actually contained in the middle part of that description ("Tell them"), and that doesn't provide any structure at all.

A related structure businesspeople are tempted to follow when crafting a story is the one they use when writing a memo: lead with a summary of the recommendation and key ideas. It's based on the structure used by journalists to write newspaper articles. Reporters typically include all of the important information in the entire article up front, often in the first sentence. An example is "Boston, Aug. 21, 2015—A three-day search for a missing two-year-old girl found her alive and well."

After that opening sentence, called the lede (or lead), information is presented in decreasing order of importance. Journalists refer to this as the "inverted pyramid" structure because the most important information is at the top (the wide part of the upside-down pyramid), and the least important information is at the bottom (the narrow part).

News articles are written that way for a reason. A reader who doesn't have time to finish the entire article won't be left not knowing if the bank robber was captured or who won the election last night. It also helps editors know where they can cut if space is tight and the deadline is looming. They cut from the bottom. If the articles weren't in the inverted pyramid structure, the editor would have to go through much more slowly, reading each sentence and cutting a phrase here or a word there.

In their book *Made to Stick*, Chip Heath and Dan Heath recount a perhaps apocryphal explanation that the inverted pyramid was originally developed during the Civil War. They write: "All the reporters wanted to use military telegraphs to transmit their stories back home, but they could be cut off at any moment; they might be bumped by military personnel, or the communication line might be lost completely—a common occurrence during battles. The reporters never knew how much time they would get to send a story, so they had to send the most important information first."[1]

And so, for many reasons, cub reporters are often taught "Don't bury the lede," which is shorthand for "use the inverted pyramid structure like we taught you, and don't bury any important information in the middle or end of your article. No surprise endings!" The same advice, delivered in different language, falls on junior managers joining the corporate ranks.

That's all well and good for writing newspaper articles and standard memos. But for a story, it doesn't work. Can you imagine if the opening scene in *Star Wars: A New Hope* gave away the fact that Darth Vader was Luke's father or that Princess Leia was his sister? The inverted pyramid robs a story of its mystery and intrigue, and therefore part of its unique power to persuade. Fortunately, for a three-minute story in a modern sales call, you don't have to worry about an editor or telegraph lines being cut.

There are better ways.

STORY STRUCTURES THAT WORK

The oldest surviving text on literary theory is *Poetics,* written by the Greek philosopher Aristotle in the third century BCE.[2] In it, he proposes a simple three-part structure to any dramatic narrative: protasis, epitasis, and catastrophe, which could be loosely translated as setup, complication, and resolution. Since Aristotle, countless writers, novelists, philologists, and literary critics have offered their own analysis and preferred story structures. Nineteenth century German novelist and playwright Gustav Freytag popularized the five-act structure, aptly named Freytag's Pyramid, which you probably learned in high school: exposition, rising action, climax, falling action, denouement.

Both more complex and less complex structures have also been proposed. The simplest effective model is probably a two-step structure: conflict-resolution.[3] All storytelling boils down to conflict, and without a resolution, a story is unfinished at best.

On the other end of the spectrum are Blake Snyder's "Save the Cat" structure (a 15-step structure designed for screenwriting),[4] and the monomyth (or "Hero's Journey") structure first introduced by the mythologist Joseph Campbell.[5] The Hero's Journey includes a total of 17 stages and was developed by analyzing epic stories throughout history. If you're going to write your first screenplay or a 300-page novel, these structures might be for you.

In preparation for this book, I studied and considered these and more than a dozen other story structures, including ones with four, five, six, eight, and nine steps.[6] Here's my conclusion: All of them work. Unlike the inverted pyramid or "Tell them what you'll tell them" structures, all of these other structures were designed for real stories (as I defined them in Chapter 1), and all of them will work. What you need as a salesperson is one that's simple enough to easily produce short, two-minute stories, yet sophisticated enough to provide meaningful guidance.

In my first book, *Lead with a Story,* I advocated a structure on the simpler end of the spectrum with three steps designed to work with a broad set of leadership stories. That structure was context, action, result. In considering the options for sales stories, I wanted to provide something a little more advanced while at the same time be guided by what

I found in the most effective sales stories I came across in my interviews with salespeople. The resulting model includes four parts for the main story, plus additional steps for transitioning in and out of your stories and making your conclusions and recommended actions clear.

That seven-step model is shown in Exhibit 13-1 and is made up of these primary story components: context, challenge, conflict, and resolution. That main structure is preceded by a transition-in (or "hook") and is followed by a transition-out, which serves up the lesson you want the buyer to learn and/or recommended action steps. Before we get into the details of each step, let's look at the overall flow.

EXHIBIT 13-1: STORY STRUCTURE

	1 Transition in: (Hook)
MAIN STORY BODY	2 Context
	3 Challenge
	4 Conflict
	5 Resolution
	Transition out:
	6 Lessons(s)
	7 Recommended Action(s)

One good way to get a feel for the structure is to consider the questions each step answers for the listener. For now, let's ignore the name of each step. Here are the questions in the order they would be answered in the story:

- Why should I listen to this story?
- When and where does the story take place?
- Who is the main character (or hero) and what do they want?
- What was the problem or opportunity they ran into?
- What did they do about it?
- How did it turn out in the end?

- What did you learn from it?
- What do you think I should do?

Notice this starts by providing a reason the buyer should be interested in even listening to your story. The next five questions then follow a natural human progression of understanding the main events in a story. Then the final two questions are where the buyer makes meaning from the story and you, as the salesperson, recommend some action.

A second way to get a feel for the flow of this structure is a Story Spine. A Story Spine is a series of unfinished sentences that, if completed, would constitute a complete story in the desired structure. The concept of a Story Spine was originally created by playwright and actor Kenn Adams for improvisational theater,[7] but is now used by writers at Pixar and other Hollywood studios.[8] Below is a Story Spine for the structure I'm outlining here:

- "I think the best example I've seen of that was . . ."
- "Back in _____, at _____, there was _____, and they were trying to _____."
- "Then, one day _____."
- "So they _____, and then _____, and so they _____."
- "Eventually . . ."
- What I learned from that was . . ."
- "And that's why I think you should . . ."

Again, notice the first sentence gives the listener a reason to listen to the story. The next four statements walk through the main body of the story in a natural way. And the final two sentences explain the lesson and the recommended action. It's natural, genuine, and authentic. And it's the typical flow of the most effective sales stories I came across in my research.

Okay, let's put the Story Spine and questions together with the names of each step and then walk through each one. Exhibit 13-2 is your guide.

EXHIBIT 13-2: SELLING WITH A STORY STRUCTURE

STEP	ANSWERS THE QUESTION	STORY SPINE
TRANSITION IN: (HOOK)	Why should I listen to this?	I think the best example I've seen of that was . . .
CONTEXT	Where and when did it take place? Who is the hero and what did they want? Back in _____, at _____, there was _____, and they were trying to . . . (could be unspoken objective)	
CHALLENGE	What was the problem/ opportunity?	Then, one day _____.
CONFLICT	What did you do about it?	So they _____, and then _____, and so they _____.
RESOLUTION	How did it turn out (for everyone)?	Eventually . . .
TRANSITION OUT		
LESSON(S)	What did you learn?	What I learned from that was . . . (That's when I realized . . . That explains why . . . What I've since come to realize is . . .)
RECOMMENDED ACTION(S)	What do you think I should do?	And that's why I think you should . . .

14

THE HOOK
(TRANSITION IN)

THE HOOK IS a single phrase or sentence that explains why you're sharing the story. For listeners, it generates interest and gives them a reason to want to listen to it (hence the name "hook"). For you, it serves as a way to simply and smoothly transition into your story.

With all there is to learn about good storytelling, does this single phrase really warrant its own step in the storytelling structure and an entire chapter of this book? Yes. And here's why. It's one of the most confounding, awkward, and anxiety-producing steps in storytelling to many people.

It's confounding in that many people just have no idea how to do it well. In fact, one of the most common questions I get asked in my seminars on storytelling is "How do I kick off my story?" And because people don't know how to do it, they awkwardly dance around the topic of the story for several sentences, all the while building up more and more unnecessary anxiety like a novice speaker taking the podium for their first public address. And these are seasoned professionals in a room with only a few people, or even just a single buyer.

Let's start with the wrong ways to do it. There are several.

● ● ●

HOW NOT TO TRANSITION INTO A STORY

First, don't apologize for telling your story. You've seen this happen before. In the middle of a meeting, someone says something like, "I'm sorry, I've just got a quick story I'd like to share. I promise it'll just take a minute." What does that kind of language communicate? It communicates that the speaker doesn't value the story as much as what would have been said otherwise. And if that were true, then she should skip the story and get back to the bullet points on slide number 72. You don't apologize for making your sales pitch, do you? Of course not. Then don't apologize for telling a sales story.

Second, don't ask permission to tell your story. You've seen this happen also. I've even seen professional speakers ask, "Can I share a personal story?" and then proceed only after a few obligatory nods from the audience. Granted, it's a fairly safe question to ask. Your listeners aren't likely to say no. But that's probably out of politeness, not because they want to hear a story. Asking adults if they "want to hear a story" in the middle of an important meeting is like asking five-year-olds if they want to stop playing outside and come in to take a bath. In both cases, they don't actually want to. But once they get in it, they like it and don't want to get out. Don't undermine your own authority as the salesperson by asking permission to do your job.

Third, don't even tell your audience you're going to tell them a story. In Shawn Callahan's book *Putting Stories to Work*, he cleverly articulates this as "Don't use the 'S-word'."[1] In training classes, he demonstrates by asking his audience to "imagine this scenario. I'm your boss and I'm standing here in front of you to kick off a meeting. And I say, 'Okay, everyone. I just wanted to get things going here, and I thought I'd start by telling you a story . . .' Now, what's your reaction to that so far?"

What he inevitably gets from his audience are rolling eyes, groans of indignation, and frustrated tones that say, "Ugh, do we really have time for this? Can't you just give us the facts?"

Then he continues, "Now, imagine instead if I kicked off the meeting by saying something like this: 'Okay, everyone. Something really important happened a couple of weeks ago and it completely changed how I think about our business. So I wanted to share that with you . . .' Now, what's your reaction to that?"

The answer is always the polar opposite. "Well, let's hear it!" is a typical response.

In both cases, the audience hears the exact same story. So why such a difference in reaction? Many people have a negative visceral reaction to the word "story." Some think it's a euphemism for lies or fairy tales. Others get a mental image of a librarian reading children's books to a group of kids and are therefore subconsciously insulted. But I think a big part of the reason is that the phrase "Let me tell you a story" is most often used by unpracticed and uncomfortable storytellers to introduce their stories. As a result, the stories that follow are typically not very good. They're long, boring, and often irrelevant. So introducing your story with the word "story" sets up a resistance you don't need.

Last, don't introduce the story by giving away too many of the details, or the ending, or even the specific lesson. This is the kind of thing that happens in the nervous patter before getting to the story that usurps all the power from it. Imagine how neutered the Pig Island story would be if Chris Gug had started off by telling us, "Oh, the pig. Yeah, it was the darnedest thing. Apparently, the pigs had to learn to swim to get to some food dumped in the water by a local restaurant owner. Let me tell you what happened . . ."

Don't bother.

Your story isn't a newspaper article or corporate memo. Avoid using the inverted pyramid. Your one-sentence hook plus the context of the story (which we'll cover in the next chapter) is all the setup your story needs.

As you can tell from the second way Shawn Callahan introduced the story above, there are much better ways to transition into a story.

HOW TO TRANSITION SUCCESSFULLY

First of all, recognize that stories don't appear out of nowhere in a sales call. They happen in the context of the conversation. Any story you'll be telling will either be in response to a question or objection you get from the buyer, or it will be the next logical component of your sales pitch. The point is that it should flow naturally as a part of the conversation and shouldn't require a lot of additional "setup." For the most part, it should be obvious why you're telling the story based on what was said by you or the buyer immediately before you start telling it.

For example, if you've just explained how your product or service works and you want to tell a story about how one of your best customers uses it, the only transitional statement you need is "Let me tell you how one of my customers used that last month . . ." Then start telling your story. Notice there's no asking for permission, no apology, no use of the word "story," and no inverted pyramid.

Another example might be if a buyer objects that your distribution center is too far away from their warehouse and asks what happens if they place an emergency order. You get that objection a lot, so you're prepared with a story about one of your customers who places emergency orders regularly and has never been disappointed in your delivery. Your transition statement in that case is simply, "You know, the best example of that I can think of was when . . . ," and then launch into your story. Again, no apology, permission, angst over the use of the word "story," or giving away the ending.

Importantly, notice in both of these cases that not only does the hook function as your transition into the story, but it also piques your buyers' interest. It tells them that if they listen, they'll either get the answer to a question they asked or learn something else important.

As examples, in Ben Koberna's story in Chapter 3, when Quave Burton asked him if EASI could do reverse auctions for direct materials, his hook might have been, "Yes, certainly. Let me tell you what we did for a big clothing client . . ." Or in Chapter 8, when Tiffany Lopez got the objection from her prospect that they didn't have time to implement her solution right away, her hook might have been, "That's fine. But let me give you an example of what can happen if you wait . . ."

Exhibit 14-1 presents some other options to keep in your tool kit and the situations each is best suited for.

EXHIBIT 14-1. OPTIONAL HOOK PHRASES

SITUATION	HOOK
In response to a question:	"I think the best example of that I've seen was when . . ."
When asked for your opinion about something:	"The best lesson I ever learned about that was when . . ." or "That's a tough problem. Let me tell you what I did when I ran into the same issue last year . . ."
When following your own statement with an illustrative story:	"So, for instance, there was this one time when . . ." or "It might be more clear if I just told you how some of my other clients have used that product . . ." or "Let me help you understand what I'm looking for . . ."
Anytime it occurs to you that a story would be helpful:	"That reminds me of a time when . . ." "Something really important happened recently and I thought you'd like to hear about it . . ."

15

CONTEXT

THE **CONTEXT IS** the first of four main phases of your story. It answers the following questions: *Where and when does the story take place? Who is the main character? What does he or she want?* It's also where you provide any other necessary background for the rest of the story to make sense.

When done well, the context provides a number of benefits for the tellers and the listeners. It grabs the listeners' attention. It tells them if the story is going to be relevant to them and their situation. It builds on the hook to generate more interest in and excitement about hearing the rest of the story. And it helps the listeners understand the lesson in the story in a more practical fashion, so they can reapply it to their particular situation.

So it's all the more unfortunate that this is the part of storytelling business leaders most often underinvest in and sometimes skip entirely. There are many reasons context gets short shrift: The tellers already know all the background and don't realize how important it is to those who don't know it; they skip it out of respect for the listeners' time; or maybe they're excited to get to the action of the story that's most interesting to them.

Whatever the reason, the result is usually a story that's confusing or uninteresting. Let's see why that's the case by looking in more detail at the questions the context needs to answer.

WHERE AND WHEN

Clearly stating up front where and when the story took place satisfies a fundamental curiosity humans have when trying to understand something that happened. As discussed in Chapter 1, time and place indicators in a story are two of the key attributes that distinguish a story from other types of narrative. If you leave them out of a story, it creates a dissonance for the audience—an unanswered question that nags at them until they get the answer. It's so strong an urge it's not uncommon for someone to interrupt the speaker in midstory and ask questions like, "Wait, where was this?" or "Was this recently?" Until answered, those nagging questions distract the audience from listening to the rest of your story.

Another benefit of starting the story with the where and when is that doing so provides instant credibility. If I start a story by saying, "In May of this year at Coney Island in Cincinnati," what do you immediately assume about the story? That it's a true story. If, instead, my story started, "Let's say you're in the chicken business and one day . . . ," you'd immediately know the story is made up. But what if I didn't say either of those things and just started into the plot of a story? You wouldn't really be sure if it was true or not. And that's why, especially for the most remarkable stories, a speaker gets interrupted with the question "Wait, did this really happen?" Almost inevitably, that question is followed by "Where was it?" or "When did it happen?"—again illustrating the credibility-building nature of the where and when of a story.

WHO THE MAIN CHARACTER IS

This is the protagonist of your story. It's sometimes called the hero by literary theorists, although that doesn't necessarily mean the person who saves the day. It just means the person from whose perspective the story is told.

The importance of a relatable hero was detailed in Chapter 11, so I won't repeat that advice here. Just remember that the more your audience can see themselves in the hero, the more interested they'll be in your story.

For many people, the closest they've ever come to crafting a real story at work is writing a case study. And in case studies, the main character is usually a company: "The company did this . . . then the company did that," etc. As a result, I'm often asked: "Does the main character have to be a person, or can it be a department or the whole company?"

Yes, it's okay for the main character to be a company. But if possible, it's usually better to have a real person as your hero. Remember that the hero should be relatable to the audience, who are human beings, not a company. So a story about a person is always more relatable than an impersonal corporate entity.

An easy way to write a story about people is to choose one or more people at the company to serve as the main characters and tell the story from their perspective. Instead of "the company did this and the company did that," it becomes "Bob, the marketing director, did this, and Sally, the product designer, did that." Choose the people most closely associated with the activity in the story. Or, if you don't exactly know who those people are, use job titles of the people most likely involved—for example, "The product design manager did this . . ."

Another way to alter the hero of the story without choosing a different story to tell is to tell the story from the perspective of a different character. For example, you might want to tell the same story from a different perspective depending on whom you're addressing at the time.

Consider Kevin Moulton's story in Chapter 7 about battling the ATM in Las Vegas. That story was told with Kevin as the main character. And when talking to a male banker, that might be the best way to tell it. But if Kevin's audience was someone who might more readily relate to a female main character, the entire story could have been told from the perspective of Kevin's wife. The story would start with her going to bed after a hard day's work, looking forward to a restful night's sleep (perhaps without having to listen to a snoring husband because he was away on a business trip in Las Vegas). When all of a sudden the phone rings . . .

Same story. Same lesson. Different main character.

What if you only know the story from one person's perspective? In that case, you might have to do a little research to learn the details of what happened from the other people involved. That's okay. You expect to have to do some research and analysis for every other idea you share with your buyers, right? You should be willing to do the same for good stories. They're just as important to your success.

Another helpful way to alter the main character of a story is to make the customer or buyer the hero, instead of the product or service you sell. Major advertisers learned this lesson years ago. A case in point is Bounty paper towels. A couple of decades ago, it wouldn't have been uncommon to see a Bounty ad on television where a big mess gets made in the kitchen (presumably by the kids), and the Bounty paper towel comes to save the day for mom. The paper towel is the hero.

Today, you're more likely to see a similar scenario, except the entire story is told from mom's perspective. She's watching the kids play and have a good time. Then one of them accidentally spills something. The kids stop playing immediately, afraid mom's going to get mad at them. Mom confidently reaches for a paper towel. She cleans up the mess with a single swipe and a laugh that signals to the kids that all is well so they can get back to playing.

Notice the difference. In this version, mom is the hero, not the paper towel. The obvious reason for the change is that mom is a more relatable hero for the audience than a piece of paper.

If your sales stories are written with your product as the hero, consider recrafting them with your customer or buyer in the role of hero. You'll almost certainly have better luck.

► *Watch out:*

It's not uncommon for some salespeople to cast themselves as the hero and main character in most of their sales stories. A little of that is understandable when you're trying to establish your value to the prospect. But when you're the hero in most of your stories, you come across as arrogant and self-centered. Your stories also aren't as effective as they could be with more thoughtfully chosen main characters. Alan Veeck has seen that firsthand.

Alan is vice president of Denali, a procurement services company. As a procurement professional, Alan has had occasion to see lots of salespeople in action. One of the least effective he ever saw was a guy we'll call Frank. Frank spent very little of his time in sales calls telling stories, which was part of his problem. But the stories he did tell always had himself in the starring role in an ill-concealed attempt to make himself look good. Needless to say, Frank didn't last long in that role.

Don't always be the hero of your own stories.

WHAT THE MAIN CHARACTER WANTS

What is your hero trying to achieve? What is their passion or objective? Are they trying to save the world, or beat their competition? Are they trying to win the sale, or just not get fired? Sometimes the objective is simple and easy to state at the beginning of your story. For example, in Kevin Moulton's adventures in Las Vegas (Chapter 7), he just wanted to get some cash from an ATM.

In other cases, the hero's goal changes or doesn't become clear until after the challenge. For instance, Mark Bowser's original objective (Chapter 10) was to get a good night's sleep in the hotel. But once he realized he was missing his pants, his objective quickly changed to finding them.

In the simplest cases, the goal is so obvious it doesn't require stating directly. For instance, in Chris Gug's story of Pig Island, the pigs just wanted to eat and survive. In the absence of food, of course the pigs wanted desperately to eat. It's hardly necessary to explain the need and desire to eat. Similarly, sometimes the unstated goal of a main character in a business story is to make a profit or grow sales. As long as it's clear to your audience what the hero is trying to accomplish at each point in the story, you should be fine. But if and when the hero's motivation changes and it's not clear, you owe it to your audience to make it clear.

Stated or unstated, however, your hero's objective must be one your audience would deem worthy, or at least intriguing. Otherwise, they lose interest in your story.

OTHER BACKGROUND FOR THE STORY
TO MAKE SENSE

You've seen this happen countless times. Someone is excitedly telling you a story, and it's just not making sense. Eventually, they can see the sense of confusion in your eyes and stop themselves midsentence. They say, "Oh, wait, let me back up. See, I probably should have told you that . . . ," which is where they fill in the missing pieces of the puzzle that had you so confused. Once they see the spark of understanding in your eyes again, they continue their story where they left off.

What just happened is that the teller left out part of the context of the story—some vital piece of information that you needed to make sense of the story. In many cases, that vital information is the answer to one of the questions we've just discussed: where and when did it happen, who is the main character, what were they trying to accomplish. But sometimes there's other background the listener needs to properly understand the behaviors of the main character. The extra background should explain the character's motivations to act or their reactions to what happens to them.

You can see an example of that in Chapter 9 in the section on creating urgency. There, Tiffany Lopez shares at the beginning of her story that December and January were busy months for the payables department when they were closing the books, and February was their audit season. So March would be the earliest the A/P staff would be freed up for an installation project like the one involving Tiffany's product. "Come back in January and we'll sign all the paperwork, and then start work in March," the client told Tiffany.

Those few sentences, which describe why her prospect was so busy from December through February, explain why they would agree to a sale but then tell her they couldn't start until March. Without that background, it makes no sense why they would wait so long. It would be one of those nagging questions that would distract Tiffany's audience from listening to the rest of her story if she didn't answer it up front.

HOW MUCH IS TOO MUCH SETTING?

No doubt in high school you learned there are five "Ws" that need addressing in any story: who, what, when, where, and why. Notice that the context contains four of them: who, when, where, and why. The who is the main character. The where and when are obviously the where and when. And the why is the answer to the last two questions, "What does the main character want?" and "Is there any other background needed for the story to make sense?" It explains the passions and motivations that drive the character's behavior throughout the story. It explains *why* the character does what they do.

If you have material at the beginning of your story that doesn't answer one of these questions, it's probably not necessary. But it's even worse if you leave one of these questions unanswered. If you're lucky, the confused look on your audience's face will prompt you to go back and answer it. If you're not so lucky, your audience will just endure a less effective story.

The only "W" left is the what, which refers to what happens in the remaining three sections of the story (the challenge, conflict, and resolution). This helps explain why the context is so vitally important to storytelling. Four of the five Ws are addressed there. So, ironically, storytelling has its own unique version of the inverted pyramid. Much of the important information in a story is at the very top. It's just not the same important information that's called for in the journalistic version.

But that doesn't mean the context should be the longest part of the story. In fact, it's usually very short. The goal for the context is to pack all the answers to the who, when, where, and why in as few words as possible. That way, you can invest more of your words and time in the more exciting conflict section, which we'll discuss in the next chapter.

For example, in Kevin Moulton's story of his battle with the ATM, the entire context of the story and the answers to all four W questions are in the first two sentences. Those two sentences essentially say that he was in Las Vegas on a business trip a few years ago and realized he needed some cash so he found the nearest ATM. The who is Kevin. The where and when is Las Vegas a few years ago. And the why is that he needed some cash to enjoy the Vegas nightlife. That's it. Short and sweet.

16

CHALLENGE, CONFLICT, RESOLUTION

THE CHALLENGE

THE **CHALLENGE IS** the part of a story where the hero first faces the problem or opportunity. It's often called the "complication" or the "catalyst" because it's that moment that a monkey wrench gets thrown into the hero's original plans and sets off the entire series of events in the story. In other words, this is where the hero meets the villain.

In Mark Bowser's story in Chapter 10, the challenge was a problem. It was the fact that he didn't have any pants. Before he realized that, everything was going fine. In Ben Koberna's story in Chapter 3, the challenge was an opportunity—the unexpected low bid on cashmere from the Chinese supplier. Before that, everything was normal.

Here's a little test to help you distinguish the challenge from other events in the story: Ask yourself how it would impact the rest of the story if the challenge never happened. If most of the things that happen in a story never occurred, the story would continue, but things might turn out a little differently in the end. But without the challenge, the rest of the story wouldn't happen at all.

Try it yourself. Remove the part of Mark Bowser's story about his nagging feeling that he'd forgotten something, or searching the parking garage, or asking for help at the front desk, or even getting the generous loaner pair of pants from the clerk. An interesting story would have still resulted. It would just be a somewhat different story. But if Mark had never lost his pants, you would have never heard the story to begin with because there wouldn't be any story to tell. Without the challenge, nothing of interest would ever happen.

The challenge has the potential to be the shortest part of your story. The reason is that it's usually an unexpected event that happens in an instant, or that the main character realizes in an instant. So it doesn't take long to describe. It's the moment you realize that the pigs don't have any food to eat (the Introduction) or the moment Keith Krach offered Chris Powers a job at Ariba (Chapter 6). All of the messy (and probably lengthier) struggling with the villain happens next, in the conflict portion of the story. This is just the brief initiating event.

Unlike the context, the challenge is a part of the story that business leaders are typically more adept at delivering. That's because it's usually very short, and it's an obviously instrumental part of the story. In fact, try telling a story without it and see how far you get. Not far, I'll bet.

THE CONFLICT

The conflict is where the hero does battle with the villain. And as we learned, this is the heart of a story. If you were to strip everything else away from a story except the conflict, it would still be interesting to listen to. In fact, it's the only part of a story that can stand on its own and still command an audience. The context alone would be pointless. The challenge alone would be a tease. And the resolution alone would be baseless and therefore powerless to effect change. This explains why millions of people sit through even the most unpromising and poorly reviewed action movie just to watch the battle scenes.

In his book *TED Talks Storytelling*, author and performance coach Akash Karia observed, "The number one thing that makes a story irresistible—that has audience members sitting on the edge of their seats, totally captivated by your every word—is conflict."[1] So, don't make it too easy for the hero to get what he's after. Let the audience see the struggle. And remember from David Hutchens's story of Marcela (Chapter 11) that sometimes the struggle is internal.

If there was a single most important part of a story, this would be it. Invest the time to develop it well. In fact, its ultimate importance to a story is one reason the conflict is often the longest part of a story, sometimes making up half or more of it. Another reason is that this is where most of the plot plays out. In Mark Bowser's story (Chapter 10), the conflict is his anxiety-riddled search for his pants: He looks through his bag, searches the parking garage, asks at the front desk, and considers buying new ones the next morning but the store won't be open in time. It continues all the way up to when the clerk offers him a pair of his pants. The entire story is about 300 words long. The conflict is about 180 words of that, or 60 percent.

► *Watch out:*

Don't take that advice as license to ramble on in this, or any, part of your story. Some of the best advice to follow in knowing how much territory to cover in the conflict section is to "arrive late, leave early." It was first expressed this way by screenwriter William Goldman in his book *Adventures in the Screen Trade.*[2] The idea is to introduce the audience to the action of the story as close to the climax as possible, and then stop talking as soon as you've shared enough to make your point.

For example, in Kevin Moulton's story, the challenge is when the ATM rejected his transaction. The conflict begins in the next paragraph, and you'll notice that he skips immediately to the part where the bank called his wife at home and woke her up. In reality, there are probably a number of things that happened right after the ATM rejected his card. He probably tried it two or three more times to make sure it wasn't just a mistake. He probably let out a few foul words. He might have even hit the machine in frustration, or maybe he took a cab to another ATM down the street to try it and see if it worked any better. And perhaps he finally just gave up and went back to his hotel room because he didn't have enough money to continue his evening out. All of these things could have (and probably did) happen before the phone call was made to his wife, and they certainly happened before he found out about the call to his wife.

But Kevin doesn't share those parts of the story. He knows that the real climax of the conflict with the bank was during the call to his wife and his frustrating call to the bank the next day. So he lets you, his audience, "arrive late" in the conflict, right as the exciting part is about to start. And then when he finishes telling you about his call to the bank, he moves immediately to the resolution and lesson. He doesn't tell you about how he ended up canceling the card and getting a new card from a new bank, or about how his wife teased him for a week about his late-night escapades in Las Vegas. He lets you as the audience "leave early" in the story, thus sparing you those less interesting events. Arrive late, leave early.

THE RESOLUTION

The resolution is where you explain how everything turned out in the end.[3] Did the hero win or lose? Did the plan work? Did the villain get caught or did he escape? It's there that you may also explain how things (including the characters) were forever changed as a result of the ordeal.

The resolution in Chris Gug's story about Pig Island is that the pigs finally learned to swim so they could eat (the heroes won!). It's also there you find out that Big Major Cay has been known ever since as Pig Island (how things changed as a result of this ordeal). In the cashmere auction story (Chapter 3), the resolution is that all the suppliers lowered their bids. The resolution is also where, in the same story, you find out that's when the chief procurement officer first earned a seat at the decision-making table (how things changed as a result).

How do you know if you've adequately wrapped up the story in the resolution? The work of educational philosopher Kieran Egan offers some insight. In his book *The Educated Mind*, he reports the result of his research that suggests "we know we have reached the end of a story when we know how to feel about the events that make it up."[4] So here's the test: The resolution is complete when the audience knows how to feel about what happened in the story. If you haven't provided enough information for the audience to have an emotional conclusion, you're not done with the story.

Consider Chris Powers's story in Chapter 6. At the end of the story, he decides to take Keith Krach's offer and join Ariba as a sales rep with the explanation that "It was a no-brainer. I signed up and traded in my partnership to become employee #92 . . ." And that's where the resolution and the story could have ended. But it isn't emotionally satisfying yet because the audience doesn't know how to feel about the outcome. We don't know if we should be happy or not because we don't know how Chris felt about the decision.

Fortunately, Chris finished the story with the words " . . . in a company that grew to over 2,000. And it was absolutely the best decision I ever made." That last sentence and a half helps us know how to feel about the outcome. The fact that the company grew from 92 employees to 2,000 tells us that the company has done well and that Chris got in on the ground floor of something big. And the assurance that it was the best decision he ever made gives us an unambiguous license to feel good about the outcome, because he feels good about the outcome.

17

LESSON AND ACTION (TRANSITION OUT)

THE STORY IS technically over at this point, but your work as a storyteller isn't. Now it's time to "get out" of the story and make use of it—to make meaning with it and drive action. The three most productive things you can do immediately following the story are: (1) explain the lesson, (2) recommend action, or (3) just listen. And you might do all of them. Let's talk about each one.

EXPLAIN THE LESSON

For most things of value, there is a price to be paid. Storytelling is of great value in sales for all the reasons discussed in Chapter 2. But here's the price to be paid for it: There's a risk that the audience may not draw exactly the same lesson from the story that you intended them to. As a result, it's usually a good idea to clarify what you think that lesson should be. This is your reflection on or assessment of the whole experience, and it should tie directly to your main message and objective in telling the story to begin with.

Admittedly, this isn't normally done in other types of storytelling. For example, David Hutchens observes that making "this kind of overt connection is unwelcome in most entertainment stories, where it may be seen as moralizing. But in leadership storytelling, our mandate is not to entertain but to align."[1] True. And in selling stories, our ultimate goal is to sell something. It's okay to make sure the buyer connects the dots the right way.

As examples, the lesson from the Pig Island story was that it answered my original question by explaining why Chris Gug was able to get a picture of a pig in the ocean—because the pig learned to swim up to approaching boats in search of food. The lesson from the Iceland volcano story (Chapter 5) was more of an assessment of the whole story, which could be summarized as "This is the kind of partnership Microsoft is looking for with our suppliers."

The easiest way to share the lesson of your story is to start like this: "I think what I learned from that story was . . ." and then complete the sentence. This method has a couple of benefits. First, by telling the audience what *you* learned from the story, you're still giving them the freedom to draw their own conclusions, but guiding their thinking in the direction you want it to go. This shows respect for the audience and lets you leverage one of the strengths of storytelling, which is to get your message across without arrogantly telling your listeners what to think.

The second benefit is that it's a short, simple way to signal that the story is over and now it's time for both of you to talk about it. Transitioning out of the story for some people is just as awkward as transitioning in. They end up hemming and hawing and waving their hands around in a tongue-tied attempt to signal the end of the story. But using this kind of a transitional phrase into the lesson makes it easy.

Below are some other transitional phrases you can use, depending on which fits best with your story, lesson, and personal style:

- I think what I learned from that was . . .
- That's when I realized . . .
- So, that explains why . . .
- What I've since come to realize is . . .

RECOMMENDED ACTION

Recall that stories are just components within your overall sales process. Not all of them will end with a recommended action or ask for the sale. But some will. And for those, this is the place to make that recommendation.

For example, in the Pig Island story, there was no recommended action that followed naturally from the story. In fact, it might have seemed crass for an artist to follow that story with "So, therefore, I think you should buy my photo." In Ben Koberna's story of the sludge removal contract (Chapter 8), there would be no recommended action unless that story happened to be delivered as the final step in the sales pitch prior to asking for the sale.

However, in Kevin Moulton's story of his battle with the ATM (Chapter 7), he follows the story with the recommendation, "You could send a onetime password to your customer's cell phone." In Tiffany Lopez's story in Chapter 9, she recommended the prospect implement her solution now and not wait, which was the point of the entire story.

JUST LISTEN

The final option for what to do when transitioning out of your story sounds like the easiest, but in practice it's the hardest one to pull off. That's unfortunate because it might also be the most effective. And that is to just listen. We're so enamored of our own voice that it's hard to turn over the reins of the conversation to someone else. Let the story sink in and give your listener a chance to respond to it. After all, you're having a conversation. Giving your partner a chance to talk is a requirement, and right after you've told a story is a good time to do that.

Recall from Chapter 5 that your story might prompt your prospects to tell their own story, which is always a good thing. The other thing they're likely to do is to tell you what they think the lesson in the story is. That's ideal. Chances are, because you chose the right story to tell, they'll come to exactly the same conclusion you wanted them to. In that case, you're better off letting them come to that conclusion themselves than having to tell them about it.

As mentioned above, you may choose to pursue one, two, or all three of these options after transitioning out of your story. The story structure template in Appendix C has space for the first two options that involve planning your words. And the online resources for this book include a Story Database containing 24 blank story templates, one for each of the sales stories you need. (Download free copies at www.leadwithastory.com/resources).

To help you get a feel for story structure and for how to use the story structure template, Exhibit 17-1 shows an outline of three of the stories presented earlier in the book. Read down through each column to get a feel for the flow of the stories. Then read across each row to help improve your sense for what each step sounds like.

EXHIBIT 17-1. EXAMPLES OF HOW TO USE THE STORY STRUCTURE TEMPLATE

STEP	PIG ISLAND	ATM IN LAS VEGAS	"THESE ARE NOT MY PANTS!"
OBJECTIVE/ MAIN MESSAGE	Explain why there are pigs in the ocean.	Illustrate how a bank's security protocols can harm customers.	Great customer service makes loyal customers.
TRANSITION IN: (HOOK)	[Unnecessary, since we asked Gug to tell us a story.]	"Let me give you an example of the kind of problem I can help you fix."	"Hello, I'm Mark Bowser, and these are not my pants!"
CONTEXT	Picture taken off Big Major Cay in Bahamas A few years ago, local entrepreneur brought pigs to island for bacon farm.	A few years ago In Las Vegas on a business trip Needed some cash	Late 1990s Indianapolis, IN Hyatt Regency To conduct a seminar on customer service
CHALLENGE	No food for pigs.	Went to the ATM, and it rejected transaction	Nagging feeling . . . "I don't have any pants!"

Table continues

STEP	PIG ISLAND	ATM IN LAS VEGAS	"THESE ARE NOT MY PANTS!"
CONFLICT	Struggles and weren't thriving. But restaurant dumped food. Pigs had to venture into water to get it.	They called my wife! Woke her up. Pissed me off. I called them Monday to ask why. They said, "It's our policy."	Looked in bag, garage, car, no pants! Asked at front desk, no pants! Retail store opens too late to get pants in morning. Clerk offered, "Do you want to borrow my pants?"
RESOLUTION	Pigs learned to swim. Now called "Pig Island"	Left me wondering why they even have my cell phone number.	Took the clerk's pants. Didn't fit perfectly. But were better than nothing. Wore them all the next day
TRANSITION OUT			
LESSON(S)	That's why it was easy to get the picture. The pigs swim up to the boats now.	Banks need better security protocols.	Most amazing customer experience of my life. I became a loyal Hyatt customer.
RECOMMENDED ACTION(S)	None.	Ask the customer, "What's your mother's maiden name?" We can do that for you.	None.

STORY CLINIC:
THE UNWELCOME BUSINESS CARD

The goal of this book is to be a practical guide to storytelling, not an academic or theoretical treatise. As such, here I present a Story Clinic as an opportunity for you to apply the tools and techniques you learn. I'll introduce an idea for a story here, and then, throughout the rest of the book, you'll get a chance to improve its effectiveness.

The story that follows, which serves as the basis for most of the Story Clinics, is fabricated. However, it's formed from the combined facts of two true stories in a way that will give us the opportunity to explore all of the story tools.

The protagonist in the story is a man we'll call Bob Jacobson, who's a vice president at his company. The audience is a department of people reporting to him. It's a story of the sort we ran into at the end of Chapter 10, used to summarize the lessons from a particularly insightful sales call.

Let me tell you a story about how to handle a sales call. Apparently, you shouldn't give your business card to the buyer unless you're on the sales team. If buyers can call headquarters directly to get stuff done, they don't need the sales team. That's exactly what happened at my last job.

I'd been with the company almost a decade—first as a sales rep, then D12 manager, and then finally as VP of Bay-ops. I liked moving around a lot so I kept raising my hand for every assignment that came open in an interesting place. I didn't know that would help me get promoted faster too, but I'm sure that had something to do with it.

Anyway, there was this one time I was asked to fly out from headquarters to join the sales team for a meeting with the buyer. It was an uncomfortable meeting for sure, but when the yelling was over, I handed my business card to the buyer and told her she could call me directly, anytime.

And that's exactly what she did. That buyer came straight to me with all her questions for several months. I thought I was being a team player and showing her how important she was to our business.

But that's not how it worked out. Since she didn't need the sales team anymore, she stopped accepting meetings with them. Sales dropped big time, and everyone knew exactly why. About six months later, I was asked to resign.

It was a powerful lesson for me. Sales is a relationship game. Without a relationship, not many sales happen.

This isn't a bad story as is. But it could be a lot better. Let's work through the story template in Appendix C, one step at a time, to see what we could do to improve it. You can make a copy of Appendix C and take notes as we go, or just follow along as I describe how you would use the template. My answers are shown in Exhibit 17-2 later in this chapter. As with any time you're using the story structure template, just fill it out in outline or bullet point form. There's no need to write out full sentences. Think of this as your story outline. You'll turn it into a full story later.

One of the things you should notice right away is that you have a lot of questions about what happened. And since you're not Bob Jacobson, you don't know the answers to them. So you won't know exactly what you can add to the story to make it better, but you should have an idea for the kind of questions you'd like to ask Bob to help improve his story. That's good. Write those questions down. I'll answer them below. This is good exercise to go through because you'll have to ask the same kind of questions when developing your own stories, whether they're about you or other people.

STORY CLINIC ASSESSMENT

We'll start at the top of the template in Exhibit 17-2 and work our way down, filling it out with what we know already from the story as written. Then we'll see where we don't have complete answers to the questions each section should address. Those questions are in the first column of the template. See the story spine in the second column for additional guidance.

Objective/Main message. If you asked Bob, he would indicate that his purpose in telling the story is to give a warning to any visitor asked to join a sales call to not try to be a hero. You'll disempower the sales team. Your job is to make their job easier.

Transition in (The Hook)—The first problem you're likely to notice is that the story starts off with the words "Let me tell you a story . . ." Unless Bob is telling his story to a group of kindergarteners, this isn't a good idea. Check the Story Spine column and Exhibit 14-1 for better ideas.

Recommendation: Replace the first sentence with "I think the best lesson I ever learned about going on a sales call was . . ."

Context—A quick look at the opening paragraph makes it clear the context is almost entirely missing. Consider the questions the context is supposed to answer: Where and when does the story take place? Who is the hero and what does he want? Is any other background necessary to understand the characters' motivation and behavior? The only one of those things we know is that Bob Jacobson is the main character. We don't know when or where it all happened. We don't know what the purpose of the meeting was. And we don't know why Bob was asked to fly out to attend it.

In brief, here are the answers: (1) The meeting happened last year at the company Bob used to work for. (2) The meeting was called at the request of the customer because they were angry about a price increase Bob's company had just pushed through. (3) The customer asked for a senior executive of the company to attend so they would have someone important to complain to.

Recommendation: Rewrite to add these facts in the first paragraph.

Also, look at the second and third sentences as they're written now ("Apparently, you shouldn't give your business card to the buyer . . . they don't need the sales team."). That seems like the lesson Bob learned.

Recommendation: The lesson doesn't belong in the first paragraph. It belongs at the end. Move it.

Challenge—Recall that this is the catalyzing moment (or the monkey wrench) that sets the rest of the events in motion. For Bob, that moment has to be when he was chosen as the sacrificial executive to send to the customer meeting. And until that moment, Bob's purpose and motivation was unclear and less important. But at this point, it's important for the audience to know what his objective is. In other words, what role is he supposed to play in this meeting? In talking to Bob, he explains to you that his goal was damage control—smooth things over with the customer.

Recommendation: State that in the story.

Also, the second paragraph (which is where the challenge belongs) seems self-serving and irrelevant to the rest of the story. All that talk about Bob's career path might be interesting to Bob, but it probably won't be nearly as interesting to the audience.

To figure out if this is essential or not, go through all the questions a story is supposed to answer (why are you telling me this story, where and when did it take place, who is the hero and what does he want, is there any background I need to understand the character's motivations, what was the challenge, what did you do about it, how did it turn out in the end, what did you learn, and what do you think I should do). If the text doesn't answer any of those questions, it's probably not necessary to the story. In this case, it doesn't seem to answer any of them and really just seems to serve Bob's ego rather than the needs of the audience. That's a common mistake in storytelling.

Recommendation: Delete the whole paragraph.

Conflict—As discussed in Chapter 11, this is where we should see an honest struggle between the hero and the villain. In this case, the only indication of a struggle is that the meeting was "uncomfortable," there was some yelling, and then it was over. That's too easy. Here's where you might have to do some detective work.

An obvious place to look for more conflict would be to ask Bob what all the yelling was about. But in this case, there's an even more productive option. The real turning point in this story is when Bob gave his business card to the buyer. That's what caused all the trouble that followed, up to and including his getting fired. Surely there's an interesting struggle there. And if you don't see it, remember that a hero's struggle is often internal as he debates what decision to make or suffers to make productive sense of a bad decision. In this case, it was the latter.

If you talked to Bob, he would tell you that the toughest

moment for him wasn't the yelling in the meeting or getting fired later. It was the moment right after the meeting when one of the sales reps confronted him and told him how bad he made the sales team look.

Recommendation: Add details of the confrontation with the sales rep after the meeting.

Resolution—We know three things resulted from the customer meeting: (1) The buyer went straight to Bob with all her questions and stopped accepting calls from the sales team, (2) sales dropped, (3) Bob got fired. This nicely summarizes the fate of all the main characters in the story: Bob, the sales team, the buyer, and the business results.

Recommendation: None.

Transition Out—Go back to Bob's objective in telling this story. It's to provide a specific warning to visitors in a customer meeting for how to behave. So he clearly is interested in both drawing a lesson from the story and making a specific recommendation.

The Lesson—Looking at the story the way it's written, we have two contenders for the main lesson. The first is the admonition to not give your business card to the buyer unless you're on the sales team. This is the part we found in the first paragraph and decided to move to the bottom where the lesson belongs. The second is the concluding paragraph that says, "Sales is a relationship game. Without a relationship, not many sales happen." And as a platitude, that's certainly true enough.

But do either of these options really capture the wisdom that could be gained from this story? The business card advice seems too specific and narrow. And the relationship commentary, while pithy and memorable, seems too broad and not really related to what happened in the story. It's not like the problem resulted from a lack of a good relationship between buyer and seller.

If you've done a good job of identifying your objective and main message, you'll already have a clear line of sight to what the lesson in the story should be. It's that even well-intentioned behaviors in a customer meeting can have unproductive consequences, specifically behaviors that make you out to be valuable at the expense of the sales team.

Recommendation: Remove both the business card and relationship lessons and replace with the right one.

Recommended Action—As written, this story has no specific recommended action. But we've agreed that it should. There are many ways that could be articulated. Here's one: "The role of the visitor should not be to impress the buyer at the sales team's expense, but to make the sales team's job easier. Offer help. But don't do it in a way that disempowers the sales team. That does more harm than good."

Recommendation: Add this specific recommendation action to the story.

See Exhibit 17-2 for a completed story structure template for this story.

EXHIBIT 17-2. COMPLETED STORY STRUCTURE TEMPLATE FOR "THE UNWELCOME BUSINESS CARD."

STEP	ANSWERS THE QUESTION:	STORY SPINE	UNWELCOME BUSINESS CARD
OBJECTIVE / MAIN MESSAGE	What do you want the audience to think, feel, or do as a result of hearing your story?		If you're a visitor on a sales call, don't try to be the hero. You'll disempower the sales team. Your job is to make their job easier.
TRANSITION IN: (HOOK)	Why should I listen to this story?	I think the best example I've seen of that was . . .	I think the best lesson I ever learned about going on a sales call was . . .
CONTEXT	Where and when did it take place? Who is the hero and what did they want? Other background needed?	Back in ____, at ____, there was ____, and (s)he were trying to . . . (could be unspoken objective)	• Last year at the company I used to work for . . . • Customer upset about our price increase, wanted an executive to complain to.
CHALLENGE	What was the problem/opportunity?	Then, one day ____.	• I was asked to attend a meeting with the customer for damage control.

Table continues

STEP	ANSWERS THE QUESTION:	STORY SPINE	UNWELCOME BUSINESS CARD
CONFLICT	What did you do about it? (Show the honest struggle between hero and villain. Can't be too easy.)	So they _____, and then _____, and so they _____.	Yelling in the meeting. Team calmed customer and gained their understanding. I handed my card to the buyer and told her she could call me anytime. Afterward, one of the reps told me what a terrible mistake I had made.
RESOLUTION	How did it turn out (for everyone)? (How are things/characters changed as a result?)	Eventually . . .	Buyer stopped accepting calls with the sales team. Sales dropped 30 percent over 6 months. Bob got fired. (Irony that I had joined the sales meeting to make things better.)
TRANSITION OUT:			
LESSON(S)	What did you learn?	What I learned from that was . . .	Here's what I learned . . . Unintended consequences of making yourself too valuable. Visitor's role isn't to impress the buyer. It's to help the sales team be the hero.
RECOMMENDED ACTION(S)	What do you think I should do?	And that's why I think you should . . .	Offer help, but don't do anything to disempower the sales team.

18

EMOTION

PEOPLE **WHOSE LIVELIHOOD** depends on selling something have known this instinctively for centuries, if not millennia. Emotions play a critical role in decision making. But it's only been in the last few decades that science has shed some light on exactly how that works.

Enormous amounts of research in psychology, behavioral economics, and neuroscience concludes that human beings make rapid, subconscious, and emotional decisions in one place in the brain (the limbic and root brain areas), and then justify (or possibly adjust) those decisions more slowly, logically, and rationally in another area of the brain (the neocortex).[1]

That may sound like bad news, but it's not. For centuries, conventional wisdom has held that emotions cloud our judgment and represent a barrier to good decision-making. But science is finding that's not always the case. In fact, it can often be just the opposite. Antonio Damasio is a professor of neuroscience at the University of Southern California and the author of the book *Descartes' Error: Emotion, Reason, and the Human Brain*. In it, he concludes, "When emotion is entirely left out of the reasoning picture . . . reason turns out to be even more flawed than when emotion plays bad tricks on our decisions."[2]

Damasio's extensive research with patients suffering damage in the emotion centers of the brain supports this conclusion. But a little self-reflection can also tell you this is true. After all, we have a name for people who don't seem to use emotions when making decisions. We call them psychopaths.

Finally, research by education professor Kerry Mallan showed that "emotional engagement is why [information] presented in the structure of a story is more easily remembered."[3] And since good decision making requires accurate recall of pertinent information, emotion again plays a positive role in the decision-making process.

The obvious conclusion from this is that if you want to influence buyers' decisions, you need to influence them emotionally, not just rationally and logically. And it's difficult to influence people emotionally with only facts and logic and data. Fortunately, we have a tool to tap into people's emotions quite effectively: a story.

In fact, emotional impact is such an important component of storytelling that many story experts consider it a defining characteristic of a story. Novelist E.M. Forster, for example, defines a story as a fact plus an emotion. And he gives this brilliantly simple example.[4] If I were to tell you, "The king died, and then the queen died," well, that's not a story, is it? It's just a fact. But if I were to tell you, "The king died, and then the queen died *of grief*," now *that's* a story! And why is it a story? Because you can immediately imagine what might have happened. You might think that the queen must have so loved the king that when he died, she stopped eating and just withered away. Or maybe she was so distraught that she took her own life! All of those stories immediately come to mind just because of the last two words, "of grief." The emotion turned the fact into a story.

Here's what this looks like in a selling situation, or in this case in particular, for fund-raising.

As the chief development and marketing officer for Children's Hospital Los Angeles, one of DeAnn Marshall's jobs is to raise money for the hospital. As such, she's learned the hard way that telling a story is usually more effective than spewing out a bunch of statistics on the hospital's accomplishments and needs.

Not surprisingly, storytelling is commonplace in the fund-raising business, especially for organizations that visibly help groups that we easily hold compassion for, like sick children. Tired of the typical sick-child-gets-cured-at-Children's story, DeAnn decided to take a risk at one event and share a rather different kind of story. She shared a story that celebrated no cure.

She told the audience about a time she was walking through the hospital lobby when through the glass walls and doors she noticed a white minivan pull into a parking spot. The driver, a woman, got out and walked around to the back of the van. Then, in what was probably a strategically chosen spot where she could conceal herself, the woman stopped. The look on her face changed instantly from calm to abject anguish. She raised her hands to cover her face, bent over slightly at the waist, and burst into a sobbing fit of tears. DeAnn watched from a distance, unsure if she should go over and comfort the woman, or let her have what she thought was a private moment in dignity.

A moment later, the woman stood up, wiped the tears from her eyes, straightened her blouse, and steeled herself up for whatever it was she had to do next. Then she continued around the minivan to the passenger side. She opened the door and with a smile on her face, she helped a baby girl (presumably her daughter) out of the van and into a stroller. With her newfound positive demeanor, the woman pushed the stroller across the parking lot and into the main doors of the hospital.

And that's it. That was the end of DeAnn's story. She doesn't know who the woman was, what ailment her daughter suffered, or what treatment she was there for. She doesn't know if the girl recovered quickly or succumbed to her disease. She never saw either of them again.

What she does know, however, is that as a parent, she could relate to that agonizing moment at the back of the van—that moment when a mother indulged herself in a brief cathartic release of the pain she had surely been keeping bottled up inside to stay strong for her daughter on this and perhaps countless other drives to Children's Hospital.

What DeAnn could relate to was knowing that "no parent ever wants to be at our hospital. Because if you're here, it doesn't mean *you're* sick. It means you have a child who's sick." But she also knows that not every city is lucky enough to have a hospital like Children's with the resources and staff of experts dedicated to treating children. And so she knows if you're ever unlucky enough to be bent over sobbing at the back of your minivan over a sick child, you're going to want it to be in her parking lot.

Let's notice a few things about that story. First, if you consider it a story about the woman driving the minivan, then the story seems to be missing many of the critical elements of a story. It lacks a complete context since we don't know who the woman is, or her daughter, or why they were at Children's. The challenge is unclear because we don't know exactly what made the woman cry. And the story lacks resolution since we don't know how it turned out in the end. We essentially see only a brief moment of conflict at the back of the van.

But here's another way to look at the story. It's not a story about the woman driving the minivan. It's a story about DeAnn. The context is that DeAnn was walking through the hospital lobby when she saw a minivan pull into the parking lot. The catalyzing event (the challenge) was when she saw the woman break down in tears behind the van. The conflict began with DeAnn's internal struggle to decide whether she should go out to comfort the woman or not. And it continued as her inner dialogue empathized with the woman's struggle to conceal her anguish in front of her daughter.

The resolution is how DeAnn was changed by the event through that introspection and relating to the woman as a parent. And the lesson at the end was that if you are unfortunate enough to be reduced to tears over your child's medical condition, your best odds of relief will be found at Children's Hospital.

The core of DeAnn's story, the conflict, was brought about because of the highly emotional moment she saw at the back of the minivan. The emotion turned the facts into something worthy of being called a story. The fact that the woman stopped behind the van to cry made it a story. If she had stopped behind the van to sneeze, there would be no story.

TECHNIQUES

Here are a few techniques to enhance the emotional potential in your stories.

Start by identifying the emotional moments and what those emotions are or could be. Do this by going back through your story structure template to highlight the places where the characters (or the audience) should be feeling some emotion. Make note of each emotion (joy, sadness, fear, angst, pride, etc.). Not every bullet point has to have an emotion associated with it, but it's a good exercise to go through anyway. This gets you in touch with the emotional flow of the story and gives you practice identifying emotions.

You won't be able to use every technique or highlight every emotion, so it helps to prioritize. Identify one or two emotions that you believe, if developed well, will have the biggest impact on moving the audience to your desired outcome.

Finally, go through each emotion you identified and pick one technique to apply to each. Again, you can skip the least important ones.

The techniques follow.

Technique #1: Tell Me

This is the first of a good-better-best set of three emotional delivery vehicles. The simplest method, which is good, is to just tell your audience how your main characters feel. Stating "I was shocked" or "He was scared out of his wits" or "She was so excited" is better than nothing. But you can do better.

Technique #2: Show Me

Better is to *show* your audience how the characters feel. Describing the woman crying behind the minivan in the story above is a perfect example. DeAnn didn't tell you the woman was distraught. She showed you through the woman's behavior. Another example is in the story of the sludge contract in Chapter 8 when you read that the incumbent showed up at the meeting yelling and kicked over a chair. Nobody had to tell you he was angry. You inferred that from his behavior.

Technique #3: Make Me Feel

Best is to actually make your audience feel emotion without having to tell about or show the emotion in the characters. In his book *The Hook*, playwright and former USC screenwriting professor Richard Krevolin provides insightful advice about how to do that.[5] He identifies three positions your audience can be in relative to your main characters: superior to, inferior to, or equal to. Each has a unique way to create an emotional response.

In *superior position*, your audience knows more than the characters do. This is the case, for example, if you tell your audience that unbeknownst to your hero, there's a man with a knife hiding in the closet waiting for him to come home. When the hero comes home and walks closer and closer to the closet, your audience starts to feel angst and tension, even though the main character doesn't.

Compare this to *inferior position*. This is often used in detective novels where, say, Sherlock Holmes has already figured out whodunit, but Watson and the reader haven't caught up yet. This helps create curiosity and anticipation and keeps the reader turning pages even though no such emotions exist in the characters.

Last is *equal position*, which might be the most powerful one of all. This is where the audience knows as much as, but no more and no less than, the main characters. This position allows the audience to experience the same emotions as the characters by finding out the same emotion-causing information in the same way they do in the story.

For example, consider Kevin Moulton's story of his battle with the ATM in Las Vegas (Chapter 7), specifically the part about the bank calling his wife in the middle of the night. Relative to Kevin in the story, we—the audience—were in a superior position. He told us early in the story that the bank called his wife. As a result, it was kind of funny when we heard the details of it happening.

But imagine instead if that story was in "equal to" position. We wouldn't have heard about the phone call to his wife until Kevin found out about it. That might have been when she called him the next morning, or maybe not even until he got home and she met him at the door with a scowl. He might have asked her, "How were things while I was gone?" To which she might have replied, "Oh, everything was fine until 3 o'clock this morning when the bank called. What on Earth were you doing getting cash in Las Vegas in the middle of the night anyway?!"

Now it's not funny. It's embarrassing and even rage-producing, and as the audience, we feel that embarrassment and rage along with our hero.

Choose which position to put your audience in based on which emotion you're trying to evoke in them.

Technique #4: Let the Audience Get to Know Your Main Characters

If your audience doesn't know anything about the characters, it's difficult for them to care about what happens to those characters. Richard Krevolin calls this the "Stormtrooper Effect." He explains, "Remember all those guys in white Stormtrooper uniforms in [the original] *Star Wars* movies? And remember what you felt when Luke or Han Solo shot them and they died? NOTHING! You felt nothing, because you didn't know them. Beyond them even being bad guys, they're faceless, nameless creatures. As a result, you have no connection to them and no strong emotional response to their death."[6]

If your story starts out, "There was this guy I used to work with who got fired . . . ," we don't care. But instead, you could start your story, "There was this guy named Matt I used to work with in California who was my favorite coworker. He used to get to work before everyone else and turn on the coffee pot. He'd always cover for me when I needed to take a day off. And he'd been there longer than anyone else, so if I ever got stuck and didn't know what to do, I could always ask him so I didn't have to admit to the boss that I didn't know what I was doing. Then I came to work one day and found out he'd gotten fired." Now you care. And you care because you know Matt and you like him. And it only took a few sentences.

Technique #5: Use Dialogue

Instead of you telling the audience what the characters feel, let them hear that directly, even if it's words your characters are thinking without saying them out loud. For example, instead of telling the audience that the hero was feeling nervous and unprepared for her new job, you could share her inner thoughts this way: "She shook the interviewer's hand and said, 'Thank you so much for the job offer. I won't let you down.' But inside, she was thinking, 'Oh my God, I have no idea how to do this, I'm going to get fired on my first day!'" (I'll have more to say on the use of dialogue in Chapter 20.)

TWO IMPORTANT WARNINGS

Watch Out #1: Be Aware of the Intimacy Threshold

Emotion is such a powerful tool it warrants coming with its own warning label—or in this case, two warning labels. Here's the first: *The level of tolerance for emotional content in stories varies across cultures.*

In David Hutchens's storytelling seminars, he often shows a video produced by a major U.S. airline designed to motivate and inspire its employees.[7] It includes short vignettes of passengers telling a story about a recent flight and how the company went above and beyond their expectations to help them send off a loved one, welcome a returning one, or just be able to afford to come home and surprise mom for Christmas. It's a touching and moving video that's hard to watch without tearing up a bit.

But at the end of one particular showing of this video in Paris, David's audience sat unmoved, with arms folded, scowling at him. They said things like, "That was too fake . . . too sappy . . . too much music" and, perhaps most telling of all, "too American."

David's conclusion is that all effective storytelling needs an emotional component. But how much and how it's delivered can vary by culture. He aptly describes it this way: "Every time a group comes together, whether it's a board of directors, or a family of four sitting down to dinner, there is an intimacy threshold. It's an invisible, unspoken, but collectively held boundary of how much intimacy we're willing to extend to one another."[8] David's observation, as well as mine and those of other storytelling experts, suggests that the intimacy threshold is often lower in Europe than in the United States. And I would speculate that in some places in Latin America, that threshold might be higher than in the United States.

Everyone is different, so it's important to know your audience. The good news is that if you're paying attention, your audience typically lets you know. If they're uncomfortable with the level of emotional intimacy, they look uncomfortable and sound uncomfortable. And if you don't take the clues, they'll change the subject.

The point here is not to frighten you away from using emotion in your stories—just to make you aware of the risk. The payoff is worth taking a risk. Just keep your eyes open for hints that you've crossed your audience's intimacy threshold.

Watch Out #2: Avoid Improper Emotional Manipulation

Storytelling is an art. Like all art forms, such as music or photography or cinema, it has the ability (some would say the obligation) to evoke strong emotions in the audience. Said another way, storytelling (like all forms of art) is an emotion manipulation device.

And as we discussed earlier, emotions are a powerful force in human decision making. Make sure you wield that power responsibly. If you don't, you could leave your audience feeling improperly and unfairly manipulated.

The difference between proper and improper emotional manipulation is whether or not your audience welcomes that manipulation. Consider the following examples. When you listen to a full orchestral performance of Wagner's "Ride of the Valkyries," or watch Shakespeare's *Romeo and Juliet* performed live, you are being supremely and uncontrollably emotionally manipulated. And like everyone fortunate enough to experience those works of art, you welcome that manipulation. The reason is that you will have lived a fuller life and I dare say be a better person because of it.

Now, I'm not suggesting that your sales stories need to compete with Shakespeare or Wagner in terms of their contribution to humanity. But I am saying that beauty is in the eye of the beholder. If your audience feels unfairly manipulated by your story, then they've been unfairly manipulated.

Short of turning your stories into timeless masterpieces, there are two ways to make sure the emotional punch in your stories doesn't land unwelcomed. The first is to make sure your purpose is to benefit your audience (the buyer). No doubt you will benefit from the sale also, as well you should. But if you're selling someone something that you know they don't need or can't afford, your efforts will clearly be unwelcomed and your emotional content deemed inappropriate.

The second way is to make sure that your story's emotional payload doesn't distract your audience from more important decision criteria. In his book *Attacking Faulty Reasoning*, T. Edward Damer, a philosophy professor at Emory and Henry College, names and deconstructs several dozen types of fallacies used in argumentation and persuasion. A handful of them fall under the heading of "irrelevant emotional appeals," including appeal to pity, use of flattery, appeal to self-interest, guilt by association, and playing to the gallery.[9] The defining characteristic of all of these fallacies is that they distract listeners from more important decision criteria and lead them to make a decision at odds with that better criteria.

For example, let's say you're selling a raw material used by your customers in their manufacturing process. You know their decision criteria are based on the quality and price of your product. Knowing your company's product doesn't measure up to their quality standards, you tell the buyers an emotionally laden story about some financial problems you're having trying to care for your sick parents while getting your kids through college, and how making this sale will get you through another year. It might work. But you've distracted the buyers from more important criteria, and you've misused the power of story.

SOLUTIONS

Given both of the above warnings, here are some ideas to make sure the emotion in your story is both effective and welcomed by your audience.

▶ *Know your audience, and watch for clues you've crossed the intimacy threshold.*

Uncomfortable facial expressions, loss of eye contact, strained voices, and attempts to change the subject may all be indications you need to rein in the emotion.

▶ *Have emotional content, not emotional delivery.*

As an extreme example, imagine crying while delivering that sob story to your buyer about your financial woes. If the story didn't cross the line of emotional manipulation already, your tear-filled delivery certainly would.

Ira Glass is the host of public radio's wildly popular *This American Life*. In an ABC News interview about his success as a storyteller, he addressed this exact topic. He concluded, "When you're telling an emotional story, you can't play it emotionally. You have to be as flat as possible. The more emotional it is, the more neutral you have to be. Otherwise it's so corny."[10] Precisely. Let the story do the work, not the delivery. This is a sales call, not an acting class.

Another reason this is good advice is that when you display the emotions in your delivery, you prescribe exactly which emotions your listeners should be experiencing. That robs them of the opportunity to assign their own emotional value to the story.

▶ *Go easy on the music.*

For stories produced on video, keep the musical background to a minimum. Doubtless it was one of the factors that made David Hutchens's audience in Paris cry foul at the airline video. In general, avoid making it too easy for the audience to become aware of the devices you're using to convey the emotion.

▶ *Give listeners space to draw their own conclusions.*

With a particularly emotional story, instead of transitioning from the resolution directly into the lesson and recommended action, just listen. If it's as powerful a story as you think, it will lead the audience to the conclusion and action you're after anyway. Give them a chance to reach that conclusion on their own. If you follow a powerful emotional climax with a recommendation, it increases the likelihood it will be seen as manipulative.

▶ *Provide an emotional palate cleanser.*

Avoid moving directly from your emotional story to closing the sale. Instead, save one final, short topic to discuss prior to the close. Give your buyer something rational and logical to think about for a few minutes prior to making a decision. You'll still get the benefit of the emotional impact, but with less risk of your buyer feeling manipulated at the critical moment.

▶ *Invite the listener to talk about the story.*

When you ask people to participate in a dialogue about a story, they have an explicit invitation to ask questions, to challenge, to investigate your motives in telling the story, and most importantly to create their own meaning from it. David Hutchens summarizes this idea nicely in the pithy phrase, "it's not manipulation when there is participation."

STORY CLINIC:
THE UNWELCOME BUSINESS CARD

Step #1: Identify Emotional Moments

Go back through the story template and highlight the places where the characters (or the audience) should be feeling some emotion, noting which emotion.

See Exhibit 18-1, where I've indicated in parentheses the emotions I think are likely at play. For simplicity, I've only included the two relevant columns of the story structure template.

EXHIBIT 18-1. EMOTIONAL MOMENTS IN
"THE UNWELCOME BUSINESS CARD."

STEP	THE UNWELCOME BUSINESS CARD
OBJECTIVE/ MAIN MESSAGE	If you're a visitor on a sales call, don't try to be the hero. You'll disempower the sales team. Your job is to make their job easier.
TRANSITION IN: (HOOK)	I think the best lesson I ever learned about going on a sales call was . . .
CONTEXT	Last year at the company I used to work for . . . Customer upset about our price increase and wanted an executive to complain to. **(angry, disappointed)**
CHALLENGE	I was asked to attend a meeting with the customer for damage control. **(nervous, apprehensive)**
CONFLICT	There was yelling in the meeting. **(angry, frustrated)** Team calmed customer and gained her understanding. **(calm, hopeful)** I handed my card to the buyer and told her she could call me anytime. **(relieved, helpful, connected)** Afterward, one of the reps told me what a terrible mistake I had made. **(Sales rep = angry; Bob = shocked, guilty, embarrassed)**

Table continues

STEP	THE UNWELCOME BUSINESS CARD
RESOLUTION	Buyer stopped accepting calls from the sales team. **(discouraged)**
	Sales dropped "big time." **(guilty)**
	Bob got fired. Ironic since he had joined the sales meeting to make things better. **(sad, ashamed)**
TRANSITION OUT:	
LESSON(S)	Here's what I learned . . .
	Don't make yourself the hero. **(humble)**
	Visitor's role isn't to impress the buyer. It's to help the sales team be the hero.
RECOMMENDED ACTION(S)	Offer help, but don't do anything to disempower the sales team. **(resolute)**

Step #2: Identify the one or two most important emotional moments

This step requires some judgment. Which emotional moments do you think were the most salient for the characters in the story? Which do you think will be most compelling for your listener? Make sure you do a thorough job enhancing these emotional moments. Enhance other moments if you have time and space.

In this case, I've chosen as the most important the moment at the end of the conflict where the sales rep confronts Bob with his misstep. Recall from the Story Clinic in the last chapter that I mentioned Bob had said that was the toughest moment for him.

Step #3: Explore each emotional moment and apply one or more of the techniques

There's no right answer here. You'll eventually develop a comfort level with each technique. For illustration, here's what I chose to do for each:

Context: Customer upset about the price increase—Use the "tell me" technique.

Recommendation: Add "We had just pushed through a major price increase, and one of our biggest customers was absolutely livid over it." (It helps to have a good thesaurus.)

Conflict: Angry yelling in the meeting—Use the "show me" technique.

Recommendation: Add "The meeting was brutal. It was the first time in my career that I'd seen that kind of red-faced tirade in a customer meeting." Obviously, you can't have a red-faced tirade unless you're pretty angry about something.

Conflict: *Bob's guilt and embarrassment when confronted by the sales rep.* Recall that we've decided this is the most important emotional moment. So let's use both the dialogue technique as well as the "make me feel" (equal position) technique so that the audience feels the same emotions that Bob did.

First, to put the story in proper equal position, notice how it's currently written. The audience is told that Bob gave his business card to the buyer and told her to call him anytime. In the very next sentence, we find out that that is exactly what she did, essentially cutting out the sales team. But that's not how it actually happened for Bob. Bob didn't find out until months later how bad the impact was on the sales team. The way Bob found out he'd messed up in the first place was in the embarrassing hallway conversation with one of the sales reps right after the meeting. So that's the way we should tell the story to our listener, and we can do so using dialogue to make it more powerful.

Recommendation: Add "One of the sales reps later described the meeting this way. She said, 'Everything was going fine, right up until the end when you gave the buyer your business card and told her that we were basically a bunch of idiots who can't even pass along messages to headquarters properly. It'll probably take us six to nine months to rebuild the trust you just lost us in 10 seconds.'"

Resolution: *Bob getting fired*—Note that by virtue of the fact that we don't learn of Bob's firing until near the end of the story, we've used the "Let the audience get to know the main character" technique. If we had fired Bob in the beginning of the story, the audience might not care about him very much yet, and therefore not feel sorry for him (Stormtrooper Effect).

The remaining emotional moments are probably low priority, so I've skipped them. But note that we've used each of the five emotion techniques at least once already.

19

SURPRISE

IT'S PROBABLY NO surprise to you that surprise is an important element in storytelling. We all enjoy the surprise ending in a mystery novel or the unexpected turn of events in our favorite movie. And for the same reason we so enjoy them in books and movies, surprises in your sales stories can make them more entertaining.

But there's actually a more important reason to include something unexpected in your sales stories: It makes them more effective. Admit it. It's taking every ounce of discipline you have to keep from checking email in the middle of reading this sentence. Well, your buyer feels the same way when you're talking. Surprises keep things interesting. And they play a different role depending on where in the story you place them.

A surprise at the beginning gets your audience to pay attention to your story instead of thinking about the last call they had or the memo they have to write this afternoon.

A surprise in the middle gets the audience to focus and think more deeply about your story. Psychologist Jerome Bruner found in his research on cognition that "the more unexpected the information, the more processing space and time it is given."[1] For example, you pay very little attention to most two-legged people on the street because you expect people to have two legs. You pay a little more attention to someone with only one leg, since that's not what you expect. But you'd pay an enormous amount of attention to someone with three legs, since it's not even within the realm of what you thought possible.

But a surprise at the end of the story is the most powerful one of all, because it actually helps your audience remember the lesson they learned from your story. That's a bold claim, so it deserves a little explanation. Memories don't form instantly in the brain like a digital photograph. They form over a period of time shortly after the event happens, more like old-fashioned film photos when they're developed in a darkroom. Psychologists call that process "memory consolidation."

I learned about memory consolidation the hard way at the age of 16. I was playing a game of pickup football in an empty field in my neighborhood. No helmets or pads, just a bunch of teenage boys in jeans and sneakers. Teams were chosen using the time-honored "eeny meeny miny moe" method and the game was on. I happened to catch the ball in the opening kickoff and was running it back up the field at full speed. A boy of 19—and much bigger than me—tackled me head-on. My head hit the ground hard, causing what my doctor later confirmed was a concussion. I didn't lose consciousness. But when I got up, I knew something was wrong. I walked over to the huddle that was forming to listen in on the next play. When I got there, the other players looked at me like I was insane and yelled, "Smith, get back on your side!" I'd accidentally joined the wrong team's huddle! I knew every boy on the field by name but couldn't remember what team I was on. The reason was that my concussion happened less than a minute after teams were chosen. The rosters hadn't permanently formed in my memory yet. My concussion interrupted the memory consolidation process.

The scientific proof of this was first shown by James McGaugh, a neurobiologist at the University of California at Irvine.[2] While training rats to navigate a complex maze, he discovered they could remember the patterns more quickly if given a mild stimulant. That might not be too surprising. A cup of coffee makes most of us pay attention better. Only in McGaugh's experiment, he gave the rats the stimulant *after* they finished running the maze, not before. After the stimulant wore off, the rats were tested on their memory of the maze pattern. The rats with the post-administered stimulant remembered the maze patterns better than the rats without.

McGaugh later discovered that adrenaline had the same effect on memory that a stimulant did. But unlike his stimulant, adrenaline is a chemical the body produces naturally. Specifically, it's released when we experience strong emotions or surprises. It helps the body prepare for either fight or flight in case the surprise is dangerous.

The conclusion: A surprise at the end of your story helps your audience remember it better because adrenaline will be present in the brain during the important memory consolidation period.

Let's look at an example that illustrates surprises at the beginning, middle, and end of a story.

One of the most unforgettable lessons I ever learned was on the first day of my junior year in high school, 1983—Jim Owen's World History class. Class started the way most others do on the first day: The teacher introduced himself, explained what the class was about, told us how many tests there would be and how the grading would work, and so on. About 20 minutes into class, four boys burst into the room, all wearing ski masks and brandishing weapons. "Nobody move!" they shouted. They went directly to the front where they knocked Mr. Owen to the ground, took his wallet, stole the grade book off his desk, and left as quickly as they came in. It was all over in less than 15 seconds, leaving the students paralyzed in shock.

When the dust settled, Mr. Owen rose to his feet. "I'm fine. Is everyone okay?" We assured him we were. Then he said, "Relax. That was staged. Those were my students from last year.[3] Your first assignment," he continued, "is to take out a sheet of paper and write down everything that just happened in as much detail as possible."

We were all still somewhat in shock, but of course we did what he asked. A few minutes later, he collected our papers. He then stood at the front of the class and read each one aloud. And that's when the biggest shock of that class hit us. The stories were astonishing in their differences in the account of the facts. Most claimed there were four boys; some claimed there were three. Some said there were three boys and one girl. One said the weapons were all real guns; most said they looked like plastic water pistols painted black. Some insisted Mr. Owen had been hit during the mugging. Most said he wasn't touched at all. Mr. Owen continued to read while we sat and listened.

When he'd finished the last one, he put our papers down and said, "History will always be remembered from the perspective of the people who write it. As we've just seen, that can be very different, depending on the author. The victors in war will remember things differently from the vanquished. The groups in political power will surely see things differently from those not in power. Please keep that in mind as we begin our journey through world history. Now . . . open your books, and turn to Chapter 1."

That was more than 30 years ago, but I remember it like it was yesterday. Studying history taught me many important lessons that year. But the most valuable and lasting one may have been learned on that first day. History isn't a series of blind facts registered by an unbiased cosmic recording device. It's a string of very personal events experienced by emotional, fallible human beings. If you want to understand what really happened and how it impacted people, whether it was 100 years ago or earlier this morning, you might need more than one source. And for the sources you do use, it might behoove you to know a little about who they are and why they might have seen things the way they did.

Let's have a look at each surprise in this story. Notice the first surprise is at the very beginning, when you learn that masked gunmen entered the classroom. That got all of the students to sit up and pay attention. It likely had the same impact on you, the reader.

The next surprise is in the second paragraph, when you learn that the entire event was staged. We didn't see that coming and neither did you. As a result, we all remained riveted on what was happening. And for the same reason, you likely stayed focused on the story to see what would happen next.

The final surprise is in the third paragraph, nearing the end of the conflict, when you find out that all the student accounts of what happened were remarkably different from one another. That's the surprise that has kept this lesson in my memory for more than three decades, and will likely last in yours for some time as well.

Not every story, of course, has surprises at the beginning, middle, and end. And this story is an admittedly shocking one that I chose because it was so instructive of each use of surprise. But even your tamer sales stories should have some surprises in them. You've seen several in this book so far.

For example, Mark Bowser's story in Chapter 10 had a surprise at the very beginning. Recall that the first words out of Mark's mouth when he introduced himself to his audience were, "Hi, I'm Mark Bowser, and these are not my pants!" In the Pig Island story in the Introduction, the big surprise was how the pigs learned to swim, which is somewhere in the middle of the story.

And in Ben Koberna's story in Chapter 8 about finding a sludge removal company, the big surprise is at the end when you learn that the incumbent had been selling the sludge to farmers for years. Each surprise served its purpose.

CREATING SURPRISES

As with emotion, surprises aren't just something that you have to hope naturally occur in your story. There are techniques you can use to create surprises and put them where you want them. Here are some of the most effective.

Creating a Surprise at the Beginning of a Story

There are two ways to do this.

For parallel plot lines, lead with the most unexpected. When your story involves multiple events that happened more or less simultaneously, choose the more surprising one to share with your audience first. An example of that is the Iceland volcano story (Chapter 5). Chronologically, the meeting of the Microsoft executives and the eruption of the volcano happened at the same time. I chose to open the story with the erupting volcano because it was more unusual and unexpected. I could have started with the business meeting. But how surprising would it be that a big company had its executives together in a room for a meeting?

Flashback. Identify the most surprising part of the story and make it the opening scene. Then backtrack to the context and move forward as usual. An example of this is the story of Chris Powers joining Ariba in Chapter 6. In the first paragraph of that story, you learn that on the day Chris got promoted to partner, he walked into his boss's office and resigned. Who does that? It's the most shocking part of the whole story. But by paragraph three, we've backtracked all the way to when Chris was growing up playing basketball.

Notice this doesn't necessarily violate the story structure we learned in Chapter 13. I still opened with a where and when (at Crowe Horwath in 1998), introduced the main character (Chris), and told you what he wanted (to get promoted to partner). But I allowed myself to tell the story out of chronological order to create a surprise up front.

Creating a Surprise in the Middle of a Story

Skip one element of the context and let your audience figure it out on their own. Here's a sales story from speaking coach and author Michael Davis to illustrate how that might look in practice:

> One September morning in 2002, I was sitting across from my client Judy. She's a vivacious woman with a fun personality people are naturally drawn to. But not today. Today her hair is matted, her eyes are bloodshot, she's sitting slumped in her chair. She looks like she hasn't slept in days. I asked, "How you holding up?"
>
> She looked up at me. After several seconds, she said, "I don't know, Michael. I feel lost. This wasn't supposed to happen. I'm the one who's sick. This wasn't supposed to happen to him."
>
> After I took in a long breath, I replied, "I know. Fifty-two-year-old men aren't supposed to have an aneurysm in the shower."
>
> She stared down at her coffee for a long while. Then she looked up and with an angry tone said, "What am I going to do? I've never run a business by myself before. He handled all that. I just took care of the books. Now I've got payroll due next week. Michael, what am I going to do?" After a long pause, with great fear in her voice she added, "I'm so scared."
>
> Her words hung in the air for what seemed like an eternity. Finally, I broke the silence. "Judy, I can help you there. I know the last month has been traumatic. And you probably forgot all the work we did several years ago in case something like this happened." Then I reached into my coat pocket, pulled out a $600,000 check, and handed it to her.

She took it, and I watched a wave of emotions cross her face. Shock. Sadness. Surprise. I watched all this for what felt like an eternity. Finally, she looked up and said, "I forgot how much we had. He died so quickly. Michael, I'm going to be able to make payroll next week. I can keep the business. My guys can keep their jobs." After another long pause, she said, "I think I'm going to be okay. Thank you for all the work you did with us. This has saved me."

Until that moment, I'd never really understood or appreciated the real power of life insurance. Until then it was just a product I sold. In fact, I used to be embarrassed to say I sold life insurance. But on that day, Judy taught me that it wasn't about life insurance. It's about the lives and businesses that can continue when someone dies unexpectedly.

Notice how Michael's story did *not* start. It did not start, "I was in a settlement meeting with one of my life insurance clients" or "I was a life insurance salesman sitting with a client the month after her husband died." In the normal structure of a story, the context would have included that basic information. But in this case, Michael withholds those parts of the context and lets them dawn on the audience slowly as the story progresses. By the time he actually mentions that the husband died or that he was delivering a life insurance check, the audience has probably already figured that out for themselves, somewhere in the middle of the story.

This method turns a story into a mystery that the listeners get to solve themselves.

Yes, by the way, this admittedly violates the structure outlined in Chapter 13. Storytelling is an art form, like music, dance, painting, or poetry. The guidelines laid out in this book are not meant to be unbreakable rules. As the artist, give yourself license to play with your stories.

Creating a Surprise at the End of a Story

Move one key piece of information from the context to the end. Here's an example:

One evening, a nine-year-old boy named James was in the kitchen with his aunt having tea. While his aunt was enjoying her tea, James stood at the stove watching the tea kettle boil. It seems he was fascinated with the steam coming from it. He held a silver spoon over the jet of steam and watched as drops of water formed on the spoon and ran down the handle. Over and over again he studied this simple phenomenon.

Frustrated with his apparent laziness, his aunt barked out at him, "James, I never saw such an idle boy! Take a book or employ yourself usefully. For the last hour you have not spoken one word, but taken off the lid of that kettle and put it on again. Are you not ashamed of spending your time this way?" she scolded.[4]

Fortunately, the boy was undaunted by her admonishment. Two decades later, in the year 1765, the now 29-year-old James Watt invented a new kind of steam engine that helped usher in the Industrial Revolution.

I first read that story in a book titled *James Watt*, written by Andrew Carnegie in 1905. To me, it was no surprise the story was about James Watt. But to you, it probably was. Why? Because I didn't tell you his last name. In my version, I simply moved his last name from the beginning of the story to the end. Presto! Surprise ending.

STORY CLINIC:
THE UNWELCOME BUSINESS CARD

Let's investigate each of these techniques and see if we can add some surprise to the Unwelcome Business Card story.

For parallel plot lines, lead with the most unexpected

This one is probably not applicable for this story, since there's only a single plot line.

Flashback

The part of the story with the most natural potential to be surprising is when Bob gets fired. But the way the story's told, this isn't too unexpected because we lead into that with a description about how sales dropped over six months and everyone knew it was his fault. Getting fired seems to be at least a plausible ramification. But since someone getting fired is a rare event in any one person's life, it would be much more surprising on its own, the way it would be using flashback.

The story could start like this: "Unless it's ever happened to you, it's hard to understand what it feels like. You're sitting there in your boss's office, thinking maybe you've been called in to get a raise, or better yet, a promotion. And instead, you find out you're getting fired. It's indescribable. But, given the chain of events that led up to it, maybe I shouldn't have been too surprised. It all started about six months earlier . . ."

Skip one element of the context and let your audience figure it out on their own

A good choice here might be to skip the part where we explain that Bob was asked to fly out from headquarters and just get right into the action of what happened in the customer meeting. Most listeners would naturally assume he was just part of the sales team like everyone else. Then, as we're describing the tense discussion with the sales rep after the meeting (where she tells him how badly he messed things up for the team), it will slowly dawn on the listener that Bob wasn't even part of the team at all. He was an invited guest who became an unwelcome interloper.

Move one key piece of information from the context to the end

Following the example of James and the tea kettle, we could withhold the information about exactly who the main character is in the story until the very end. Instead of Bob saying, " . . . I was asked to fly out from headquarters to join the sales team for a meeting . . . ," he could say, " . . . the vice president was asked to fly out to a meeting with the customer." The entire story could be about an unnamed VP, including the VP's handing his business card to the buyer and getting fired over the drop in sales. It could end with a very humble Bob admitting, "By the way, that vice president—was me. And I won't ever make that mistake again."

Once you've brainstormed all these options to add surprise to a story, you have to choose which ones to implement. Sometimes you can use all of them. Other times you have to choose since using one will logically preclude using another. For example, if we use a flashback and Bob describes in intimate detail what it was like to get fired, it would be difficult to also make it a surprise ending that he was the one who got fired—in this case.

Recommendation: This last option will be the most productive surprise technique with this particular story. Replace Bob as the main character in the story with "one of the VPs" everywhere in the story. Then reveal in the end that the VP was actually Bob.

20

DIALOGUE, DETAILS, AND LENGTH

NOVELISTS, SCREENWRITERS, AND playwrights have several tools in their writer's tool kit to help make stories more compelling. Many of them are just as effective and appropriate for sales stories. Some are not. Below are a few of the most important ones you can put to use.

DIALOGUE

Dialogue is the most engaging literary device you can put in a story, for a number of reasons. It's the most natural way humans tell stories, even from a young age. Listen to a kindergartener at the end of the day talk about what happened at school, and you're likely to hear, "Johnny said . . . and then Jane said . . . and then the teacher said . . ."

Second, dialogue can turn a dry account of the facts into a story about the impact the facts had on real people. People say what they think and feel. When you quote people in stories, you share what they think and feel. As a result, dialogue delivers the majority of the emotional content in your stories.

Third, dialogue grabs the listener's attention. There's something magical that happens in that brief pause after you say, "And then my boss said . . ." that focuses the listener's attention with anticipation of what's coming next.

Fourth, it makes it easy to craft the story. If you rely on what was said by the people involved, you'll have less of a need to create your own historical account.

Last, using dialogue allows you to add some vocal variety by changing the pitch and pacing of your voice. That makes for a more dynamic and engaging narrative.[1]

As an example, let's look at part of Michael Davis's story from the last chapter. Early in the story he asks Judy, "How you holding up?"

She replies, "I don't know, Michael. I feel lost. This wasn't supposed to happen. I'm the one who's sick . . . What am I going to do? I've never run a business by myself before. He handled all that. I just took care of the books. Now I've got payroll due next week. Michael, what am I going to do? I'm so scared."

If we were to try to explain that in third-person narrative, it might sound like this: Michael asked how she was doing, but she didn't really know how to respond. Having been the one who was sick, it just didn't seem right to her for this to happen to him. . . Plus, she'd never run a business by herself before. Her experience was limited to the accounting. Now she had to make all the decisions and make sure all the employees got paid on time. She was at a real loss, and honestly afraid.

See how much more stale and clinical that sounds compared to the dialogue? Plus, when shared orally instead of in writing, the dialogue can be delivered with feeling and emotion, giving the audience a front row seat to what it must have been like to be there at the time. The third-person narrative is much more limited in its delivery options.

There are actually two types of dialogue: outer and inner. Outer dialogue is the type we've discussed so far—where you as the storyteller relate what the characters in your story actually said to one another. Inner dialogue reveals the unspoken thoughts of characters—sometimes called their inner monologue. This type of dialogue is especially useful at clarifying the character's motivations, passions, desires, and secrets.

Of course, in order to create inner dialogue, you need to actually know what your main characters were thinking. When that main character is you, that's easy. When it's someone else, you have to ask to find out. But the investigation is worth it. Inner dialogue can be some of the most interesting and insightful parts of your stories.

DETAILS

In the spring of 2014, my wife and I took our two boys on vacation to the Grand Canyon. While there, we coaxed Bob Woolley, an expert on the geology of northern Arizona, to take us on a day trip to see a mile-wide hole in the ground known appropriately as Meteor Crater.

With a story, Bob took us back in time 50,000 years describing what it would have looked like in the sky when a 150-foot-wide iron meteor hurtled toward the desert near Flagstaff. He described in breathtaking detail how fast it was traveling, how it would have glowed from the friction with the air and the pressure wave building up in front of it, and exactly how and when pieces of it might have broken off during its descent.

As he was describing every minute detail, three of us faced him, riveted with attention to his story. But my then nine-year-old son Ben was staring off dreamily into the sky at the spot where our guide was pointing. I thought he was daydreaming until I heard him say softly under his breath, "Wow, that looks cool." Clearly, he'd been listening just as closely as the rest of us. In fact, he'd been doing more than listening to the story. He was *watching* it.

A good story made the whole scene sound cool. But the exquisite details made it look cool. It's the details that help your audience *see* the story in their mind's eye. And there are other benefits as well.

First, several studies have shown that story details (especially sensory details like the sound, smell, and feel of the scene) make a story more memorable.[2] Second, details also lend credibility and authenticity to a story. This is also backed up by research but it should ring true to most people without that.[3] As we discussed in Chapter 13, just starting your story with a specific time and place makes it more believable.

So, having some sensory detail in your stories can help make them more effective. But there are good and bad ways to go about that. Let's start with the bad ones.

How *Not* to Add Details

Some of the most common pieces of advice you're likely to come across for adding details to your stories are: (1) use as many of the five senses as possible, and (2) if nothing else, give a clue as to what season it was.

If you're writing your first novel, that's probably great advice. But for a business story, and a sales story in particular, it can lead you wildly astray. In fact, I see this all the time from my new storytelling clients. Early attempts by most people to follow those two pieces of advice all sound the same. And it's awful. Imagine yourself as a buyer in a meeting with a salesperson. Then think about your reaction if in the middle of the meeting, the salesperson answered one of your questions by saying this: "Well, that's an interesting question, Bob. You see, it was a warm September morning, and the leaves on the trees outside our Dallas office were finally starting to change color. The smell of lilacs wafting through the lobby was almost strong enough to make us forget about the traffic noise from the highway out front. . ."

At best, you've checked out of the story already. At worst, you've shown the salesperson to the door. Not much will make buyers roll their eyes and disengage faster than overly descriptive language that sounds like it belongs in a 19th-century romance novel.

"Okay," you might say. "All of that was a bit much. But surely some of it was good, right?"

Perhaps. Let's look and see. What would it sound like if we took out everything about the leaves, the lilacs, and the traffic noise? Now it looks like this: "It was a warm September morning . . ." That's better, right?

Sure. But go back and put yourself in the buyer's position again. If at any point in the meeting you hear the words "It was a warm September morning," what reaction would you have? If you're like most people, those words make it sound like the beginning of a creative writing exercise for a high school English class. They make it painfully obvious that your buyer is listening to a story instead of having a conversation. In other words, it's kind of like saying, "Let me tell you a story . . . ," which as we discussed in Chapter 14 is the death knell of storytelling.

The problem with that opening, and why it sounds so blatantly contrived and lacking in authenticity, is that the details that it provides are probably irrelevant to the rest of the story. Does it really matter that it was warm that September morning instead of cold? Does it matter that it was in the morning instead of the afternoon? If so, by all means, put those details in. For example, if the story is about you testing your company's newest line of winter coats by wearing one of them outside, then the fact that it was unexpectedly warm could be very important to the story. But if it's not relevant, it just makes it sound like you're trying too hard.

Ironically, that first phrase is lacking one important detail: the year. Mentioning that the story happened in September isn't very helpful without knowing if it was last September, or 15 years ago in September. So in this case, the better opening to the story would be "Well, that's an interesting question, Bob. In September of last year, we . . ."

Details: A Better Way

Here are five techniques to add detail to your stories that won't get you in trouble.

▶ Add details that explain the main character's motivations.

It wasn't the length of the flowery "warm September" prose above that made it inappropriate. It was that it was irrelevant to understanding what was going on in the story. Here's another example that's just as long, but more relevant:

It was already 4 o'clock in the afternoon, and Jack hadn't had any coffee since breakfast. He was a three-cup-a-day guy—9, noon, and 3. You could set your watch by him. But this meeting had been running late all day, the coffee machine was broken, and nobody had the time to make a run to Starbucks. It started to show by about 1 o'clock. You could hear Jack's heel tapping on the hardwood floor in the conference room as his right leg was nervously bouncing up and down. You could see his eyes getting bloodshot and ears flushing red the more irritated he got. His voice was getting more and more shrill, and he'd been fidgeting in his chair since lunch . . . and then finally, he just snapped! . . ."

In this case, the story is obviously about someone who was about to suffer a mental breakdown. All the detail about his nervously tapping heel and bloodshot eyes and shrill voice give the listener some insight into how he felt and why (he hadn't had two of his three daily cups of coffee). And it shows the buildup to his emotional breakdown. (But hopefully you can see that all that detail would have been a complete waste of time if instead of Jack snapping, the story had continued, ". . . and then Jack approved our recommendation and we all went home.")

▶ Replace general words with specific ones.

If the height of a main character is important, instead of saying, "He was really tall," say, "He was at least 6-foot-4." If your main character's choice of automobile says something important about who she is, instead of saying, "Then she got in her old used car and drove off," say, "Then she got in her '82 Toyota Corolla with the missing headlight and headed home." And whenever possible, refer to your characters by name instead of just job titles. It's easier for your audience to care about "Julie, from accounting" than it is to care about "the accounts payables clerk."

▶ Show, don't tell.

Instead of describing what's happening to your audience, show them the evidence of it and let them draw the conclusion for themselves. Here's an example from Richard Krevolin, again from his book *The Hook*.[4]

Take a look at this sentence, "Frank was stressed out and nervous." Now, grammatically it's sound, but it tells the reader about Frank's emotional state without letting the reader determine what that emotional state is. Now, look at this sentence, "Frank wrapped and unwrapped the telephone cord around his ring finger." This sentence conveys the same information as the previous sentence, but the reader has to visualize Frank's actions and then, as a result of using their imagination, the reader can, on their own, determine that Frank is stressed-out and nervous.

▶ Pick one important scene and describe it in vivid detail.

As an example, in one of my training classes a woman shared a very personal story about a health issue she'd been battling. She took us back to a specific date in January 2015 as she was preparing to leave work. She was scheduled to go to the hospital the following morning for exploratory surgery to uncover the specific condition. She had already given her doctor consent to continue with any procedure necessary based on what she found. Her doctor had explained that the more dire possibilities ranged from a bowel resection to ovarian cancer surgery.

Since she didn't know how long she'd be gone, she decided to pack up her personal belongings and take them home. When she'd finished packing her box, she paused for a moment and looked up from her desk. Directly out the window of her 29th-floor office was the most amazing sunset. She described dramatic wisps of clouds sweeping across the entire sky, each one catching a slightly different shade of sunlight, from dark red, to reddish-orange, to yellow, all set against a still bright baby-blue sky. It was so beautiful she instinctively snapped a picture of it.

As she stood there admiring the view, she couldn't help but reflect on the metaphor it presented to her. "Is this the sunset of just another day," she wondered, "or of my career . . . or of my life?" The truth was, she had no idea if she would be home in 24 hours recovering from an uneventful procedure, or still in the hospital coming to grips with a cancer diagnosis that might or might not be treatable.

It turned out she did have cancer, and she spent the next few months in chemotherapy. The fact that this woman was present and healthy in class to share her story perhaps foreshadowed the happy ending, which was that she was now in remission. But that reflective moment at the window watching the sunset with her box of personal items was really the emotional climax.

When commenting on her story, one participant articulated what many were surely thinking when he said that he could "see the sunset" as she was describing it. Others concluded it was the most memorable part of the story.

Compare that to the flowery "warm September" opening scene with the lilacs and traffic noise. Both are vivid descriptions of a single scene. But in this case, that sunset scene was chosen because it served as an important metaphor in the main character's struggle. If you're going to invest your effort and your audience's time in vivid sensory detail, pick an important scene.

▶ *Use a metaphor.*

A metaphor helps your audience understand an abstract idea in concrete and more familiar terms. In this way, it's similar to adding details to your story, except in this case the metaphor communicates the detailed understanding using fewer words, not more. It works because a metaphor is simply a reference to something similar your audience already has a detailed understanding of in their head.

In their book *What Great Salespeople Do*, Michael Bosworth and Ben Zoldan suggest, "Metaphors are particularly useful for expressing intangible feelings and emotions. Let's say you're telling a story that involves a major deadline at work. You might describe the deadline as a noose around your neck, getting tighter every day. Or maybe it's more like a dark cloud, a black hole, the edge of a cliff, an eighteen-wheeler bearing down on you, or a gun to your head."[5]

With a little creativity, you can come up with all kinds of metaphors to bring the details of your story to life for your audience, without adding a lot of words.

STORY CLINIC:
THE UNWELCOME BUSINESS CARD

Let's go through our story template (in Exhibit 18-1) and look for opportunities to add dialogue and details.

Step 1. Outer Dialogue

There are three obvious places where our outline actually makes reference to things being said out loud. Look through the template and see if you can find them.

Here's what I come up with: (1) whatever it was they were yelling about in the meeting, (2) when Bob told the buyer to call him directly, and (3) when the sales rep told Bob how bad he'd made the sales team look. All three are in the conflict section.

To find other candidate spots for outer dialogue, or to prioritize the ones you have, think about the most emotional or surprising moments in the story. Could dialogue be used to deliver them in an even more engaging way? For example, instead of being told that Bob was fired, perhaps we could recount the words his boss used to fire him. After all, those words are probably seared into Bob's memory. Why not sear them in the audience's memory as well? Or maybe in the challenge, when Bob was selected as the sacrificial VP? How was he asked? The actual words of that invitation could lay out his objective in the meeting instead of us just telling the audience that "his objective was damage control."

Recommendation: In this case, we've already learned from Bob that the most emotional part for him was the conversation with the sales rep after the meeting, so we should definitely include that quote. And since exactly what he said to the buyer is what caused the problem to begin with, that quote is also important. Let's say we've learned that quote was: "Your business is very important to me. Here's my number. Sometimes things can get lost in translation back to headquarters, so feel free to call me directly anytime." You can add these quotes directly into the appropriate place in your story template.

Step 2. Inner Dialogue

To find places for inner dialogue, look for scenes where you imagine the main characters' thoughts or feelings that did not adequately make it into the verbal conversation. Put yourself into the shoes of the characters and ask yourself: "Where am I being silent when inside I want to scream or cry?" If you are the main character of your story, this should be easy. If not, you might need to make a phone call to your main character to find out what they were thinking.

In this story, a good candidate might be what Bob was thinking after the sales rep told him what a problem he'd caused. If you were Bob, what you'd probably be feeling at that moment was how desperately you wish you could take back those words to the buyer, and thinking about what you wish you'd said instead. Here's what he probably wishes he had said: "Your business is important to us. So we've put one of our best sales teams right here. If there's ever anything you need, just let these folks know. They know how to get things done, even if that means getting me, the president, or the CEO involved."

Recommendation: Insert the words Bob wishes he would have said in the template.

Step 3. Add Details That Explain Motivation

Look for elements of the story plot that might confuse a listener, and make them more clear with some detail. Let's say you've told this story several times, and about half the time, one of your listeners seems confused about what Bob did that was so bad. In that case, you might add a little clarification.

Recommendation: Add "He was trying to be helpful. But he did so by making himself look important while throwing the sales team under the bus—something he managed to do on just about every visit."

Step 4. Replace General Words with Specific Words

Recommendation: In the resolution, replace "Sales dropped big time" with "Sales dropped 30 percent over next six months."

Step 5. Show, Don't Tell

Recommendation: In describing the tense moment when Bob finds out what he'd done, describe the awkward silence and sideways glances that must have been exchanged between the sales team members while someone worked up the courage to tell him.

Step 6. Pick One Important Scene and Describe It in Vivid Detail

Clearly, one of the two most important scenes is when Bob commits his blunder and hands his card to the buyer. The second is after the meeting when he's talking to the sales rep and finds out what an awful position he'd put the team in.

Recommendation: For this example, I'll pick the second scene and build on the recommendation from Step 5 above by adding the following detail: "After the meeting was over, the sales team regrouped in the lobby to debrief. The VP was absolutely beaming. He turned to the team and said, 'Well, that went pretty well, don't you think?' But they just stared back at him like he was from Mars. And then one of them finally spoke up and said . . ."

Step 7. Use a Metaphor or Simile

Looking through the story as we've been changing it, notice that we already have a few well-placed metaphors and similes. In the conflict, getting "lost in translation" is a great metaphor, and the VP is being looked at "like he was from Mars."

In the lesson section, however, one of the sentences we decided on back in the first Story Clinic in Chapter 17 can probably be replaced with a metaphor. The sentence was "The role of the visitor should not be to impress the buyer at the sales team's expense." That could be replaced by a simple but more memorable metaphor: "Don't steal the spotlight."

Recommendation: Replace it.

LENGTH

According to the National Center for Voice and Speech, the average adult speaks at around 150 words per minute.[6] With that as background, how long should your sales stories be? Let's look at some data.

As a benchmark, the 112 leadership stories documented in my first book, *Lead with a Story*, had a median length of just over 600 words each, and most ranged from 450 to 750 words. That means those leadership stories would each take an average of around four minutes to tell orally, with most falling into the range of three to five minutes.

But how do these leadership stories, collected from more than 100 CEOs and executives at dozens of organizations around the world, compare to sales stories? Before conducting the research for this book, my hypothesis was that sales stories would be shorter than leadership stories, but I hadn't a clue by how much. My reasoning was this. First, most leadership stories are told to people who either report to or work closely with the person telling the story. In other words, the listener has either a hierarchical or social incentive to listen more patiently than a typical buyer might listen to a typical salesperson.

Second, leadership stories are usually delivered in the somewhat forgiving time and place of the office where both teller and listener work—in hallway conversations, over the lunch hour, in staff meetings that occur on a weekly or sometimes daily basis. In contrast, a salesperson often has to travel long distances to conduct a meeting with a buyer that then takes place in a short, fixed window of time. For salespeople, every minute counts. Therefore, everything a salesperson says (stories and nonstories) has to be more succinct.

So I wasn't surprised at the end of my interviews to see that sales stories were, indeed, shorter than leadership stories. Specifically, it turns out, they're shorter by half. Considering the roughly 30 sales stories you've seen in this book so far, the median length is approximately 280 words, with most (one standard deviation) falling between 140 and 420 words. At 150 words per minute, that means these sales stories would take an average of just under two minutes to tell orally, with most falling into the range of one to three minutes.

Given the expected relationship with leadership narratives, and the career success of the salespeople interviewed, I recommend a target range of one to three minutes for your sales stories as well.

The ideal length for any particular telling, however, depends on a number of factors. How much time do you have left in your meeting? What's the attention span of this particular buyer? How did they react to the first 20 seconds of your story, especially the hook? Do they look interested in hearing the rest of it?

As such, it's good to have short, medium, and long versions of your most common stories, and be able to modulate from one version to the other at the last moment or even midstory.

HOW SHORT CAN A GOOD STORY BE?

The shortest sales story in this book is 70 words long. It was the story from Jo Zulaica of Backroads (Chapter 10) illustrating how the company's leaders get customers to think more creatively about how Backroads can design a trip. That story is shown again below with each part of the story identified.

> [HOOK and CONTEXT] Last week (when), we had a guest (who) who was really interested in golfing and fishing (what the hero wanted) even though [CHALLENGE] that wasn't part of this trip. [CONFLICT] So on the layover days, he found a local operator who could take him fly fishing (what he did). And on a couple of other days, we set up a tee time for him at the nearest golf course (what we did). [RESOLUTION] We drove him to the course right after breakfast to get started.

Note that the hook, context, and challenge are all delivered in the first sentence. In this case, the context shows a fellow guest facing the same situation as the audience of the story—he doesn't necessarily want to do what everyone else is scheduled to do tomorrow. That *is* the hook. The audience always wants to hear a story about someone like them facing the same challenge they're facing right now. The shortest, most engaging stories start by introducing a relatable hero, seeking a worthy objective, confronted by a relevant challenge.

The conflict is the next two sentences, which answer the question, "What did the main characters do about the situation?" The resolution is that the following morning the guest was taken to get started on his first custom-designed vacation day.

After telling that story, the leader might transition out with this recommended action: "So, don't be bashful about telling us what you'd really like to do tomorrow."

STORY CLINIC:
FEBREZE

In all the other Story Clinics, we're working through the construction of a full-length story. So let's take the opportunity in the following Story Clinic to practice cutting a story down to size.

The longest story in this book involves the creation of Febreze in Chapter 7, which clocks in at around 580 words (about four minutes to tell). Let's take that story and see if we can cut it in half to an average-length two-minute story (300 words). Then we'll cut it down again to a short one-minute story (150 words). Start by re-reading the story on page 63 to refresh your memory.

One strategy for shortening a story is to begin with the full story and start removing individual sentences that seem like the least valuable until you get to the desired length. A better strategy is to use the story structure template to determine the most important parts of the story, and build up the story from there until you reach the desired length. Exhibit 20-1 is an attempt to do that. I populated the last column the same way you would for a new story, by answering the questions each section is supposed to answer. And for the conflict section (usually the longest), I included only the main points. Try filling out your own template on a separate piece of paper and see how similar your answer is to mine. Read through Exhibit 20-1 before proceeding to the next part of the Story Clinic.

EXHIBIT 20-1. STORY STRUCTURE TEMPLATE
FOR FEBREZE STORY

STEP	ANSWERS THE QUESTION:	FEBREZE
OBJECTIVE/ MAIN MESSAGE	What do you want the audience to think, feel, or do as a result of hearing your story?	This is the kind of thing my company can do for you.
TRANSITION IN: (HOOK)	Why should I listen to this story?	Let me give you an example of what can happen when you get the need-state wrong and when you get it right.

Table continues

STEP	ANSWERS THE QUESTION:	FEBREZE
CONTEXT	Where and when did it take place? Who is the hero and what do they want? Other background needed?	In 1996, P&G invented a new odor-trapping spray Launched Febreze in lead markets with strong marketing campaign Targeted at people with heavy odor problems like smoky bars, house pets, teenage boys
CHALLENGE	What was the problem/ opportunity?	It flopped. But why?
CONFLICT	What did they do about it? (Show the honest struggle between hero and villain, even if internal. Can't be too easy.)	Realized that with constant exposure to bad odors, you become desensitized, so you don't notice it as much Interviewed heavy users to find out why they liked it Heavy user in Scottsdale just used it for normal cleaning, as a "nice final touch." Videotaped her "mini-celebration" when done. That was the breakthrough! Other videos confirmed that women were enjoying a moment of satisfaction for a job well done. Febreze was a great way to give whatever they're working on that just-cleaned smell, worthy of celebration.

Table continues

STEP	ANSWERS THE QUESTION:	FEBREZE
RESOLUTION	How did it turn out (for everyone)? (How are things/characters changed as a result?)	Two years later, Febreze was restaged to be a reward. Sales doubled in first two months. Today it's a billion-dollar brand.
TRANSITION OUT:		
LESSON(S)	What did you learn?	P&G was focusing on the wrong need-state. That second round of more creative research identified the right need-state.
RECOMMENDED ACTION(S)	What do you think I should do?	Shane's proprietary need-state discovery model uses some of the exact same methods used on Febreze, plus some others, to find the right need-state the first time. Which is why I think that's what you should use on your next project.

Notice that if you just read down through the last column, depending on how close your bullet points already are to full sentences, you already have a cogent story. The Story Spine phrases can help turn your bullet points into sentences. If I take the bullet points in Exhibit 20-1 and stitch them together into full sentences and paragraphs, it looks like this:

Let me give you an example of what can happen when you get the need-state wrong and when you get it right.

In 1996, P&G invented a new odor-trapping spray product called Febreze and launched it in lead markets with a strong marketing campaign. The brand was targeted at people with heavy odor problems like smoky bars, house pets, or teenage boys.

Well, it was a complete flop, which raised the obvious question: "why?"

After some research, they realized that with constant exposure to bad odors, you become desensitized, so you don't notice the smell as much. They decided to interview heavy users (people who loved Febreze) to find out why they used it so much.

One woman in Scottsdale told them she just used it for normal cleaning, as a "nice final touch." She said, "Spraying feels like a little mini-celebration when I'm done with a room." And that was the breakthrough! Other interviews confirmed that women were enjoying a moment of satisfaction for a job well done when they finished cleaning something. Febreze, apparently, was a great way to give whatever they're working on that just-cleaned smell, which made it something worthy of that mini-celebration.

Two years later, Febreze was restaged to be a reward. Sales doubled in the first two months. And today it's a billion-dollar brand.

It turned out that P&G had been focusing on the wrong need-state. That second round of more creative research identified the right need-state.

Our need-state discovery model uses some of the exact same methods used on Febreze, plus a few others, to find the right need-state the first time. And that's what I'm recommending you use for your current project.

That story is about 280 words, just below the 300-word goal for our two-minute story—close enough that we could call ourselves done on that version. But if we wanted to take advantage of another 20 words or so to improve the story, we'd look to some of the other story elements. What other emotions, surprises, dialogue, and details could we add to the story?

For example, instead of just saying a "strong marketing campaign" in the first sentence of the second paragraph, we could make that more specific with the detail "two flights of television commercials, product samples and advertisements mailed to homes, and huge displays of product in grocery stores." That has the added benefit of making it even more surprising that the first launch flopped.

Or, to add more emotion to it, we could include the quotes of the researchers as they discovered the new insight: "Did you see that!" and "There it is again!" Notice that the quotes *show* their excitement, which is more powerful than just adding the words "they were excited."

Now let's look back and see what was in the four-minute version of the story (presented in Chapter 7) that didn't make it into our two-minute version. A lot of it turns out to be details that elaborate on the basic facts that are in our two-minute version: the details of the marketing campaign; comments like "If they don't notice Fluffy's stinky litter box, they don't need Febreze" that elaborate on the problem; and some of the dialogue from the women in the research.

But the biggest part of what got left out were specifics on how the second round of research was conducted: watching the women as they cleaned their homes, videotaping them, then reviewing thousands of hours of videotape to identify the insights.

So, does that mean all those details weren't necessary anyway, and now that we have a two-minute version, we would never need the four-minute version? Certainly not. Refer back to the original objective in telling the story. It's to illustrate the kind of research Hotspex can do for clients. For a prospective buyer who's interested, the longer story actually shows more of the research process (watching the cleaning, videotaping, reviewing of tapes, etc.). It would actually give the buyer a better understanding of the process being recommended. It also includes more emotion, surprise, and dialogue, which all add to the effectiveness of a story.

Okay, how do we turn this into a one-minute story? For that, let's go back to the story template in Exhibit 20-1. Go through each section and remove anything that can be removed while still leaving an answer to the basic questions each section requires. It's important to do this in the template and not in the text of your written story. The reason is that using the template ensures you don't inadvertently delete everything in one entire section. That would leave the story incomplete. So, delete something in each section, but also leave something in each section.

There's no right answer to this exercise. Try it yourself and see what you come up with. See my answers in Exhibit 20-2, where I've indicated the parts I would remove.

EXHIBIT 20–2. EDITING DOWN THE FEBREZE STORY

STEP	ANSWERS THE QUESTION	FEBREZE
OBJECTIVE/ MAIN MESSAGE	What do you want the audience to think, feel, or do as a result of hearing your story?	This is the kind of thing my company can do for you.
TRANSITION IN: (HOOK)	Why should I listen to this story?	Let me give you an example of what can happen when you get the need-state wrong. ~~and when you get it right.~~
CONTEXT	Where and when did it take place? Who is the hero and what do they want? Other background needed?	In 1996, P&G invented a new odor-trapping spray Launched Febreze ~~in lead markets with strong marketing campaign~~ Targeted at people with heavy odor problems ~~like smoky bars, house pets, teenage boys~~
CHALLENGE	What was the problem/ opportunity?	It flopped. ~~But why?~~
CONFLICT	What did they do about it? (Show the honest struggle between hero and villain, even if internal. Can't be too easy.)	Realized that with constant exposure to bad odors, you become desensitized, so you don't notice it as much Interviewed heavy users to find out why they liked it

Table continues

STEP	ANSWERS THE QUESTION	FEBREZE
CONFLICT *continued*		~~Heavy user in Scottsdale just used it for normal cleaning, as a "nice final touch." Videotaped her "mini-celebration" when done.~~ That was the breakthrough! ~~Other videos confirmed,~~Women were enjoying a moment of satisfaction for a job well done. Febreze was a great way to give whatever they're working on that just-cleaned smell, worthy of celebration.
RESOLUTION	How did it turn out (for everyone)? (How are things/ characters changed as a result?)	Two years later, Febreze was restaged to be a reward. ~~Sales doubled in first two months.~~ Today it's a billion-dollar brand.
TRANSITION OUT:		
LESSON(S)	What did you learn?	P&G was focusing on the wrong need-state. ~~That second round of more creative research identified the right need-state.~~
RECOMMENDED ACTION(S)	What do you think I should do?	Shane's proprietary need-state discovery model uses some of the exact same methods used on Febreze, plus some others, to find the right need-state the first time. Which is why I think that's what you should use on your next project.

The resulting 150-word story follows on the next page.

ONE-MINUTE VERSION OF FEBREZE STORY.

Here's an example of what can happen when you get the need-state wrong.

In 1996, P&G invented a new odor-trapping spray called Febreze, targeted at people with heavy odor problems.

Well, it was a complete flop.

They realized that with constant exposure to bad odors, people don't notice them. So they interviewed people who love Febreze to find out why they used it so much.

Those women were enjoying a "mini-celebration" with a fresh smell by spraying Febreze when they finished cleaning something. And that was the breakthrough!

Two years later, Febreze was restaged to be a reward. And today it's a billion-dollar brand.

It turned out, P&G had been focusing on the wrong need-state.

Our need-state discovery model uses some of the same methods used on Febreze, plus a few others, to find the right need-state the first time. And that's what I'm recommending you use for your current project.

21

DELIVERY

MANY OF MY clients breathe a sigh of relief when they show up at my storytelling course and realize it's not a course on public speaking or oral presentations. They're relieved because some arrived expecting to be videotaped giving a speech and having to watch it over and over again as their peers critique every imperfection and count every stutter or stray "um" and "er" in their delivery.

My hope is that you, the reader, will breathe a similar sigh of relief when I tell you that this book is not about, nor does it even contain, a deep dive on how to deliver your stories in front of an audience. The reason is this (and this is where you can let out your sigh of relief): Your delivery is not nearly as important as everything else we've covered so far.

As mentioned before, it would be far better to tell the right story in a mediocre fashion than tell the wrong story with a stunning performance. A story that delivers the right message, of appropriate length, with the proper structure, emotion, surprise, details, and dialogue, will compel an audience to act even if you fail to make good eye contact, slouch in your chair, fidget with your hands, stutter occasionally, use filler words ("ums" and "ers"), forget to smile, or have little enthusiasm or inflection in your voice.

Will your stories be more effective if you learn to master those oral delivery and body language components? Of course. But they can still be quite effective without them. The story is more important than the delivery.

Having said that, here are a (very) few words on oral delivery.

A PERFECT DELIVERY IS NOT PERFECT

Your goal in delivery is to be conversational, not perfect. A typical salesperson might use five or six filler words per minute in normal conversation during a sales call.[1] Your stories should be the same. It's more genuine and authentic without being distracting.

DeAnn Marshall, whom you met in Chapter 18, astutely observed, "The key to having a prepared presentation is that it doesn't look prepared." That doesn't mean you don't prepare. It means you prepare by preparing the right things. And memorizing your story is not one of the right things. A story should sound and feel organic, as if it's the first time you've ever told it. There are many stories I've told literally hundreds of times in front of an audience. Each time they come out slightly different. Therefore, each time it sounds like the first telling—because it is.

GOOD STORYTELLING IS INVISIBLE

A story should blend into the conversation seamlessly, without drawing attention to the fact that it's "a story" that's being told. If your tone of voice changes when you move into your story like a kindergarten teacher addressing a group of five-year-olds, you're doing it wrong.

GOOD SALES STORIES DON'T DRAW ATTENTION TO THE STORYTELLER

If you go to a storytelling festival (and I recommend you do), you see professional storytellers excitedly moving all over stage like a one-person Broadway show, waving their arms, jumping in and out of different characters, and speaking with a volume and clarity that would make a Shakespearean actor proud. At the end of the performance, you might hear thunderous applause and comments like "Wow, she was a great storyteller!" And that would be a genuine compliment.

But if you hear that same comment at the end of your sales presentation, it's not at all clear that it's a compliment. If the buyer is so focused on your "performance" that they don't engage in the sales pitch, you've failed as a salesperson.

My assumption is that your sales stories will be delivered in person, mouth to ear. My reason for this assumption is that that's how most sales stories are delivered—live, in the buyer's office or on the phone.

But it's also because that's the most effective way to share a story. Oral storytelling is just more impactful than storytelling delivered any other way. Kendall Haven reports on the results of a 1994 study of fourth-grade students.[2] The researcher delivered the same story to each of four different classes. In the first class, he read the story to the students. In the second, he handed out copies of the story and asked the students to read it themselves. In the third, he showed a video of the story. And in the fourth, he just told the story extemporaneously.

The study concluded that the "students who were the most enthusiastic and excited about their recollection of the story, who most readily recalled the story without prompting, who held the most vivid and expansive images of the story, and who were best able to verbalize their memory (and version) of the story were those from the class to whom he told the story."

But that doesn't mean stories can't be effective when delivered in a memo, an email, a letter, on presentation slides, in brochures, in print or online articles, through social media, in books, in television commercials, or on the radio. They can, of course.

WRITTEN DELIVERY

Since many of those formats involve the written word, here's my advice about committing your stories to writing: *Write the way you'd like to speak.*

In other words, write the way you think you might speak if you were speaking your best—without all the filler words and starts and stops, but with all the charm of a conversational tone. To understand this advice, let's look at the difference between how people write and how they speak. And let's use the one-minute version of the Febreze story from the last chapter as our case study.

Let's look at how you might actually deliver that story orally, in a buyer's office, without the benefit of notes:

> So, you remember back in '96 when Febreze came out? . . . Well, what you probably didn't know is that it was a complete flop.
>
> I mean . . . well, apparently, they originally made it for people with *serious* odor problems. But it turns out, I guess, you just stop noticing smells after a while if you're constantly surrounded by them.
>
> Anyway, they decided to interview people who just loved the stuff to figure out why they were so into it. Turns out they were using it like, uh, some sort of a, of a "trophy" when they finished cleaning. The smell was like their little reward. And that turned out to be the real breakthrough.
>
> A couple of years later, they restaged it as a reward. Now they sell a billion dollars' worth of that stuff a year. They were focusing on the wrong opportunity.

First of all, notice a few filler words, an unfinished sentence, short pauses, and a repeated phrase as the speaker struggled to find exactly the right word. If that's how your stories come out, relax. That's how they should sound—like a normal conversation. I'm not suggesting you should plan and practice to put fillers, pauses, and aborted sentences in your stories. I'm just suggesting that if some of that naturally finds its way in, that's okay.

Now, what if you were asked to write an official company memo with the Febreze story? You might submit something like this:

> In 1996, Procter & Gamble invented a new odor-trapping spray technology targeted at consumers with heavy odor problems, and marketed under the brand name Febreze. Revenues in the initial launch fell significantly short of expectations.
>
> A natural desensitization that accompanies continuous exposure to malodors was determined to be the cause of lackluster sales. In response, heavy users of Febreze were interviewed to ascertain why their usage patterns were unusually high.

The research concluded that heavy users often used Febreze at the end of a cleaning task as a celebratory signal of completion, with the fresh smell serving as both signal and reward.

Two years later, Febreze was restaged to be a celebratory signal of completion, and today it is a billion-dollar brand.

It turned out Procter & Gamble had been focusing on the wrong need-state.

Notice how different this version is compared to the spoken version. It's still a story, but the written version sounds so much more formal—a little too formal, in my opinion. And if you hadn't already read the same story a number of times in the preceding pages, you'd recognize how much more difficult this version is to understand. You might even have needed to read it a little more slowly to make sure you followed it all.

Let's look at how the spoken version of the story differs from the written version. The spoken version:

Uses shorter sentences. The written version averages 20 words per sentence. The spoken version averages just 12 words per sentence.

Uses simpler words. The written version uses words like "ascertain" and "celebratory" instead of simpler equivalents like "figure out" and "a reward." Simpler usually means shorter. In the written version, 17 percent of the words were greater than two syllables. In the spoken version, only 8 percent were. But simpler doesn't have to mean shorter. "Figure out" has the same number of letters as "ascertain," but most of you can recognize it as a less sophisticated phrase. As Mark Twain once said, "Don't use a five-dollar word when a fifty-cent word will do."

Uses active voice. In a memo you might write, "Our proposal was rejected by the committee." But you'd never say those words out loud to another human being. You'd say, "The committee rejected our proposal." The first sentence is in passive voice. The subject of the sentence (the proposal) is being acted on. The spoken version is in active voice. In it, the subject (the committee) is doing the acting. Passive voice makes your story sound pretentious and unnatural, even in writing. Notice several passive voice sentences in the written Febreze story above. There are none in the spoken version.

Gets to the verb quickly. Have a look at this sentence in the written version: "A natural desensitization that accompanies continuous exposure to malodors was determined to be the cause of lackluster sales." The verb in that sentence is "was determined," and you don't run into it until the tenth word in the sentence. That means your brain has to keep those other nine words in active short-term memory before figuring out what's happening to them.

Compare that to the same part of the spoken story: " . . . you just stop noticing smells after a while if you're constantly surrounded by them." The verb in that sentence is "stop noticing," and it's only three real words into the sentence. (All the words preceding "you" are filler and stammering words and can be completely forgotten without loss of meaning.)

So, how *should* we write a story? Just because it's written doesn't mean it should sound like a stodgy corporate policy memo. It should feel somewhere in between the two versions above. In fact, it should read the way you'd like to sound if you had to make a speech in front of a small audience, but you could magically get rid of all the mistakes and filler words yet keep some of the conversational tone of the spoken version. Something like this:

> In 1996, P&G invented Febreze, an odor-trapping spray for people with serious odor problems. But despite a strong product and launch plan, it was a complete flop.
>
> That's when they realized that if you have a constant odor problem, you don't even realize it because you eventually stop noticing the bad smell.
>
> Some customers did love Febreze, though, so P&G filmed them using it to find out why. That's when they had a much bigger realization. These women were using Febreze as a "mini-celebration" when they finished cleaning. The fresh smell didn't say, "No odors." It told them, "Great job!"

Two years later, the company relaunched Febreze as a reward, and today it's a billion-dollar brand.

It turned out P&G had been focusing on the wrong opportunity.

This version maintains the simple words, active voice, and early verb sentence structure of the spoken version. But it has 15 words per sentence and no filler words or pauses. It's written the way you'd like to speak.

So, here's a good set of targets for written stories:

- 15–18 words per sentence
- Fewer than 10 percent of words greater than two syllables
- Fewer than 10 percent of sentences in passive voice
- The verb in the first one-third of the sentence (first five to six words)

▶ *Practical Tip*

Counting words and sentences is a tedious task. Fortunately, many word-processing programs have writing diagnostics that can do that automatically. In addition, some can even score your writing style on standardized writing scales as a benchmark. (Check "Spelling and Grammar" options in Microsoft Word, or visit www.readability-score.com for free scoring.)

One of the more popular scales is the Flesch-Kincaid grade level, which is based on the number of words per sentence and syllables per word. The result is the estimated grade a reader would need to have completed to understand your writing. But that doesn't mean a higher score is necessarily better. The score doesn't reflect the intelligence of your ideas, just the complexity of your writing style.

Granted, too low a score could insult and bore your reader. But I've never seen that happen in practice. The more common problem is too high a score. Writing that scores above a 15 generally has to be read more than once to be comprehended well. Anything over 20 reads like a pompous, rambling, run-on mess.

For comparison, articles in the *New York Times* and *Wall Street Journal* typically score between a grade level 8 and 10 on the

Flesch-Kincaid scale. Popular fiction writers like John Grisham and Tom Clancy write at around a 7 or 8 on this scale. The book you're reading right now is about an 8.

Looking at our Febreze case studies, the spoken story example above scores a 6 on the Flesch-Kincaid scale. That's not unusual for spoken language, but it might be a little low for a written document. The more formal written version scores a 13 on this scale, which is probably too high. The last version above is an 8, which is closer to where you want to be.

I recommend most business writing be in the *New York Times/Wall Street Journal* range of 8 to 10. But for written *stories*, where you want to have a more conversational feel, I suggest staying in the John Grisham/Tom Clancy range of 7 or 8.

STORY CLINIC:
THE UNWELCOME BUSINESS CARD SOLUTION

In this final Story Clinic, let's reveal what our unwelcome business card story looks like after applying all the tools we've covered so far. Changes are indicated in [IN BRACKETS], and each part of the story structure is indicated in all caps.

[HOOK] I think the best lesson I ever learned about going on a sales call I learned [CONTEXT] at the company I worked at last year (where and when). We had just pushed through a major price increase, and one of our biggest customers was absolutely livid ("tell me" emotion) over it. The buyer wanted to complain to one of our executives [CHALLENGE], so the VP (who is the main character?) had to fly out to the meeting for damage control (what do they want?).

[CONFLICT] Well, it'd been a while since I'd seen that kind of red-faced tirade ("show me" emotion) from a buyer. But the team did a masterful job of getting the customer to calm down and understand why the price increase was necessary.

As they left the meeting, the VP—who'd been silent up to that point—shook her hand, gave her a business card, and said, (dialogue) "Your business is very important to me. Here's my number. Sometimes things can get lost in translation (metaphor) back to headquarters, so feel free to call me directly anytime." (details that explain motivation) He was trying to be helpful. But he did so by making himself look important while throwing the sales team under the bus (metaphor)—something he managed to do on just about every visit.

(One scene described in detail) After the meeting was over, the VP was absolutely beaming. He met the team in the lobby and said, "Well, that went pretty well, don't you think?" But they just stared back at him like he was from Mars. Jennifer (name), one of the sales reps, spoke up and said, (dialogue) "Sure, everything was going fine, right up until the end when you gave the buyer your business card and told her that we were basically a bunch of idiots (emotion) who can't even pass along messages to headquarters without something 'getting lost in translation' (emotion). It'll probably take us six to nine months to rebuild the trust you just lost us in ten seconds."

[RESOLUTION] And she was right. That buyer went straight to the VP with all her questions for several months and stopped accepting meetings with the sales team entirely. Sales dropped 30 percent at that customer over the next six months (details). And the VP lost his job over it.

[LESSON] Here's what I learned. I think what the VP should have said was, (inner dialogue) "Your business is important to us. So we've put one of our best sales teams right here. If there's ever anything you need, just let these folks know. They know how to get things done, even if that means getting me, the president, or the CEO involved."

[RECOMMENDED ACTION] Don't steal the spotlight (metaphor). The role of the visitor is to make the sales team's job easier. Offer help. But don't do it in a way that disempowers the sales team. That does more harm than good.

By the way, that vice president—was me (surprise ending). I won't make that mistake again. And neither will anyone I work with, because they'll have all heard this story.

In addition to better story structure, emotion, surprise, dialogue, and details, the story also now fits our guidelines on delivery. It's around 480 words long, or about three minutes to deliver orally. The average sentence length is 15 words. It's written in active voice. Only 7 percent of the words are larger than two syllables. And it has a Flesch-Kincaid reading level of 7, which is just right.

22

TELLING STORIES WITH DATA

ONE OF THE realities of our increasingly data-driven world is the need to influence with numbers and analysis. Salespeople and non-salespeople are often expected to support their recommendations with sophisticated statistics or financial analysis. That presents an obvious question. Do you have to turn off your storytelling when it's time to present your data?

The answer is "not necessarily." It's okay if you do. Remember, you're not expected to tell stories constantly. But there are ways to put the same storytelling techniques to use with data that you do with words, people, and events. This chapter presents two of the most useful techniques I've found.

"HOW WE GOT HERE" STORY

This method works by walking the audience through the data in chronological order, illustrating how you've arrived at the situation you're in now. Here's an example.[1]

In June 2000, Andrew Moorfield founded bfinance, a London-based online lending platform for small businesses. As happens with many start-ups, at one point cash flow wasn't strong enough for him to meet the payroll for his fledgling twenty-five-person company. He obviously had to decide what to do about the situation and had to inform his employees. Most people in that situation would do exactly that, and in that order—decide what to do, then inform the employees of the decision. But that's not what Andrew did.

Instead, he pulled all twenty-five employees into a conference room and did the following. He wrote a number on the whiteboard and said, "That was our bank account balance at the beginning of the month." Below that he wrote a few other numbers and said, "Those are the revenues we expect to get this month and the expenses we have to pay to keep running the business." And he explained each one. Then he drew a line underneath, added them all up, and wrote the result at the bottom. Then he said, "That's what we'll have left at the end of the month to pay salaries," and he circled the number.

Just to the right of it, he wrote another number and circled it. "That's how much your monthly salaries add up to." Then, Andrew paused and let the audience assess the stark dilemma in front of them. The number on the right was three times as big as the number on the left.

And then he asked this question: "What do you think I should do about this?"

After some deliberation, the surprising and humbling answer he got from his team was that two-thirds of them volunteered to go without any pay so that the remaining one-third could receive their paychecks in full.

Let's look at how Andrew turned a few simple numbers into a story. First, notice how Andrew walked the audience through each number, from the bank account balance at the beginning of the month to the balance at the end of the month. Didn't that feel like the context at the beginning, some challenge and conflict in the middle, and a result at the end?

Second, notice the element of surprise when he revealed that the bigger circled number on the board was payroll, and the surprise ending that two-thirds of employees volunteered to go without pay so the remaining third could collect their whole paycheck.

Third, notice the emotional impact of the dramatic pause he took as he let his audience assess their dire situation.

Fourth, notice that he used the literary device of showing, not telling. He showed them the cash flow and let them figure out there was a problem, instead of simply telling them there was a problem.

Let's compare all that to what Andrew could have done instead. He could have simply told the audience, "We're really short on cash this month, and I think I'm only going to have enough for about one-third of the payroll. Here's what I've decided to do about it . . ." That's what most of us would probably say in that situation. But notice—it's not a story. It's just a statement. And it's not nearly as effective as the story he told with the data.

This method also works well with time-series data, especially when it shows the result after some intervention. Imagine a sales trend chart showing revenues in four consecutive quarters, Q1 to Q4: $30M, $30M, $26M, $33M. You could explain this by saying, "As you can see, the intervention we put in place at the end of Q3 completely reversed the decline in sales. Let me explain what we did . . ." That's fine. But it's not a story.

Instead, you could explain it in story form. You'd start by explaining how quarterly sales had been steady at $30M through Q2 (that's context). And then in Q3, you had a 13 percent decline (that's the challenge). So you and your team developed and implemented a plan to reverse it (this is the conflict). "Here's what we did . . . And as you can see (resolution) sales are now up to record levels."

THE DISCOVERY JOURNEY STORY

The second method works by walking your audience through your personal journey of discovery as you conducted your analysis that led you to your recommendation. This is the same type of story we talked about in Chapter 8, but instead of you announcing your discovery, you allow your audience to draw that conclusion themselves. Notice a couple of things about this method.

First, unlike the "How we got here" story above, the main character in this story isn't the business. It's you (or whoever conducted the analysis). In both stories above, you're walking the audience through data showing what happened in your business from beginning, to middle, to end of some time period. In this method, you're walking your audience through the work you did up to the point that you had your aha moment of discovery.

Second, notice this is not the way we're generally taught to make a presentation. Most of us were taught to start a presentation with the recommendation up front, then explain the reasons for that recommendation, followed by the data or evidence that supports that rationale. Recommendation, reasons, evidence.

This technique, though, is precisely the opposite of that. Let's look at an example to see how it works.

In the summer of 2000, I worked in Procter & Gamble's diaper business where we made and marketed the Pampers and Luvs brands. I was given a unique opportunity that summer to develop and present a five-year strategy recommendation to the president and leadership team.

After a few weeks of analysis and preparation, I had my big moment with the leadership team. They were probably expecting a traditional presentation where I would stand up, tell them what my recommendation was, and then justify that recommendation with the details of my analysis. But that's not what I did. Instead, I told them the following:[2]

> Every one of you in this room has been taught since you joined the company that if you deliver the sales volume, the profits will follow. And our strategy in this business unit reflects that belief. All of our plans are directed at selling more diapers. Period. So in preparation for this meeting, I decided to do some research to find out if that assumption was true.
>
> I looked back over our nearly 40-year history making disposable diapers in the United States, and here's what I found. For the first 21 years, 1961–1982, there was a nearly perfect correlation between sales volume and profits. Every year as sales went up, profits went up. When sales went down, profits went down. It seems that assumption about higher sales leading to higher profits was true, and this data is probably the reason why we'd all been taught this mantra.
>
> But when I looked at the data since 1982, it told a very different story. From 1983 to 2000, there has been absolutely no correlation between sales volume and profits whatsoever. None. Over those 18 years, profit growth years have been just as likely to accompany sales growth as sales declines. The same is true for profit declines.
>
> The scatter plot of this data is shocking, so I showed it and paused

there while the audience took it in. I then asked the audience this question: "What do you think could have happened around 1983 that forever changed the nature of this higher-sales-equals-higher-profits industry?"

Someone answered, "Is that when Kimberly-Clark launched Huggies?"

"That was my first guess, too," I said. "But I checked, and Huggies launched several years earlier. Any other ideas?"

"Is that when commodity costs got out of control?" someone asked.

"Another good guess," I said. "I thought about that, too. But it turns out that happened in the late '70s. Anyone else?"

I continued to let the audience throw out guesses, most of which I had considered myself. And at some of the quieter moments, I mentioned a few of the other dead-end hypotheses I had chased. But with each question and answer, I gently guided them along the path I took until eventually, someone in the room said, "Is that maybe when the market reached full penetration?"

"Bingo!" I yelled. "That's it! Before we launched disposable diapers in the early '60s, everyone used cloth diapers. But it's not like once disposable diapers came out, everybody switched from cloth immediately. It took years for that to happen. In fact, it turns out it took exactly 21 years.

"By 1983, the market for disposable diapers had essentially reached 100 percent of households with kids who wore diapers, and cloth diapers had almost entirely vanished from the marketplace. Up to that point, everyone making disposable diapers had rapidly growing sales numbers, and the rapidly growing profit numbers to go with them. The cloth diaper makers, of course, were going out of business.

"What that means is that the disposable diaper business in the United States went from a 'developing market' to a 'mature market' in 1983. And apparently, we failed to notice it. We're still following the same basic 'sell more' strategy we've been using during the developing market period."

Of course, an appropriate business strategy for a developed market is usually very different. And my audience knew it.

But I never got to say any of that in my presentation. As soon as someone got the point about market penetration, there was a very audible and collective "Ohhhh" in the room. And right after that, all of my conclusions started pouring out the mouths of my audience like a well-rehearsed screenplay. And right after that, my recommendations started coming out of their mouths. I never even got to my recommendations slide. And I didn't have to. My recommendations had become their recommendations. It was undoubtedly the most effective presentation I made in my 20 years with the company. All of my recommendations were adopted immediately.

Why was it so successful? Because human beings are naturally more passionate about pursuing their own ideas than they are about pursuing your ideas. Inadvertently, I had turned my ideas into their ideas. And this discovery journey story, as I call it now, is why.

Let's see how that data became a story.

First, all the background of my project and the early data I found was the context. The challenge came when I found the strange relationship between sales and profits that changed in 1983, and I obviously wanted to know why. The conflict was all the work done to solve that mystery. It was thinking up hypotheses, testing them out, and finding that they didn't seem to work. Then, there was thinking up another solution and finding out it didn't work either. The result was the final discovery of the right answer. We then transition out of the story to the lessons, which were the conclusions of the analysis, and finally to the strategy recommendations. It's every single part of the story structure we covered in Chapter 13.

Only notice this twist. When I got to the conflict, instead of just telling them about my struggle to find the right answer, I let them struggle with it themselves. And I let them continue to struggle with it until they found the solution I had found. I gave them the gift of discovery that I'd had. And that's what turned my recommendations into their recommendations.

To use this method, you certainly don't have to give your audience all the data that you had or take them through all the wrong turns and dead ends you went through. Just give them enough of the wrong turns for them to see you struggle a little, and just enough of the data for them to struggle a bit themselves before finding the right answer. You may have to help them along like I did.

23

STRETCHING THE TRUTH

ONE OF THE most common questions I get in my seminars is "Does my story have to be true?" When I dig a little deeper, I find out it's generally one of two types of questions. One is "Can I make up an entire story?" The other is "Does every detail in my story have to be accurate?"

We discussed the first type in Chapter 12, where you read my perhaps surprising answer that "Yes, it's okay to make up an entire story," but under one condition. And that condition is that your audience knows you made it up. Otherwise, you risk losing all credibility.

A few well-chosen words at the beginning of your story lets your audience know. Kicking it off with "Let's suppose . . ." or "Imagine . . ." is usually enough to do the trick. But if you really want to be sure, you can use something more direct, like saying, "Okay, I'm totally making this up, but bear with me, I think it'll help you understand . . ."

Having said that, I'll remind you that making up a story should be the last resort when looking for the right story to tell. You should first be looking in your own past and the past of others you work with. We'll cover other great hunting grounds for stories in Chapter 24. If you're making up stories without trying all these other options first, you're doing yourself and your audience a disservice.

EMBELLISHMENT

Let's turn to the more difficult question: "Does every detail in my story need to be accurate?" Sometimes this question is phrased, "Is it okay to embellish my stories? And if so, how much?"

This is a complex issue. It would be easy to stand on the moral high ground and say, "Everything in your stories needs to be 100 percent true or you're a liar." On the other side, when you review much of what's been written on this topic, you find that many people are quick to trot out quotes attributed to famous people to justify all manner of fabrications. For example, Mark Twain is credited with saying, "Never let the truth get in the way of a good story," and Sir Robert Armstrong is said to have remarked, "There may be times when it's in everyone's best interests to be economical with the facts."

Here's my conclusion: I think you can err on both sides of the issue—meaning, when it comes to guarding the integrity of the facts in your story, I think you can be both too aggressive and too cautious.

The dangers of being too aggressive are obvious. The farther your story strays from what actually happened, the more likely you are to mislead your audience, violate their trust in you, and permanently spoil the relationship.

The dangers of being too cautious are not so obvious. So as an example, let's talk about the use of dialogue in a story. As mentioned in Chapter 20, dialogue is the single most engaging literary device. But in my experience with salespeople and other business leaders, dialogue is woefully underused. When I ask them why, the main reason people give is that they don't think they can remember exactly what the characters said. And being afraid to misquote someone, they opt out of dialogue entirely. This is a huge mistake. It's a missed opportunity to fairly strengthen your stories.

Here's an illustration. In the Pig Island story at the beginning of the book, I wrote that once I'd decided to buy the picture, I handed Chris Gug my credit card and said, "We'll take it!" But am I absolutely sure I said "We'll take it," instead of "I'll take it" or "Let's do it" or even "Sold!"? Of course not. That was months ago. I think that's what I said, but I'm not 100 percent sure. What I do know for certain is that I said something short, definitive, and exclamatory that basically meant "please take my money and give me that picture right now." The words "We'll take it!" capture all of that truth whether they're precisely correct or not.

The same goes for other details in other stories. For example, take Ben Koberna's story about the sludge contract (Chapter 8). It stated that the bids from the incumbent supplier dropped from $250,000 to $240,000 to $200,000 to $150,000 to $0. Is it possible Ben misremembered and the true pattern of bids was $250,000, $220,000, $180,000, $100,000, $50,000, and $0? Sure, that's possible. But who cares? It doesn't change the conclusion of the story or the lesson learned.

But if Ben were to take out those specifics (which were recounted in a slow, dramatic fashion in the original story), he'd have to replace it with something like " . . . and then they started dropping their bid until it got to zero." That way of describing it underrepresents the truth of what actually happened, because what happened was a set of specific, incrementally lower bids that created a dramatic, surprising, and confusing afternoon for the people it actually happened to. Using specific bid amounts, whether or not they correspond exactly to the ones actually submitted, better reflects the reality of the experience for the people involved. That means using the perhaps incorrect numbers actually gives the audience listening to the story a more accurate picture of what it was like to be there than if Ben had used the more correctly stated, but indefinite, description.

In storytelling, accuracy is important. Precision is not.

If you let the fear of imprecision be a barrier to using dialogue or other specifics in your storytelling, ultimately all you'd be able to say is, "I woke up, did some stuff, and then came home. The end."

An attempt to use only rigorously supportable statements either neuters your stories of anything interesting or riddles them with qualifiers and hedges.

BEING TOO AGGRESSIVE

As for being too aggressive, we all have to draw our own lines. Here's my advice on how to decide where to draw it.

As a first-order approximation, you shouldn't be any more willing to embellish stories than you're willing to embellish facts.

Notice a few things about this idea. First, it recognizes that facts and stories are both things you tell other people. Just because one of them is "a story" doesn't mean you have more license to be deceitful with it. Second, it recognizes that in many cases, most of us are willing to be less than precise with facts, and justifiably so. A 14.7 percent sales increase gets rounded up to 15 percent. An 11 percent price increase gets played down as "only about 10 percent." A 93 percent improvement in quality ratings would be celebrated by almost everyone as "We doubled our quality rating!" And nobody would fault us for making those slight adjustments to the facts.

But not many of us would feel the same way if the 14.7 percent sales increase was touted as 25 percent, or the 11 percent price increase was swept under the rug as "only 1 or 2 percent." The magnitude of the difference matters. And if you're willing to make only minor changes to the details of facts, you should be willing to make only minor changes to the details of stories.

I say this is a first-order approximation because in the messy reality of life and business, exactly where you draw the line will vary and depends on a number of things. In particular, I think it should depend on the following three criteria.

Audience expectations.

There's a broad spectrum of expectations people have about the factual integrity of a story. If you're watching a Harry Potter movie, you don't expect anything in the story to be true. If you're in the jury box listening to the testimony of a witness, you're expecting all of it to be true and precise. But what about a work story you hear on the golf course, or a fishing tale over a beer, or the story from your boss about the biggest sale she ever made? In each situation, the audience has different expectations of accuracy.

The point is that as long as your story is within the degree of accuracy your audience expects, you're in comfortable territory. If your fishing buddy tells you he caught a 10-pound catfish this weekend, and you find out later that it was only 8 pounds, it's probably not going to damage your friendship. But if you find out that he didn't even go fishing this weekend, he'll have some explaining to do.

Clearly, people don't have high accuracy expectations in a movie theater, but they generally do in the office. But how much? Here are two additional things that generally affect people's expectations about the accuracy of the story you're telling:

How much time has elapsed. If you tell people something happened a few days ago, they expect more accuracy than if you told them it happened 15 years ago when you first joined the company.

How many mouths it's passed through. If you're telling a story about something that happened to you personally, your audience expects a higher degree of fidelity than if you're telling a story passed on to you through six intermediate people.

Intentionality of the embellishment.

Are you changing the story on purpose, or is it happening by accident, organically, over time? Research shows (as common sense will confirm) that each time you try to recall a story, you find you can't remember all the details. Then, usually unbeknownst to you, when you tell the story your mind creates additional details to fill in the missing spots. When this happens, you can't distinguish between the original details and the new ones. You remember it all as if it were true.[1] It's like the childhood game of telephone, where a message gets changed as it's whispered around a circle of kids, mouth to ear. The only difference is that in this case, all of the children are you.

When this happens, you're actually being completely honest, to the best of your ability. For these types of embellishments, it's fair to let your line drift a bit farther. You have little control over them anyway, and your audience would likely forgive you such honest mistakes. However, if you've intentionally changed the details of the story, you should hold yourself to a stricter account.

You may ask, if the story gets changed either way, does intent really matter so much? Absolutely. The justice system of most countries is based on intent. If your grill tips over in the backyard and accidentally sets your neighbor's house on fire, you owe him a huge apology. If you intentionally set his house on fire because you don't like him, then you're an arsonist and you'll be going to jail.

And last, yes, it's probably true that your audience will never know if the changes you've made are intentional or accidental—or if you've made changes at all. But you'll know. And the more you know you've changed a story, the more difficult it is to deliver it with passion and conviction. It also makes it harder to remember. ("Now which part did I change last time?")

What's getting changed.

Changing minor details in the context or conflict doesn't matter much. But changing the resolution of the story or the lesson are much more substantive changes, and you should be less willing to make them.

For example, in the Iceland volcano story (Chapter 5), let's say out of excitement John Stephens ended up exaggerating the number of executives as 360 instead of the correct number of 180, or we found out he went only 24 hours without sleep instead of the 48 that he told us. In relative terms, those are huge embellishments—double the correct numbers.

But the size of the embellishment doesn't matter much because the fact getting embellished doesn't matter much. Whether it's 360 executives or 180, it's still a lot of people to have to get home during a volcano.

However, if the truth is that John and his staff failed to get all those executives home quickly, and instead they got home no more quickly than if they'd just rebooked on commercial flights, that would be a big deal. Now you've changed the entire conclusion of the story.

SOLUTIONS

Given those three criteria, here are some solutions.

Set Expectations Up Front

Give listeners some indication up front of how true to the facts they should expect your story to be. If you start off, "I saw something interesting yesterday . . . ," they'll expect a near-perfect recitation of the facts. If you say, "I have a vague recollection from my childhood about . . . ," they'll expect something much less accurate.

For tales that aren't yours where you're naturally less certain of the facts, you can use phrases like "I've heard that . . ." or "Company legend has it . . ." or "A guy once told me . . ." And if you're skeptical of the story yourself, you can be even more direct and say, "This story is probably apocryphal, but I thought you'd get something out of it anyway . . ."

Litmus Tests for Accuracy

Here's my acid test: Imagine you just discovered that someone who listened to a story you told was actually there when the story originally happened. Then ask yourself these two questions: (1) Would they be offended? (2) Would you be embarrassed? If you answer yes to either of those questions, you've probably changed too much. If not, you're fine.

This is an especially good practice to get into because it can actually happen. I was in the audience of one of Michael Miller's Primo Solutions sales training classes a couple of years ago when Mike told a story about an early prospect of his named Harry. When he finished telling the story, an elderly man in the back of the room raised his hand and said, "Hi Mike. It's nice to see you again. I'm Harry." And it was! After the initial shock wore off, Mike said he'd been telling that story for years and wondered if he'd been telling it right. Harry said, "Yeah, that's pretty much how I remember it, too."

Can you imagine how embarrassing it could have been if Mike had embellished too much and crossed the line?

In his book *All Marketers Are Liars*, Seth Godin offers his own acid test consisting of these two questions you should imagine the buyer asking you: (1) "If I knew what you know, would I choose to buy what you sell?" (2) "After I've used this and experienced it, will I be glad I believed the story, or will I feel ripped off?"[2]

What Not to Change

Since an audience is more sensitive to changes in some parts of a story than others, it's helpful to distinguish which parts belong in which group. In his book *Story Theater Method*, Doug Stevenson offers the following division, which I'll make some parenthetical comments on.[3] I call those inviolable parts you shouldn't monkey around with "hard points," and those where you have more leeway "soft points."

Hard points (don't change)

- Essence of the story
- Event or situation (although you could mask details to protect anonymity)
- People (although you could omit names to protect anonymity)
- Obstacle (the challenge)
- Process used to overcome (not all the details of the conflict, just the overall approach you took)
- Resolution
- Lesson learned

Soft points (more leeway)

- Time or location
- Names and descriptions of people
- Puffery (exaggeration so big it's obviously fake)
- Resequencing events
- Quotes and dialogue

But these are just a guideline. If you're ever uncertain about changing any particular detail, go back and use the acid test. If someone who was there hears me tell the story this way, will they be offended or will I be embarrassed?

24

FINDING GREAT STORIES

TO **FIND GREAT** stories, it helps to know what stories you're look-ing for. Fortunately, you already have a starting place. Appendix A lists the 25 stories every salesperson needs. Use that list and check off the ones you already have great ideas for. Add any unique stories you think you need. This is your "wish list" of stories. As you find sto-ries or realize you need new ones, keep this list up to date.

Now that you have your wish list, there's an almost limitless set of sources you can go to in order to fill it. Below are 14 reliable places to look, starting with you.

SEARCH YOUR OWN PAST AND PRESENT

Interview yourself. If you haven't already done so, ask yourself all the questions in the Exercises sections at the end of each chapter in Part I.

Take the West/Anthony challenge. In their book *Storyselling for Financial Advisors*, authors Scott West and Mitch Anthony ask, "What would happen if you had to start selling investment prod-ucts . . . without the use of statistics, charts, rankings, or ratings?

No Morningstar rankings, no Lipper averages. Would you go mute?"[1] And the answer is, of course, no. You'd start drawing pictures, using metaphors, and yes, telling stories. Take the challenge yourself. If you no longer had access to your most common selling tools, what would you do in the buyer's office? What stories, pictures, or metaphors would you need?

Keep a sales story journal. Whenever you hear a great story, or see one happen, write it down in your journal. Use your favorite note-taking method, whether it's pen and paper, an electronic tablet, or your computer. I personally use Evernote because I can access the same journal from my computer, tablet, or phone, whatever is closest when a story strikes me.

Stalk product reviews. Look through the online or offline reviews of your products, wherever they happen to be.

GET STORIES FROM OTHER PEOPLE

Ask around. Interview other sales reps, executives, and colleagues from customer service, marketing, product development, and consumer insights. Set a goal of interviewing one person a week until your story wish list is exhausted. And if you're the boss, you can do more than "ask" for stories. You can demand them. Do you require your employees to turn in monthly expense reports or progress memos, and do you track who does and doesn't comply? Then you can do the same thing with stories.

Share your wish list. Send your wish list to anyone and everyone who might be able to help you fill it. You'll be surprised how willing people are to share their stories when they know someone is actually looking for a story they have. Plus, the more people who know what you're looking for, the better your odds of finding what you need.

Go on regular "story hunts." In his book *Leadership*, management guru Tom Peters notes, "As I see it, an effective leader, as she makes the rounds at her organization, must ask one—and only one—question: 'Got any good stories?'"[2] One person who makes good use of this technique is Pam King Sams, chief development officer at Children's National Medical Center in Washington, D.C. She regularly walks the halls of the hospital just to get stories. She stops and meets the kids and their parents. Just hearing about their experiences usually produces great stories. She also stops and talks to the doctors, nurses, and staff and asks, "Tell me about something that touched you this week."

Follow up with customers. Jord, the maker of wood watches, maintains an email database of all its customers and specifically asks them for stories as part of its after-the-sale communications. As explained by Waqas Shah, special projects advisor for Jord, the intent is to "get the customer to reminisce about an encounter with someone who noticed the watch." You can see an example of one of their customer-submitted stories in Chapter 1 (test narrative #4).

And remember, the customer success stories you capture don't even have to be your own. See Shane Skillen's use of the Febreze story in Chapter 7.

FIND VENUES FOR CREATING AND SHARING STORIES

Look on your company website. Many companies overtly ask for customer stories on their websites and let other customers and prospects see them there.[3]

Share at client conferences. BizLibrary, an online employee training provider, hosts an annual conference for its clients to get together and share ideas on how to leverage BizLibrary's products and services. According to Becky Claggett, senior account executive, those sessions are great sources of customer success stories.

Discuss at staff meetings. Have storytelling be a standing agenda item in each meeting. Rotate who's responsible for sharing a story each week.

Host weekly story circles. Have small teams get together once a week for an hour. Sit in a circle facing each other, and ask everyone to take turns sharing stories. For the most productive way to plan and conduct story circles, refer to Chapter 2 of David Hutchens's book *Circle of the 9 Muses.*[4]

Use the buddy system. Assign every junior sales rep a senior sales "buddy." Have them meet once a month to share stories. According to Tia Finn at Pearson, this is a great way to train new salespeople and reinvigorate the more experienced ones who no longer feel as challenged.

Hold a contest. According to sales VP Rich Snodsmith, Backroads active travel company invites all its customers to share the story of their vacation through videos and photos at the end of their trip.[5] The best three submissions are chosen each year and shared on the Backroads website.[6] Winners receive a $5,000 credit on a future Backroads vacation.

CONDUCTING THE INTERVIEW

Identifying people to interview for stories is one thing. Getting them to actually tell you stories is another. Having personally conducted hundreds of one-on-one interviews, I can tell you some techniques work better than others at eliciting useful stories. Let's start by looking at what doesn't work very well.

First, asking yes-or-no questions, or questions that require only short answers, is not a good way to get stories. If you ask, "What are the best kind of stories to tell in a sales call?" you might get an answer like, "Oh, usually something where the product is the hero or where I get to talk about how much better our service department is. Those tend to work pretty well." Your question was answered. But you didn't get any stories.

Another technique I've had mixed results with is asking directly, "Tell me your best story." As discussed in Chapter 5, people don't really think about their experiences as "stories." They think about them as experiences. Asking for "stories" won't necessarily tap into the events you're looking for.

Another problem with asking for stories is that it sets up an expectation with your interviewees that they're being asked to perform and deliver a well-crafted, well-rehearsed set of lines. David Hutchens describes this with the observation that storytelling "withers under the harsh glare of self-conscious awareness." He explains it this way: "Imagine we're at a cocktail party, standing around a high-top table with drinks and a group of friends. Imagine I point at you and say: 'You know, a social engagement like this is a great opportunity to deepen our bonds through oral storytelling. I'd like for each of us to think of a 3-minute story that provides a humorous perspective on today's events at work. I'd like for you to go first, Paul. Ready? Begin.'"[7]

That's too much pressure.

Another problem with asking for someone's "best stories" is that it's just too general of a question. Would that be my funniest stories? The ones that are the most effective? The ones I like telling the most? Or something else?

Having said all that, I can tell you that of all the people I've asked that question, the only group I've had any luck with are salespeople. In all my work with business executives at all levels and across all functions, with parents, and with children, that question has failed to deliver. But with salespeople, it sometimes works. My hypothesis is that salespeople use stories more purposefully than other people, so they have a better instinct about what a story is. Plus, most of them would assume "best story" means the one that has the best track record at delivering a purchase order.

So, when you're interviewing product development people, marketing managers, executives, or customers, don't expect to get much use out of the "best story" question. But if you're interviewing other sales reps, go ahead and try it. Sometimes it works.

INTERVIEW TECHNIQUES THAT WORK WELL WITH EVERYONE

We covered some of the basics in Chapter 5 when we discussed how to get buyers to tell their stories. Those techniques work just as well with other people, so let's review the most relevant ones:

Shut up and listen. If you spend 30 minutes talking in a one-hour interview, you've cut your odds of getting a good story in half. Listening is one of the hardest things to do, especially for naturally gregarious, outgoing people. Resist the urge to take over the conversation.

Ask open-ended questions. Avoid yes-or-no or short answer questions. Instead, use open-ended questions like "How did you first find out your original material wasn't working well?"

Ask about specific moments in time. Use questions that refer to specific times, like "Tell me about a time when a customer called to say 'thank you.'"

Use problem prompts. For instance, say, "Have you ever noticed that . . ." and then follow it with the kind of problem other people in their roles have that might make a good story for you.

Tell your story first. Tell the kind of story you want to hear. This uses the "Hey, something like that happened to me once" phenomenon to prompt your interviewee to share a relevant story. But this takes up valuable interview time, so try the other methods first.

QUESTIONS TO USE WHEN INTERVIEWING SALESPEOPLE

Here are some of the questions I found most productive when interviewing salespeople for this book. This line of questions is designed to elicit stories that other salespeople are already telling. So, in this case, referring to them as "stories" works fine.

- What's the most effective story you've ever told during a sales call?
- What's the least effective story you've ever told during a sales call?
- What's one of the most interesting stories you've ever heard from a buyer?
- Tell me one of the legendary sales stories in your company or your industry.
- Here are some specific stories I'm looking for. Can you share examples of stories you tell when:
  - Networking and introducing yourself
  - Building rapport and a relationship with the buyer
  - Explaining who you are
  - Explaining what you do for a living
  - Explaining whom you work for
  - Explaining what your product or service is and why someone should buy it
  - Giving an example of a customer success
  - Giving an example of a customer failure
  - Demonstrating your understanding of the buyer and her problems
  - Talking about price (negotiating)
  - Handling objections
  - Closing the sale
  - Describing how your customer service works

QUESTIONS TO USE WHEN INTERVIEWING CUSTOMERS

These questions are designed to elicit stories that aren't necessarily being told yet. Note that the word "story" isn't used in the questions. Also, notice that they generally start with or include the words "Tell me about a time when" or "Tell me what happened."

- What was the best experience you've ever had with our company? Tell me about it.
- Tell me about the worst experience you've ever had:
  - With us
  - With our competitors
  - With anyone in the industry
- Tell me about a time when you were completely surprised by something we did for you. Tell me about a time when you were completely surprised by something one of our competitors did for you.
- When did you first know for sure that working with us helped your bottom line (or however you measure success)? Tell me what happened.

PLANNING AND EXECUTION

Here are three final pieces of advice on conducting a story interview.

Let the interviewees see the questions ahead of time. This gives them time to think of good stories. It also avoids David Hutchens's cocktail party problem mentioned above. In working on this book, I generally sent questions to interviewees a week ahead of time, and it was obvious who had looked at them ahead of time and who had not. The ones who did had lots of stories to share. The ones who did not had very few.

Record the interview (but get permission first). Most of us can't write or type fast enough to keep up with all the details of a story.

A recording allows you to go back and fill in details later without bothering your interviewee with endless follow-up questions.

For in-person interviews, I used the "voice memo" app on my iPhone. I found it easiest to mention the recording when I sent the questions instead of waiting until just before the interview. Asking people if you can record what they say can be off-putting. It's better to get them past that emotional barrier early, so it's not hanging over them during the interview. I included this statement with the questions I sent a week before the interview: "I'll be recording our conversation to help me with note-taking and no other purpose. I promise it won't end up in anyone else's hands."

Get permission to use the story. If you do uncover a story you'd like to use, give your interviewee the opportunity to review how you captured it and make any corrections. This also serves as their opportunity to make it clear that they're okay with you using their story for your purposes. If it's someone in your company, a verbal okay usually suffices. For a customer or supplier, it's best to get it in writing or in an email response. I discovered the hard way that asking permission to use stories can create a lot of stress and bureaucratic machinations, especially when the external relations department gets involved. And that's understandable. One big PR nightmare can get the company in a lot of trouble and get your interviewee fired, while the upside for them in your using the story is probably very low.

Ultimately, I found that stories that reflect favorably on a company and its employees move through the approval process quickly. Unfavorable or neutral stories do not. If the story paints an unflattering picture, you might be better served leaving out the names of the characters, brands, and company involved and making it a completely anonymous story. For a more thorough discussion on how to navigate the permission waters, see Chapter 5 of Casey Hibbard's *Stories That Sell.*[8]

25

PRACTICING AND SAVING YOUR STORIES

ONE OF THE more interesting questions I asked procurement professionals was "What makes a sales pitch sound like a sales pitch?" The answers I got were telling.

Some had to do with the structure of the sales pitch. Specifically, I was told, conversations that begin "If I could show you a way to save X dollars a year, would you buy this today?" are universally met with disgust. Many find it both condescending and manipulative—a bit of verbal trickery to get them to commit to buying something before they even know what it is they're being sold. Listening to buyers explain their reactions to this taught me more creative ways to describe the act of vomiting than I hope to ever need.

Other responses referred to the obligatory canned background on the salesperson's company, usually delivered in a rapid monotone in the first five slides of a presentation. One buyer aptly described such an irrelevant waste of time this way: "The salesperson is about as invested in presenting those slides as I am in listening to them."[1]

Still others mentioned obvious attempts to find a personal connection between buyer and seller when one clearly didn't exist.

But by far the most often cited indication that a sales pitch was in progress was the moment when the tone of the discussion turned from an improvisational conversation to something that sounded scripted.

Often described as memorized, practiced, rehearsed, and passionless, these lines come across to the buyer like something that was written to be read, not spoken.

Whether the scripted tones deliver a more traditional part of a sales presentation or the kind of sales story we're addressing in this book, the reaction is the same. It's not quite as visceral as the vomit-inducing "would you buy this today" line. But it's not much better either. One buyer described it as "making the hairs on the back of my neck stand up, and think, 'Oh God, I'm being sold something here.'"

The only reason your sales stories would ever sound scripted and memorized, of course, is if you scripted and memorized them. So don't.

Professional screenwriters in Hollywood can write a script that doesn't sound like a script. And professional actors can memorize and deliver that script in a way that doesn't sound memorized. But since you're probably not a Hollywood screenwriter or actor, your best odds of delivering a story that doesn't sound like it's been memorized word for word is to not memorize it word for word. And the best way to avoid memorizing your story word for word is to never write it out that way in the first place.

The good news is that if your stories are just for your personal use, you don't need to write them out word for word. The bullet points and phrases you have written down in the story structure template should be all you need to review and remember any story you want to tell. Because you're remembering only the general outline and a few key words and phrases, most of the actual words that come out of your mouth when you tell the story will be improvised, just like any normal conversation. And that's exactly the way you want it to sound.

Having said that, some people find it builds their confidence in telling a story if they memorize a few key sentences. The best candidates for that are the first sentence, the last sentence, and any key transition points. What that might look like is writing out and memorizing the hook (the one sentence or phrase that's your transition into the story) as well as the transition out of the story at the end leading into the lesson. And if it makes you comfortable, you can do the same thing with the first sentence of the challenge, conflict, or resolution.

But err on the side of less, not more. The more you memorize, the more you risk making the hairs on your buyer's neck stand up.

PRACTICE

An Olympic swimmer practices more than a thousand hours for every one hour of actual competition. A professional football player puts in 200 hours of practice for each hour of playing time. And a professional musician might practice three or four hours for every one hour on stage.[2]

But how long does a typical salesperson practice for each hour of time in a sales call? One expert's guess is zero to five minutes.

Of course, nobody expects a salesperson, or any businessperson, to put in hours of practice before each day of work. But it raises a fair question. If you want to deliver sales stories well, should you practice them, and if so, how?

There's no unanimous answer among sales professionals. Some, like sales consultant Kristin Luck, don't practice their stories at all. She says, "I've never done it. It doesn't feel genuine or organic to me . . . I will plan. But I don't rehearse the stories. I don't want them to sound dry and unauthentic."

Salespeople fortunate enough to have several sales calls a week (or even a day) often don't even feel the need to practice. They have enough occasions to deliver their stories in actual sales calls. Each call serves as the practice and refinement opportunity for the next call.

But others, like DeAnn Marshall at Children's Hospital Los Angeles, do believe in the benefits of practicing stories. In fact, she insists that all the people on her team go through a dry run of their entire presentation (including the stories) in her office prior to the call. That gives them a chance to practice and her an opportunity to offer a critique and advice.

And many fans of practicing their stories will resonate with Mark Satterfield's comment: "You wouldn't believe how hard I work to make this sound as natural as it does."[3]

If you choose not to practice, make sure to use each call as an opportunity to refine your stories. As Shawn Callahan explains in *Putting*

Stories to Work: "The instant feedback we get when we tell a story plays an important role in how we naturally improve our stories. For example, let's say something remarkable happens and we immediately tell someone a story about it. The first version of our story will tend to be raw and rambling. The second (and subsequent versions), however, will be adapted based on how the audience has reacted and what we like about the story. In other words, the best way to improve an oral story is to tell it."[4]

If you do choose to make practice a part of your storytelling routine, here are some thoughts to help make the most of it. Let's start with one of the most common pieces of advice you're likely to encounter: practice in front of a mirror.

This is an age-old recommendation for any kind of public speaking, and many people still swear by it today. They argue it gives you self-confidence and that you can see what you're doing so you can critique yourself along the way. That may be true. And if you already use this practice technique and it works for you, keep doing it. But if not, I recommend against it for practicing stories.

Ideally, all practice should be under as close to the same conditions as possible to how the performance will happen. And *you* are the one thing you're guaranteed to never see in front of you when you tell a story to a buyer.

Practicing in front of a mirror also makes you focus on the physical performance aspects, like facial expressions and hand gestures, instead of on the content of the story. As we discussed earlier, none of these delivery elements are nearly as important as the content of the story.

As for its building self-confidence, I've never found that to be the case. Instead, all it's ever done is made me self-conscious about how I look. In fact, I find nitpicking my own appearance and movements such a distraction that I can rarely get through an entire story without stopping.

Here are some better ideas:

Walk and talk with an imaginary friend. Find a private room, hallway, or office. Stand up and start walking around, even if it's in a small circle. Then imagine you're on a casual walk with your buyer discussing business. Now, start telling your story. Out loud. Really.

Sound strange? It's not any stranger than standing in the bathroom talking to yourself in the mirror, and that's what some of you are doing now. Plus, it's much more effective. The reason is that it puts you into the frame of mind to have a casual conversation—just a couple of friends out for a walk chatting. If you practice your story in a casual, conversational manner, you'll deliver it that way.

Another reason this method works well was best described by Doug Stevenson when he observed, "When you walk and talk you integrate your movements and gestures with your material. Your body language will spontaneously evolve."[5] That doesn't seem to happen as much when you practice sitting down.

Too embarrassed to do this at work? Try at home in the shower, in the basement, or wandering in the backyard.

Practice in front of a live audience. Ditch the imaginary friend and ask a real one to listen to your stories and give you feedback. You can offer to return the favor. This method works especially well between salespeople who both have a need to practice their stories. Not comfortable doing this at work, either? Share your stories with your spouse, kids, or even the dog.

Use audio recording. Use a digital voice recorder or smartphone app to record your voice while telling the story. A recording gives you something to critique and revise later. If you don't have access to those options, call yourself on the phone and tell the story to the answering machine. If many of your sales calls are over the phone anyway, this makes an especially relevant opportunity to practice under game conditions.

Use video recording. This is one of the most powerful yet somewhat controversial options. Some experts believe video practice has the same shortcomings as practicing in front of a mirror. Storytelling authors Karen Dietz and Lori Silverman maintain that video recording "will only make you self-conscious. We can always tell who's been practicing in this manner and who's been practicing with others. The mirror/video practicers usually sound rehearsed, stilted, and less alive."[6]

I'm somewhat sympathetic to this point of view. But the benefit of being able to see and hear yourself tell your stories is so powerful, I think it's worth finding a way to salvage it. There are two options to do that.

Option one is to videotape yourself telling your story to a live person. That gets you the best of both worlds. If you can't or aren't interested in pulling that off, option two is likely to win favor among introverts. Record yourself telling your story to that imaginary friend sitting in the room with you. In other words, don't look directly at the camera while recording. Look at an empty chair across the desk and pretend. The camera will record you from, say, a 45-degree angle as if watching a real conversation between two people.

> *Use online services.* If you're comfortable and interested in video practice, there are professional online services that can help you get the most of it. For example, SharperAx (www.sharperax.com) starts by allowing you to record your sales presentations and stories using your computer's webcam. You can then watch and critique your own performance and re-record the same story multiple times until you're happy with it. It also allows you to easily share your stories with coworkers, bosses, or subordinates and solicit feedback from them as well. And if your story can be used by other salespeople at your company, you can set it as a "story guide" that others can watch, take notes on, practice, and deliver themselves.

SharperAx founder Paul McGhee says his experience with clients is that the first recording is decent. Then the next few get worse as the client explores and experiments with different ways to tell the story. Then, by the fifth or sixth effort, they have something even better than they started with. In all, Paul thinks it takes about 30 minutes to perfect a good story, and he recommends 30 to 90 minutes a week practicing.

SAVING YOUR STORIES

The modern sales professional maintains an amount of data that would have been inconceivable a generation ago. Customer relationship management programs make it possible to keep a record of every client phone call, email, or meeting, along with notes on everything that was discussed. Every presentation, proposal, price list, and product catalog is saved electronically, along with every analysis performed in preparation for each of those client engagements.

Just about everything of value to a salesperson is saved in a computer somewhere. Everything, that is, except for the most powerful tool in any salesperson's tool kit—their stories. Those are usually entrusted only to the frailties of human memory and the inevitability of attrition.

Treat your sales stories like the valuable asset they are. Once you've found your stories and crafted them (using all the techniques from Part II), database them. Below are some ideas for how to do that.

First, the good news is that you don't have to commit every word of your story to writing in order to save it. Most of your stories will only be delivered orally. As we just covered in the previous section, the best oral delivery is extemporaneous, not memorized. And the best way to avoid being tempted to memorize every word of your story is to not write it down that way to begin with.

Therefore, if your stories are for only your own personal use, the easiest way to save them is in rough outline form in the story structure templates you're using to craft them (Appendix C). For your convenience, I've created a Microsoft Word file with 25 blank story structure templates, one for each of the 25 sales stories on your wish list. It's called "Story Database" and you can download an electronic version of it at www.leadwithastory.com/resources.

If, on the other hand, you want to capture your stories in a way that they can be shared with or used by other people, you need to capture them in a more complete fashion. Here are a few options for that.

Microsoft Word (or other word-processing document). For those of you, like me, who prefer a simple solution, it doesn't get any simpler than this. Just type up your stories in your favorite word-processing program. But instead of a separate file for each story, put all the stories in a single file, one after the other. That makes it easier to search for the one you need. You can search for story titles, keywords, or character names—whatever helps you remember the stories best.

PowerPoint (or other presentation document). To people who do most of their storytelling during a slide presentation, incorporating the text of their stories into the "speaker notes" section of each slide is a more practical solution. You can start and maintain a master set of story slides that have an appropriate title, image, and bullet points on the main slide section, along with the entire text of the story hidden in the section only you or the speaker can see. Keep this file up to date with stories, and then just copy and paste appropriate story slides from it as needed into upcoming presentations.

Online story databases. These offer a more sophisticated solution with shared access for sales teams or an entire company. Zahmoo.com allows you to combine story text, video, audio, and images for each story. It's easily searchable and you can allow common access to corporate stories for multiple users. For the budget-conscious, Imastory.com is a free service. Although it's marketed a bit more for collecting family stories, it works much the same.

Audio recording. This is the method favored by journalists for the past century. And while the technology has changed, the principle is still the same. Record the originator telling their own story. Then listen to it when you need to remind yourself of their actual words. A digital voice recorder or smartphone with an audio recorder app can do the job nicely.

Video recording. This is the same idea as with audio, but with the added benefit of video. Some companies leverage an internal or outside video service to create professional-looking videos of the stories for distribution around the company. The SharperAx practicing solution discussed previously in this chapter can also serve as a database for preserving your stories. But I expect new options to come to market regularly. Email me at paul@leadwithastory.com for the latest.

26

GETTING STARTED

CONGRATULATIONS! YOU'VE COME to the end of this book on storytelling for sales. But this is just the beginning of your journey. Here's a final checklist of ideas and resources to help you along the way:

1. If you haven't already, create your story wish list. Use Appendix A as your starting point. Add to and delete stories as appropriate. Keep the list fresh and up-to-date.

2. Start hunting for and crafting stories on your list. Prioritize them and start with the most important. Always be on the lookout for the next story you need. Appendix D is a list of all the sales stories in this book. Use them as a springboard for coming up with your own similar stories.

3. Use the Selling Story Roadmap (Appendix B) and Story Structure Template (Appendix C) to develop each story. Make copies of the templates, or download electronic versions at www.leadwithastory.com/resources along with all the other tools.

4. Download and use the Story Database to develop and keep track of all your stories.

5. Make storytelling part of your organization's culture. Establish some of the storytelling venues outlined in Chapter 24.

6. Want to learn more? Explore the books in the Additional Reading section. All were useful to me in my exploration of storytelling in the sales space.

7. Want still more help crafting sales stories? Visit me at www. leadwithastory.com for access to blogs, podcasts, newsletters, and training opportunities.

8. Start telling your sales stories. Each time you share one, take note of your buyer's reaction. What worked and what didn't? What did you accidentally add or omit? Go back to the Story Database and make whatever changes you think necessary.

Last, I want to leave you with a final resource for learning to tell better sales stories that's already closer to you than any of the options above: your procurement department. My hypothesis going into the research for this book was that interviewing procurement professionals might be helpful but that my primary learning would come from salespeople. What I concluded by the end was that I learned as much, if not more, about what makes a good sales story from professional buyers than I did from professional sellers.

After all, procurement people attend more sales calls than salespeople do. Some of the salespeople they deal with are good, and some are not so good. Some tell great stories. Some tell lousy stories. And some tell no stories at all. Some they award enormous sales contracts to. Some they send away disappointed.

The company you work for probably has a procurement department. Find it. Meet some of the people who work there. Invite them to lunch. Get to know them. Share some of your sales stories and get their input. Ask them to tell you some of the best, and worst, sales stories they've ever heard.

Put that relationship to work—along with all the tools you've learned in this book—and you'll have much more success when you sell with a story.

25 STORIES SALESPEOPLE NEED

STORY TOPICS:
MY STORY "WISH LIST"

Introducing Myself to New Prospects

❒ Explaining what I do simply _____

❒ Whom I've helped and how I've helped them _____

Stories I Tell Myself Prior to the Call

❒ My personal motivation story _____

❒ To relax and take the stress out of the call _____

Building Rapport with the Buyer

▶ *Stories About Me*

❒ Why I do what I do _____

❒ I'll tell you when I made a mistake _____

❒ I'll tell you when I can't help you _____

❒ I'll go to bat for you with my company _____

❒ I'm not who you think I am _____

▶ *Stories About My Company*

❏ Founding stories _____

❏ How we're different from our competitors _____

The Main Sales Pitch

❏ My product's invention or discovery story _____

❏ Problem stories _____

❏ Customer success stories _____

❏ Two-roads stories _____

❏ Value-adding stories _____

Handling Objections

❏ Objections response stories_____

❏ Negotiating price _____

❏ Resolving objections before they're brought up _____

Closing the Sale

❏ Creating a sense of urgency _____

❏ Arming my sponsor with a story _____

❏ Coaching the breakup _____

After the Sale

❏ What's worked well in the past _____

❏ Loyalty-building stories _____

❏ Summarizing the call: Great sales calls _____

SELLING STORY ROADMAP

STEP 1: Story Selection (Chapter 12)	QUESTIONS	IDEAS FOR YOUR STORY
	A. Define objective What is your main message? What do you want your audience to *think, feel,* or *do* after hearing your story?	
	B. Brainstorm story ideas Think of examples of successes, failures, or moments of clarity involving your main message. Strike out? Use the story hunting tools in Chapter 24.	
	C. Still can't find any? Make one up Make sure your audience knows you made it up.	
	D. Choose the best one Pick the one that best delivers the main message. If all do, then pick the one with the most relatable hero, relevant obstacle, and engaging struggle.	

Table continues

	QUESTIONS	IDEAS FOR YOUR STORY
STEP 2: Story Structure	Complete the Story Structure Template (Appendix C) Follow guidance in Chapters 13–17.	
STEP 3: Emotion (Chapter 18)	A. Identify emotional moments For each bullet point in your story outline (Story Structure Template), identify which emotions the characters or audience should be feeling. B. Prioritize Which ones will have the biggest impact on moving your audience to the desired outcome? C. Pick one or more techniques below to apply to the important ones: *Tell me*—Just state the emotion ("I was scared"). *Show me*—Describe the behavior that demonstrates the emotion ("She was crying" or "He started yelling"). *Make me feel*—*Superior* position creates tension and angst. *Inferior* position creates curiosity and anticipation. *Equal* position lets audience feel the same emotions as characters. *Let the audience get to know characters* to avoid the "Stormtrooper Effect." *Dialogue*—Use inner and outer dialogue to show characters' feelings.	

Table continues

	QUESTIONS	IDEAS FOR YOUR STORY
STEP 4: Surprise (Chapter 19)	Add surprise at the beginning to get the audience's attention, and at the end to make it more memorable. Use any or all of these techniques: *Lead with the most unusual event* (like the Iceland volcano). *Use flashback*—Start with most surprising event, then backtrack to the beginning (like Chris Powers's Ariba story). *Skip one element in the context* and let your audience figure it out on their own (like the story about Judy and the $600,000 check). *Create a surprise ending*—Move one key fact from the context to the end (like the story about James and the tea kettle).	
STEP 5: Dialogue, Details, Length (Chapter 20)	Add outer dialogue: Replace scenes where you *describe what characters meant* with what they *actually said* (even if you have to paraphrase). Make emotionally high potential moments stronger through actual dialogue. Add inner dialogue—Where are your characters silent when inside they want to scream or cry? Share their inner monologue so we can hear what they're thinking.	

Table continues

	QUESTIONS	IDEAS FOR YOUR STORY
STEP 5: *continued*	Add details using these techniques:	
	Give details only when it's relevant to the conflict or explains a main character's motivations (no "It was a warm September morning . . .").	
	Replace generalities with specifics (say "He was 6'4'" rather than "He was tall").	
	Show, don't tell—(e.g., "Frank wrapped and unwrapped the telephone cord around his finger" shows he's nervous).	
	Pick one important scene and describe it in vivid detail (like the story about the cancer patient's sunset that she thought might be her last).	
	Use metaphors (e.g., a looming deadline is a "dark cloud" or a "gun to my head").	
	Length	
	Sales stories average two minutes (300 words)— and generally range from one to three minutes (150–450 words). Does yours fit this range?	
	To shorten a story—use the Story Structure Template (Appendix C) and eliminate the least critical part of each section, while leaving some content in each section.	
STEP 6: **Delivery** (Chapter 21)	Oral Delivery	
	Relax—the story is more important than the delivery.	

Table continues

	QUESTIONS	IDEAS FOR YOUR STORY
STEP 6: *continued*	*A perfect delivery is not perfect*, so five or six filler words a minute is okay.	
	Don't slip into "storytelling voice"—stay in the same conversational tones.	
	Focus on the story, not your physical performance.	
	Written Delivery	
	Write the way you'd like to speak—conversational, but without all the filler words.	
	Use short sentences—15-17 words per sentence.	
	Use simple words—< 10 percent greater than two syllables.	
	Use active voice—< 10 percent passive voice sentences.	
	Get to the verb quickly—in the first five to six words of each sentence.	
	Calculate Flesch-Kincaid grade level, with a target score of 7-8 (like John Grisham or Tom Clancy).	
STEP 7: **Stretching the Truth** (Chapter 23)	Check your story for fidelity to the truth with these guidelines	
	A. Accuracy is important. Precision is not.	
	Don't be afraid to use specific quotes and details.	

Table continues

	QUESTIONS	IDEAS FOR YOUR STORY
STEP 7: *continued*	B. Don't embellish stories any more than you would embellish facts. *Set expectations up front* about how factually precise the story will be. "I saw something interesting this morning . . ." suggests high precision. "I once heard about a guy who . . ." suggests low precision. *Litmus test*—Imagine someone who listened to your story was actually there when it happened. Would they be offended? And would you be embarrassed? If yes to either of those, you've probably changed too much. If not, you're fine. *Hard points (don't change these)*—event, challenge, process to overcome, resolution, lesson learned *Soft points (more leeway)*—time, location, names and descriptions of people, resequencing events, quotes, dialogue.	
STEP 8: **Practice and** **Save** (Chapter 25)	Practice *Don't fully script your story* unless it will be delivered in writing. Outline it, using the Story Structure Template. *Don't memorize your story word for word,* so you can deliver it extemporaneously each time.	

Table continues

	QUESTIONS	IDEAS FOR YOUR STORY
STEP 8: *continued*	*Practice options*—(1) Walk and talk with an imaginary friend, (2) live audience, (3) audio recording, (4) video recording, (5) online services. (Avoid the mirror.) Save—Database your story Use Story Database, Microsoft Word file, PowerPoint, online story database services, audio or video recording.	

STORY STRUCTURE TEMPLATE

STEP	ANSWERS THE QUESTION:	STORY SPINE	NOTES FOR YOUR STORY
OBJECTIVE/ MAIN MESSAGE	What do you want the audience to think, feel, or do as a result of hearing your story?		
TRANSITION IN: (HOOK)	Why should I listen to this story?	I think the best example I've seen of that was . . .	
CONTEXT	Where and when did it take place? Who is the hero and what do they want? Other background needed to understand characters' motivations?	Back in ____, at ____, there was ____, and they were trying to . . . (could be an unspoken objective)	
CHALLENGE	What was the problem/ opportunity?	Then, one day ____.	
CONFLICT	What did they do about it? (Show the honest struggle between hero and villain, even if internal. Can't be too easy.)	So they ____, and then they ____, and so they ____.	

Table continues

STEP	ANSWERS THE QUESTION:	STORY SPINE	NOTES FOR YOUR STORY
RESOLUTION	How did it turn out (for everyone)? (How are things/ characters changed as a result?)	Eventually . . .	
TRANSITION OUT:			
LESSON(S)	What did you learn?	What I learned from that was . . . (That's when I realized . . . That explains why . . . What I've since come to realize is . . . What I think we should have done was . . .)	
RECOMMENDED ACTION(S)	What do you think I should do?	And that's why I think you should . . .	

APPENDIX D

LIST OF SALES STORIES

CHAPTER	STORY	PAGE
Introduction	Pig Island	
1: What Is a Sales Story?	University of Leeds and HP's TippingPoint	
	Jord wood watch in the elevator	
2: Why Tell Sales Stories	Dan Huish and Kirkland Signature	
3: Introducing Yourself	"Suppose you're in the chicken business"	
	Quave Burton's "speed date"	
	The cashmere auction	
4: Stories You Tell Yourself	Biotech rep "gave me back my life"	
5: Getting Buyers to Tell Their Stories	Microsoft and the Iceland volcano	
6: Building Rapport	Why Chris Powers joined Ariba	
	Jamie Lancaster's tale of two IT salesmen	
	Xerox and Huntington National Bank	
	Teacher turned yearbook salesperson	
	Tom Hale founding Backroads	
	Sharad Madison and UBM cleaning services	
7: The Main Sales Pitch	Prentice Hall Reference Guide to Grammar and Usage	
	Battling the ATM in Las Vegas	
	Febreze	
	Selling basketball hoops	
	Andy Smith's "Story" bonds	

8: Handling Objections	More time for grant applications at the zoo	
	"Paying up front" at Excel Model & Talent	
	Discovery journey story at Amway	
	Picking up the sludge	
9: Closing the Sale	Acquisition delaying A/P installation	
	A school "just like you"	
	Coaching the breakup	
10: Service After the Sale	Sally's long bike ride	
	Tee time and fly fishing	
	"These are not my pants!"	
	"Where's the rest of the chocolate?"	
12: Choosing the Right Story to Tell	Trauma counselors at Children's Hospital	
17: Lesson and Action	"The Unwelcome Business Card"	
18: Emotion	Crying behind the minivan	
19: Surprise	Delivering Judy's $600,000 check	
22: Telling Stories with Data	Making payroll at a start-up	
	1983 in the diaper business	

ADDITIONAL READING

Storytelling in Sales

Soft Tales and Hard Asses: One Salesman's Discovery of the Art of Storytelling, by Paul Lanigan and Denis Goodbody

What Great Salespeople Do: The Science of Selling Through Emotional Connection and the Power of Story, by Michael Bosworth and Ben Zoldan

Stories That Sell: Turn Satisfied Customers into Your Most Powerful Sales and Marketing Asset, by Casey Hibbard

Story-Based Selling: Create, Connect, and Close, by Jeff Bloomfield

Storyselling for Financial Advisors, by Scott West and Mitch Anthony

The Elements of Persuasion: Use Storytelling to Pitch Better, Sell Faster, & Win More Business, by Richard Maxwell and Robert Dickman

How to Prospect, Sell, and Build Your Network Marketing Business with Stories, by Tom Schreiter

The 60-Second Sales Hook: How to Stand Out and Sell More Using the Power of Your Story, by Kevin Rogers

Unique Sales Stories: How to Get More Referrals, Differentiate Yourself from the Competition, & Close More Sales Through the Power of Stories, by Mark Satterfield

Story Selling: Hollywood Secrets Revealed: How to Sell Without Selling by Telling Your Brand Story, by Nick Nanton and J.W. Dicks

The Hidden Power of Storytelling: Persuading with Story Telling: How to Write and Tell Magical Stories That Sell Your Product and Yourself, by Pierre Provost

Told Gold, Sales-Based Storytelling, by Richard Harris

Sales and Customer Service

New Sales Simplified: The Essential Handbook for Prospecting and New Business Development, by Mike Weinberg

Selling with Noble Purpose: How to Drive Revenue and Do Work That Makes You Proud, by Lisa Earle McLeod

To Sell Is Human: The Surprising Truth About Moving Others, by Daniel Pink

Positively Outrageous Service: How to Delight and Astound Your Customers and Win Them for Life, by T. Scott Gross

The Brain, Decision-Making, and Emotion

Story Proof: The Science Behind the Startling Power of Story, by Kendall Haven

Descartes' Error: Emotion, Reason, and The Human Brain, by Antonio Damasio

The Righteous Mind: Why Good People Are Divided by Politics and Religion, by Jonathan Haidt

Thinking, Fast and Slow, by Daniel Kahneman

ENDNOTES

INTRODUCTION

1. It turns out there are other theories about how Pig Island got its name, but this is the one Chris Gug heard and the one that he shared with me. Not that it matters. The truth is there is no situation in which a pig would find itself in the Caribbean Ocean happily swimming its sand-covered snout up to a camera lens that would *not* be entertaining. I was just happy to hear one of them.
2. Paul Smith, *Lead with a Story: A Guide to Crafting Business Narratives That Captivate, Convince, and Inspire* (New York: AMACOM Books, 2012).
3. Paul Smith, *Parenting with a Story: Real-Life Lessons in Character for Parents and Children to Share* (New York: AMACOM Books, 2014).

CHAPTER 1: WHAT IS A SALES STORY?

1. University of Leeds HP TippingPoint Solution Case Study, YouTube video, 4:04, posted by HPE Technology, February 5, 2011, www.youtube.com/watch?v=0pYzCUGXnPY.
2. Kevin Canfield, *Mastering Sales: 19 Years at the Intersection of Procter & Gamble and Walmart* (Fayetteville, Arkansas: Main Street Media USA, 2010), Kindle Locations 885-896.

CHAPTER 2: WHY TELL SALES STORIES?

1. Kevin Rogers, *The 60-Second Sales Hook: How to Stand Out and Sell More Using the Power of Your Story* (Middletown, Delaware: CreateSpace, 2014).
2. Annette Simmons, *Whoever Tells the Best Story Wins: How to Use Your Own Stories to Communicate with Power and Impact, Second Edition* (New York: AMACOM Books, 2015), p. 59.
3. Jonathan Haidt, *The Righteous Mind: Why Good People Are Divided by Politics and Religion* (New York: Pantheon, 2012), p. 328.
4. For example, J.M. Mandler, *Stories, Scripts, and Scenes: Aspects of Schema Theory* (Hillsdale, NJ: Lawrence Erlbaum, 1984); J.M. Mandler and N.S. Johnson, "Remembrance of Things Parsed: Story Structure and Recall," *Cognitive Psychology 9* (1977): pp. 111-151; G.H. Bower and M.C. Clark, "Narrative Stories as Mediators for Serial Learning," *Psychonomic Science 14* (1969): 181-182.

5. Chip Heath and Dan Heath, *Made to Stick: Why Some Ideas Survive and Others Die* (New York: Random House, 2007).
6. Andrea first became aware of this story through German communications trainer Vera F. Birkenbihl.
7. About the Significant Objects Project, significantobjects.com/about/. See also Rob Walker and Joshua Glenn, *Significant Objects* (Seattle: Fantagraphics, 2012).
8. Paul Lanigan and Denis Goodbody, *Soft Tales and Hard Asses: One Salesman's Discovery of the Art of Story Telling* (Middletown, Delaware: CreateSpace, 2013), Kindle Locations 2344-2347.
9. Craig Wortmann, *What's Your Story? Using Stories to Ignite Performance and Be More Successful* (New York, New York: Kaplan Publishing, 2006), p. 176.
10. Ibid., p. 44.
11. Doug Stevenson, *Story Theater Method: Strategic Storytelling in Business* (Colorado Springs: Cornelia Press, 2008), p. 12.
12. "Why Don't Buyers Want To Meet With Your Salespeople," post by Mark Lindwall, September 29, 2014, blogs.forrester.com/mark_lindwall/14-09-29-why_dont_buyers_want_to_meet_with_your_salespeople

CHAPTER 3: INTRODUCING YOURSELF

1. Mark Satterfield, *Unique Sales Stories: How to Get More Referrals, Differentiate Yourself from the Competition & Close More Sales Through the Power of Stories* (Atlanta: Mandalay Press, 2010), Kindle Locations 234-240.

CHAPTER 4: STORIES YOU TELL YOURSELF

1. Adam M. Grant, "The Significance of Task Significance: Job Performance Effects, Relational Mechanisms, and Boundary Conditions," *Journal of Applied Psychology* 93, no. 1 (2008): 108-124.
2. Lisa Earle McLeod, *Selling with Noble Purpose: How to Drive Revenue and Do Work That Makes You Proud* (Hoboken, NJ: Wiley, 2013).
3. Based on certified Zig Ziglar trainer and motivational speaker Mark Bowser, www.markbowser.com.
4. Paul Lanigan and Denis Goodbody, *Soft Tales and Hard Asses: One Salesman's Discovery of the Art of Story Telling* (Middletown, Delaware: CreateSpace, 2013), Kindle Locations 1053-1057.

CHAPTER 5: GETTING BUYERS TO TELL THEIR STORY

1. Mike Weinberg, *New Sales Simplified: The Essential Handbook for Prospecting and New Business Development* (New York: AMACOM Books, 2012), p. 141.
2. Iceland Volcano: Airlines Clash With Government Over Ash, *The Telegraph*, posted by David Milward, Auslan Cramb, and James Kirkup, May 24, 2011. www.telegraph.co.uk/travel/travelnews/8534342/Iceland-volcano-airlines-clash-with-Government-over-ash.html

3. Paul Smith, *Lead with a Story: A Guide to Crafting Business Narratives That Captivate, Convince, and Inspire* (New York, New York: AMACOM Books, 2012).

CHAPTER 6: BUILDING RAPPORT

1. Simon Sinek, *Start with Why: How Great Leaders Inspire Everyone to Take Action* (New York: Portfolio/Penguin, 2009), p. 41.

CHAPTER 7: THE MAIN SALES PITCH

1. owl.english.purdue.edu/owl/.
2. "On Counting English Grammar," posted by David Crystal, April 2, 2007, david-crystal.blogspot.com/2007/04/on-counting-english-grammar.html
3. Casey Hibbard, *Stories That Sell: Turn Satisfied Customers into Your Most Powerful Sales and Marketing Asset* (Boulder, CO: Aim Publishers, 2009), p. 11.
4. Hibbard, p. 12.
5. Robert B. Cialdini, *Influence: The Psychology of Persuasion* (New York: HarperCollins, 2006).
6. Hibbard, p. 3.
7. University of Leeds HP TippingPoint Solution Case Study, YouTube video, 4:04, posted by HPE Technology, February 5, 2011, www.youtube.com/watch?v=0pYzCUGXnPY.
8. Charles Duhigg, *The Power of Habit: Why We Do What We Do in Life and Business* (New York: Random House, 2012), Kindle Locations 918-919.
9. Christine Bittar, "Freshbreeze at P&G," *Adweek*, October 1999.
10. Robert Frost, *The Road Not Taken and Other Selected Poems* (New York: Start Publishing, LLC, 2012).
11. Why Closing Is Just a Matter of Telling Better Stories, posted by Logan Strain, September, 22, 2015 www.salesengine.com/power-of-story/why-closing-is-just-a-matter-of-telling-better-stories
12. Fannie Mae refers to the Federal National Mortgage Association. Freddie Mac refers to the Federal Home Loan Mortgage Corporation.

CHAPTER 8: HANDLING OBJECTIONS

1. Jeff Bloomfield, *Story-Based Selling: Create, Connect, and Close* (New York: SelectBooks, 2014), Kindle Locations 1301-1303.
2. Paul Lanigan and Denis Goodbody, *Soft Tales and Hard Asses: One Salesman's Discovery of the Art of Story Telling* (Middletown, Delaware: CreateSpace, 2013), Kindle Locations 1462-1463.
3. "How to use your success stories to demonstrate value — Selling with Story part 3," posted by Shawn Callahan, July 31, 2015. www.anecdote.com/2015/07/success-stories-to-demonstrate-value/.
4. Paul Smith, *Lead with a Story: A Guide to Crafting Business Narratives That Captivate, Convince, and Inspire* (New York: AMACOM Books, 2012), pp. 230-232.

CHAPTER 9: CLOSING THE SALE

1. Tia learned this technique from executive speech coach Patricia Fripp. See www.fripp.com/

CHAPTER 10: STORYTELLING AFTER THE SALE

1. Mark is also the author of the book *Three Pillars of Success*. He can be found at www.markbowser.com

CHAPTER 11: ELEMENTS OF A GREAT STORY

1. Karen Dietz and Lori L. Silverman, *Business Storytelling for Dummies* (Hoboken, NJ: Wiley, 2014), p. 107. Adaptation based on original story in Dara Marks, *Inside Story: The Power of the Transformational Arc* (Studio City, CA: Three Mountain Press, 2007).
2. John D. Bransford and Barry S. Stein, *The Ideal Problem Solver*, Second Edition (New York: Freeman, 1993).
3. I am grateful to Kendall Haven for first introducing me to the Bransford and Stein quote as well as the inspiration to write the story about Bob and the socket wrench. See Kendall Haven, *Story Proof: The Science Behind the Startling Power of Story* (Westport, CT: Libraries Unlimited, 2007), Kindle Locations 729-737.
4. David Hutchens, *Circle of the 9 Muses: A Storytelling Field Guide for Innovators & Meaning Makers* (Hoboken, NJ: Wiley, 2015), p. 75.

CHAPTER 13: STORY STRUCTURE

1. Chip Heath and Dan Heath, *Made to Stick: Why Some Ideas Survive and Others Die* (New York: Random House, 2007), pp. 31-32.
2. Aristotle, *Poetics* (United Kingdom: Oxford University Press, 2013).
3. Karen Dietz and Lori L. Silverman, *Business Storytelling for Dummies* (Hoboken, NJ: Wiley, 2014).
4. Blake Snyder, *Save the Cat! The Last Book on Screenwriting That You'll Ever Need* (Studio City, CA: Michael Wiese Productions, 2005).
5. Joseph Campbell, *The Hero with a Thousand Faces* (New York: Pantheon, 1949).
6. To illustrate the diversity of structures available, here's a sample of some with six steps. Classic dramatic structure: setup, catalyst, turning point, climax, confrontation, resolution. SHARES: setting, hindrance, action, results, evaluation, suggested actions. PARLAS: problem, action, result, learning, application, suggested action. CCARLS: context, challenge, action, result, lesson, suggested action. CHARQES: context, hindrance, action, results quantified, evaluation, suggested action. Source: Dietz and Silverman, *Business Storytelling for Dummies*.
7. About Kenn Adams, Kenn Adams' Adventure Theater. www.kennadamsadventuretheater.com/About_Kenn_Adams_.html

8. Pixar storyboard artist Emma Coats created a list of Pixar's "22 Rules of Story-telling," which became a popular Internet meme. Her rule #4 was a shortened version of Kenn Adams's Story Spine. See io9.com/5916970/the-22-rules-of-storytelling-according-to-pixar

CHAPTER 14: THE HOOK (TRANSITION IN)

1. Shawn Callahan, *Putting Stories to Work: Mastering Business Storytelling* (Melbourne: Pepperberg Press, 2016).

CHAPTER 16: CHALLENGE, CONFLICT, RESOLUTION

1. Akash Karia, *TED Talks Storytelling: 23 Storytelling Techniques from the Best TED Talks* (2013).
2. William Goldman, *Adventures in the Screen Trade: A Personal View of Hollywood and Screenwriting* (New York: Warner Books, 1983).
3. I was tempted to name this segment "The Conclusion" of the story because it would make for a nice mnemonic with the other three main components, making them together the 4 Cs: Context, Challenge, Conflict, Conclusion. But I didn't want to confuse this step with the lesson. And the word conclusion has both two connotations: the "result or outcome" of the story, as well as "a reasoned deduction or inference." Both are important and deserve separate attention. Source: www.dictionary.com
4. Kieran Egan, *The Educated Mind: How Cognitive Tools Shape Our Understanding* (Chicago: University of Chicago Press, 1997), as quoted in Kendall Haven, *Story Proof: The Science Behind the Startling Power of Story* (Westport, CT: Libraries Unlimited, 2007).

CHAPTER 17: LESSON AND ACTION (TRANSITION OUT)

1. David Hutchens, *Circle of the 9 Muses: A Storytelling Field Guide for Innovators & Meaning Makers* (Hoboken, NJ: Wiley, 2015).

CHAPTER 18: EMOTION

1. Daniel Kahneman, *Thinking, Fast and Slow* (New York: Farrar, Straus and Giroux, 2011); Jonathan Haidt, *The Righteous Mind: Why Good People Are Divided by Politics and Religion* (New York: Pantheon Books, 2012); Jeff Bloomfield, *Story-Based Selling: Create, Connect, and Close* (New York: SelectBooks, 2014), Kindle Locations 488-493.
2. Antonio Damasio, *Descartes' Error: Emotion, Reason, and the Human Brain* (New York, Putnam, 2005), p. xii.
3. Kerry Mallan, "Storytelling in the School Curriculum," *Educational Practice & Theory* 19, no. 1 (1997): 75-82.
4. Jack Maguire, *The Power of Personal Storytelling: Spinning Tales to Connect with Others* (New York: Tarcher/Putnam, 1998), p. 105.
5. Richard Krevolin, *The Hook: How to Share Your Brand's Unique Story to*

Engage Customers, Boost Sales, and Achieve Heartfelt Success (Wayne, NJ: Career Press, 2015).

6. Ibid. Page 129.
7. Southwest Airlines: Our Purpose and Vision, YouTube video, 13:18, posted by Southwest Airlines, December 19, 2013. www.youtube.com/watch?v=eGxM-f88I5g4
8. A full discussion with David on this topic is available on my *Lead with a Story* podcast episode here: leadwithastory.com/the-intimacy-threshold-storytelling-differences-across-cultures/
9. T. Edward Damer, *Attacking Faulty Reasoning: A Practical Guide to Fallacy-Free Arguments*, Fifth Edition (Belmont, California: Thompson Wadsworth, 2005).
10. "This American Life creator Ira Glass on the art of storytelling," from Conversations with Richard Fidler, May 25, 2012, www.abc.net.au/local/stories/2012/05/25/3511216.htm

CHAPTER 19: SURPRISE

1. Jerome Bruner, *Actual Minds, Possible Worlds* (Cambridge, MA: Harvard University Press, 1986).
2. Richard Maxwell and Robert Dickman, *The Elements of Persuasion: Use Storytelling to Pitch Better, Sell Faster & Win More Business* (New York: Harper Collins, 2007), pp. 122-131.
3. As you might imagine, Mr. Owen had to discontinue his annual dramatization after the tragic shootings at Columbine High School in 1999 made such a specter all too real.
4. Andrew Carnegie, *James Watt* (New York: Doubleday, Page & Co., 1905).

CHAPTER 20: DIALOGUE, DETAILS, AND LENGTH

1. Akash Karia, *TED Talks Storytelling: 23 Storytelling Techniques from the Best TED Talks* (Middletown, Delaware: CreateSpace, 2013), Kindle Locations 333-336.
2. Mark Turner, *The Literary Mind: The Origins of Thought and Language* (New York: Oxford University Press, 1996).
3. Deborah Tannen, *Talking Voices: Repetition, Dialogue, and Imagery in Conversational Discourse* (New York: Cambridge University Press, 1999).
4. Richard Krevolin, *The Hook: How to Share Your Brand's Unique Story to Engage Customers, Boost Sales, and Achieve Heartfelt Success* (Wayne, NJ: Career Press, 2015).
5. Michael Bosworth and Ben Zoldan, *What Great Salespeople Do: The Science of Selling Through Emotional Connection and the Power of Story* (New York: McGraw-Hill Education, 2012), p. 125.
6. Voice Qualities, Tutorials—Voice Production, National Center for Voice and Speech, www.ncvs.org/ncvs/tutorials/voiceprod/tutorial/quality.html

CHAPTER 21: DELIVERY

1. According to Paul McGhee, founder of SharperAx, www.sharperax.com; www.saleshacker.com/prospecting/how-using-ummm-in-sales-conversations-is-losing-you-deals/
2. Kendall Haven, *Story Proof: The Science Behind the Startling Power of Story* (Westport, CT: Libraries Unlimited, 2007), Kindle Locations 1920-1928.

CHAPTER 22: TELLING STORIES WITH DATA

1. Paul Smith, *Lead with a Story: A Guide to Crafting Business Narratives That Captivate, Convince, and Inspire* (New York: AMACOM Books, 2012).
2. Ibid.

CHAPTER 23: STRETCHING THE TRUTH

1. Roger Schank, *Tell Me A Story* (New York: Charles Scribner's Sons, 1990), cited in Kendall Haven, *Story Proof: The Science Behind the Startling Power of Story* (Westport, CT: Libraries Unlimited, 2007).
2. Seth Godin, *All Marketers Are Liars: The Underground Classic That Explains How Marketing Really Works—and Why Authenticity Is the Best Marketing of All* (New York: Penguin Group US, 2009), Kindle Locations 1500-1503.
3. Doug Stevenson, *Story Theater Method: Strategic Storytelling in Business* (Colorado Springs: Cornelia Press, 2008, p. 107-108.

CHAPTER 24: FINDING GREAT STORIES

1. Scott West and Mitch Anthony, *Storyselling for Financial Advisors* (Chicago: Dearborn Publishing, 2012), p. 3.
2. Tom Peters, *Leadership* (New York: DK Adult Publishers, 2005).
3. Casey Hibbard, *Stories That Sell: Turn Satisfied Customers into Your Most Powerful Sales and Marketing Asset* (Boulder, CO: Aim Publishers, 2009), p. 39.
4. David Hutchens, *Circle of the 9 Muses: A Storytelling Field Guide for Innovators & Meaning Makers* (Hoboken, NJ: Wiley, 2015).
5. Photo and Video Contests, Backroads, www.backroads.com/photo_contest
6. Backroads Videos, Backroads, www.backroads.com/videos/guest/
7. Hutchens, p. 60.
8. Hibbard, p. 54-61.

CHAPTER 25: PRACTICING AND SAVING YOUR STORIES

1. That's unfortunate, because as we discussed in Chapter 6, stories about the founding of your company can help you differentiate yourself like nothing else. After all, nobody ever founded a company without an interesting story behind it. But this series of compulsory facts is no substitute for a good story.
2. Estimates provided by Paul McGhee, a former professional musician, lifelong

competitive swimmer, sales coach, and football fan.

3. Mark Satterfield, *Unique Sales Stories: How to Get More Referrals, Differentiate Yourself from the Competition & Close More Sales Through the Power of Stories* (Atlanta: Mandalay Press, 2010), Kindle Locations 840-843.

4. Shawn Callahan, *Putting Stories to Work: Mastering Business Storytelling* (Melbourne: Pepperberg Press, 2016), p. 39.

5. Doug Stevenson, *Story Theater Method: Strategic Storytelling in Business* (Colorado Springs: Cornelia Press, 2008), p. 270.

6. Karen Dietz and Lori L. Silverman, *Business Storytelling for Dummies* (Hoboken, NJ: Wiley, 2014), p. 187.

INDEX